Working with Walt

UNIVERSITY PRESS OF MISSISSIPPI

JACKSON

Working with

INTERVIEWS

WITH

DISNEY

ARTISTS

———

DON PERI

www.upress.state.ms.us

The University Press of Mississippi is a member
of the Association of American University Presses.

Copyright © 2008 by University Press of Mississippi
All rights reserved
Manufactured in the United States of America

∞

Library of Congress Cataloging-in-Publication Data

Peri, Don.
Working with Walt : interviews with Disney artists / Don Peri.
p. cm.
Includes index.
ISBN-13: 978-1-934110-67-6 (cloth : alk. paper)
ISBN-10: 1-934110-67-1 (cloth : alk. paper) 1. Disney, Walt,
1901–1966. 2. Animators—United States—Interviews. I. Title.
NC1766.U52D52 2008
741.5'8092273—dc22   2007031892

British Library Cataloging-in-Publication Data available

To my parents, Alice and Joe Peri,
Who first introduced me to the Disney dream

And to my wife, Sue, and my daughters, Julie and Emily,
Who continue to share it with me.

Contents

Acknowledgments

This book has been a labor of love for me, but without having met Ben Sharpsteen, this book would never have happened, so my first debt of gratitude is to him. My work with him encouraged me to seek out other Disney artists, and I will be forever grateful to them for the privilege and the honor of allowing me to interview them and for sharing their stories, their emotions, and their lives with me. They inspired me then and they inspire me still.

Didier Ghez set this project in motion when he encouraged me to contact humanities professor Thomas Inge of Randolph-Macon College with a book proposal. Didier is an author, historian, and proprietor of one of the best web sites on Disney, disneybooks.blogspot.com. His series, *Walt's People*, has fast become required reading for all those who are serious scholars of Walt Disney. Even though he and I have never met face to face, he became my champion from across the Atlantic, and this book is largely the result of his efforts.

Tom Inge was very supportive of the book proposal and his recommendation catapulted the book from an idea to reality and for that, I am deeply in his debt.

Director Seetha Srinivasan, managing editor Anne Stascavage, and editor Walter Biggins of the University Press of Mississippi have been very helpful in guiding a novice author through the steps required to turn a proposal into a book, and I am most grateful to them for their kindness and patience and professionalism.

My sister, Camille Peri, and historians J. B. Kaufman (co-author with Russell Merritt of *Walt in Wonderland: The Silent Films of Walt Disney* and *Walt Disney's Silly Symphonies: A Companion to the Classic Cartoon Series*) and Michael Barrier (*Hollywood Cartoons: American Animation in Its Golden Age* and *The Animated Man: A Life of Walt Disney*), greatly improved the introductory material with their comments and suggestions. Camille also accompanied me on some of these interviews years ago and was an early supporter of my passion for Walt Disney.

Mike Barrier helped me immeasurably by encouraging me to interview some of the subjects of this book and actually contacting some of them for me by way of introduction. He has been a mentor, a longtime friend, and the founder of another web site, www.Michaelbarrier.com, that along with Didier's web site, have become two required stops on my daily perusal of the internet.

Dave Smith of the Walt Disney Archives was most helpful to me in the early days and served as another mentor who helped guide my efforts. Rebecca Cline of the Walt Disney Archives has been very responsive to all my requests in recent years, and I appreciate her professionalism and her assistance.

And finally to my wife Sue, and my daughters, Julie and Emily, who have endured the many months of my work on this project with good cheer and support: Thank you for allowing me to pursue my passion.

Introduction

Like millions of Baby Boomers in the 1950s, I sat in front of the television set and watched *The Mickey Mouse Club* Monday through Friday. With my family, we watched *Disneyland*, the TV show, and eagerly awaited the opening of Disneyland, the theme park. I purchased my first serious paperback at about ten years of age and read *The Story of Walt Disney* by Diane Disney Miller and Pete Martin.

My lifelong interest in Walt Disney blossomed into an avocation in 1974 when I met Ben Sharpsteen, a retired Disney animator, director, and producer. Together we wrote his memoirs of his thirty years at the Disney Studio, most of which he deposited in the Walt Disney Archives, where successive scholars have utilized it. Drawing on that experience and extensive independent research, I began teaching courses in the field of popular culture, on Disney in particular and animation in general, and more significantly, I continued my research by interviewing a group of key artists from the Walt Disney Studio over the next seven years. Meeting Ben Sharpsteen—someone who *knew* Walt Disney—inspired me to seek out as many of the early Disney artists as I could find. Even as early as 1974, death had robbed the world of an alarming number of Disney artists, starting with Walt Disney himself in 1966. So on each trip to southern California, from my home in northern California, I tried to interview as many people as I could squeeze into my schedule. Fortunately, I had an opportunity to talk with all of those I sought, sometimes just shortly before they passed away.

I was lucky and privileged to have an opportunity to meet so many of Walt's people, including the fifteen who appear in this book. These remarkable people were generous to share their stories and their lives with me.

Many of the group I have chosen to include in this book have not received the attention they surely would have if they had lived long enough to benefit from the surge of interest in popular culture. They include Dick Huemer, a true pioneer in the animation field. He began his career in 1916 in New York, worked for all the major studios there, but really learned about animation from Walt Disney. His career at Disney covered a wide spectrum, including animating the first Donald Duck cartoons, participating in the musical selections for *Fantasia*, and developing stories on many films, most notably *Dumbo* with Joe Grant. Wilfred Jackson, employee number 13 (henceforth his lucky number), had some wonderful stories to tell from his long career as an animator and director, including his description of the early sound tests on what would become Walt Disney's first sound cartoon, *Steamboat Willie*. I have included not only Wilfred Jackson's detailed version, but a second first-person account from Les Clark, one of Walt's famed Nine Old Men of Animation (a designation given in jest to nine of Walt's best animators at a time when they were all young and as a play on Franklin Delano Roosevelt's derisive comment about the U.S. Supreme Court), whose career as an animator and director spanned almost fifty years. Ben Sharpsteen described his first meeting with Walt in 1929, walking through a partially developed section of Hollywood to the little studio on Hyperion, not an auspicious site for a cartoon studio. Ben had worked at all the big New York studios but felt they didn't have the proper reverence for cartoons. Walt felt differently and told Ben that his salvation was in creating cartoons so good that the public would demand to see them. As Walt said, "You can lick 'em with product." Eric Larson joined the Disney staff in the 1930s and also became a member of the Nine Old Men of Animation. Eric worked on all the features through

The Aristocats. Together with Don Duckwall—the head of the animation department in later years—they would establish a training program for animators, just in time to bridge the gap as veteran animators began to retire or pass away. Herb Ryman joined the Disney staff from MGM, where he had been an art director, and continued in that vein at Disney. Herb began in background and layout on the classic feature films, and after returning to the studio in the early 1950s, he created wonderful inspirational sketches for the theme parks. Among Disney scholars and fans, he is especially famous for having drawn the first full depiction of Disneyland, working side by side with Walt over a long weekend. Ken Anderson had a long career at Disney in a variety of roles including that of scene layout, character design, and art direction. He also contributed a great deal to the design of Disneyland. Marcellite Garner was an early inker and painter and distinguished herself as the voice of Minnie Mouse for many years. Clarence Nash was the original voice of Donald Duck. Floyd Gottfredson drew the Mickey Mouse comic strip for forty-five years. Ken O'Connor, after a brief stint as an animator, became a layout artist, most famous for his work on the "Dance of the Hours" in *Fantasia* and the "Pink Elephants on Parade" sequence in *Dumbo.* Jack Cutting was an early animator at Disney who later specialized in the foreign releases of Disney films. Harper Goff is most famous for his association with *20,000 Leagues under the Sea*, including the design of the *Nautilus* submarine, and for his extensive design work on Disney-land. Larry Clemmons began in the early 1930s as an inbetweener on short subjects, left Disney after the studio strike, and after a successful career as a writer for Bing Crosby, returned to the studio as a writer on television shows and all the later feature films through *The Fox and the Hound.* The Walt Disney Company has subsequently honored eleven of the fifteen artists I have chosen with the Disney Legends Award, given annually to acknowledge individuals whose imagination, talents, and dreams have created the Disney magic.

Most of this group were at the studio during the Golden Age of Animation (late 1920s to early 1940s), when Walt Disney was advancing the art of animation exponentially and was the darling of film critics and the public alike. Many celebrities from the world of show business, politics, and literature made their way to Disney's door to pay homage to an individual they felt was a leading artist of the twentieth century.

While many historians have been primarily concerned with the development of the animation medium, I concentrated on the people who made advances in the art and their relationships with each other and especially with Walt Disney. Topics included their entry into employment at the Disney Studio, their first impressions of Walt, their working relationship with Walt, the studio strike and their reaction to it, and their contributions to Disney output, whether in film, print, or theme park creation.

Most of the interviews were conducted at the homes of the artists, in locations from Balboa Island on the southern California coast to the Napa Valley. I interviewed Dick Huemer in a cozy den off the living room where he wrote the *Baby Weems* segment of the film *The Reluctant Dragon*. Just around the corner, Dick had painted Disney characters from the 1930s on his sons' bedroom walls. (Just recently, new owners demolished the house, but before they did, ASIFA Hollywood, the Los Angeles chapter of the International Animated Film Society, removed the walls; Dick's son Richard has made them available to the Walt Disney Family Foundation for display in its museum scheduled to open in fall 2009.) Some of the artists I interviewed lived modestly, others in grandeur, but they all shared one thing in common: a deep devotion to the memory of Walt Disney.

If I ever needed a reason to pursue the people who knew and worked with Walt Disney, Herb Ryman summed it up very nicely when he said to me, "So each person that you talk to and each person you interview will have a little part of the puzzle, the jigsaw puzzle, that goes into the portrait of Walt Disney. But it's of such a vast scope—the picture of Walt—and I would also like to go on record as saying that Walt was not a deity. Walt was not a superman. Walt was just a regular, live, flesh-and-blood person. . . . It is for people like yourself to have the privilege and the duty of presenting Walt as a human being and a person who can be known, a person who you can be close to."

When I began working with Ben and throughout this early interview period, few books had been written about Walt and the studio. I read everything I could find, starting with the references in Christopher Finch's bibliography in *The Art of Walt Disney*. Mike Barrier, a preeminent animation historian, became a mentor for me, supplying contacts and in some cases helping set up my interviews. As I gathered information and taped interviews, my motivation was that I wanted to, needed to, learn as much as I could about Disney. A serendipitous result of all this was that I had an opportunity to meet many wonderful people—unknown to most of the public then—who helped make the difference at the Disney Studio. To be honest, I did not try to cover the whole spectrum of people, with their divergent personalities and points of view, who worked at the studio. I focused on those people who had long careers there and, with very few exceptions, were loyal to Walt. I could have sought out, for instance, those artists who left during the studio strike of 1941, but for the most part, I chose not to. There were books in print even then which presented the more negative views of Walt. The people in this book are not unbiased. They admired, respected, even loved Walt Disney, and yet all of them experienced the full force of Walt's personality. The word most often used to describe their feelings about Walt is "awe." They were then, and for the rest of their lives remained, in awe of him.

In this book, you will meet the group of people I met and interviewed just as I met them. I learned as I moved forward. I would have liked to have begun this journey knowing enough that I could always grasp the significance of people and events that came up in the interviews. But many times, it was years later before I came to appreciate the significance of a remark or an anecdote. Each person had his own way of remembering people and events and that is what I am presenting here. For instance, Dick Huemer thought of Walt as a paternalistic figure, but Ben Sharpsteen thought just the opposite. Some had more contact with Walt, especially in the early years, and consequently they offer more of an analysis of working with Walt than some of the others. Wilfred Jackson, Ben Sharpsteen, Les Clark, and Jack Cutting certainly fall into this category.

The interviewing process was for the most part very positive. Sometimes, though, I felt a tinge of sadness as I drove away after an interview.

Some of my interviewees were retired and living modestly, but for the time we were together, they generously poured out their memories of working with Walt. I would *see* them in the present but *hear* them in their youth. I sometimes felt that I had taken more than I had given. On the flip side, I had sought them out and I was able to ask them informed questions. I was interested in them and in hearing their stories. Most of these interviews were conducted before popular culture studies brought some of these people into prominence among the increasing fan base.

Each trip to southern California was a wonderful foray into the world of Walt Disney as the people I met revealed facets of Walt's personality and his style. I was discovering that each person had his or her own Walt Disney. No two people saw him in the same way. But collectively, these people describe a person who became a dominant force in their lives. They reflect the immense impact Walt Disney had on his staff. Part of the reason they were so affected by Walt was their devotion to work that they knew was on the cutting edge of animation advancement. They cared deeply about their contributions, and Walt's opinions about their work affected how they viewed their role. Those at the studio in the 1930s experienced the excitement of advancing a new art form with each discovery made and the camaraderie of sharing those heady times with Walt and with each other. Collectively, that excitement is conveyed through these interviews. With each interview as I learned more about Walt and his relationship with his staff, I realized that completely understanding the man would be an elusive dream. Yet I wanted to continue to pursue this dream.

I had a 1956 copy of *The Mickey Mouse Club Annual*, a hard-bound book containing selected articles from the club's magazines. I had treasured that book as a child and practically memorized every page. I was especially drawn to two photographs near the front of the book. One was of the animation building at the studio. How I dreamed of what it must be like to work there! When I made my first visit to the studio in 1975, it looked just as it had in the photograph, the citadel of Disney-style animation.

The other photograph was a composite of Walt Disney and Mickey Mouse. I studied that picture and wondered what Walt Disney was really like. I saw him host his TV show each week and thought of him as

a warm and genial man with an endless supply of curiosity. For years, I
had only that image of Walt. After I began working with Ben and interviewing more and more people, my fascination with Walt grew.

Walt Disney was born in Chicago on December 5, 1901. In 1906, he
moved with his family to Marceline, Missouri, where he spent his early
childhood living in a rural and small-town America. In 1911, the family
moved to Kansas City, Missouri. Walt had many jobs as he moved from
childhood to adolescence, most notably as a newspaper boy and vendor
on passenger trains. After service in the Red Cross as World War I came
to a close, Walt worked briefly as a graphic artist for Pesmen-Rubin,
where he met graphic artist and future animator Ub Iwerks—whose
career would be forever linked with Walt's—and then worked at the
Kansas City Film Ad Company where Walt became fascinated with animation. He formed Laugh-O-grams Pictures and produced a few films
before bankruptcy closed down the fledgling studio.

At the time Walt Disney entered the world of animation, the art
form had grown by leaps and bounds from the novelties of J. Stuart
Blackton (*Humorous Phases of Funny Faces*, 1906) in America and Emile
Cohl in France (*Fantasmagorie*, 1908) to Winsor McCay's triumph,
Gertie the Dinosaur, which appeared as part of an interactive performance
with McCay himself in 1914. New York became the center of the animation business, and the industry. Many early innovations were becoming
standard industry practices. The use of clear plastic celluloid sheets (cels)
on which animated drawings on paper could be traced and then overlaid
on an opaque background drawing replaced the labor-intensive process
of drawing each animation scene and background on single sheets of
opaque paper. Tiny Laugh-O-grams studio was dwarfed by the output
of Pat Sullivan, with his immensely popular Felix the Cat, Paul Terry
and his Aesop's Fables, Max Fleischer and the Out of the Inkwell series,
and a host of other studios producing animation fare for theater bills.
It is safe to say that Walt was influenced by the work of these giants,
and he chose for his Alice series, to reverse the novelty used in the Out
of the Inkwell series. Walt recalled, "They had the clown [Koko the
Clown] out of the inkwell who played with live people. So I reversed it.
I took the live person and put him into the cartoon field. I said, 'That's a
new twist.' And I sold it. I surprised myself" (*The Quotable Walt Disney*).

As prolific as the New York studios were at producing short subject cartoons, the cartoons were not seriously regarded by most of the filmmakers themselves or the distributors. For the most part they were just fillers on a theater program, even though some characters, notably Felix the Cat, became quite popular.

With a working print of *Alice's Wonderland*, Walt headed for Hollywood. In 1923, he and his brother, Roy O. Disney, formed the Disney Brothers Studio, renamed Walt Disney Productions in 1926. The studio produced fifty-six Alice comedies which combined live action and animation, from 1924 until their popularity waned in 1927, and then they produced the animated series Oswald the Lucky Rabbit. In 1928, Walt lost the rights to the character Oswald and most of his studio staff to the series' distributor, Charlie Mintz. With only Ub and a small staff remaining, Walt launched his next cartoon creation, Mickey Mouse.

Mickey and Minnie debuted in *Steamboat Willie* on November 18, 1928, the third animated Mickey film but the first of the series with sound. The film was an enormous hit and began what would become the Golden Age of Animation at the Disney Studio. At the time, Walt was in desperate need of staff to meet his production goals, so in addition to hiring raw local talent—Les Clark, Wilfred Jackson, and Jack Cutting, among others—he recruited animators with experience from the New York studios, including Ben Sharpsteen, Dick Huemer, and many other artists who were invaluable to the development of the animation medium. In 1929, Walt launched a second series, the highly innovative Silly Symphonies, with the debut of *The Skeleton Dance*. This series, unlike the Mickey Mouse cartoons, did not have continuing characters and placed an emphasis on music and rhythm. Ub Iwerks, who animated almost all of that first cartoon, left the studio to go into business for himself in 1930, but in 1940, with his independent efforts as a producer less than successful, he returned and, for the rest of his career, remained at the studio, where he made many outstanding technological contributions to animation and live-action production.

With the success of his cartoon series, Walt constantly pushed for better draftsmanship and more realism, and he took advantage of each innovation that came along, beginning with sound and then color

(*Flowers and Trees*, 1932) and later the multiplane camera (*The Old Mill*, 1937) that added three-dimensional depth to animated cartoons. He stressed story development and personality development at a level that was unique at the time. *Three Little Pigs* in 1933 is the first outstanding example of his success in creating characters with distinct personalities. He wanted audiences to believe that his characters were real, and the reception of his short subjects proved that he was on the right track. His success at branding the Disney characters was so great that *Life* magazine ran a cartoon in which a dejected would-be movie patron turns away from the box office and the caption reads, "What? No Mickey Mouse?" In just a few years, Walt had almost singlehandedly raised the quality of cartoons from a novelty to an art form. Almost every significant advance came from his studio. His prophesy to Ben Sharpsteen at their first meeting had come true. Other cartoon producers—Max Fleischer, Paul Terry, Harman-Ising, Van Beuren—produced cartoons that in some cases rivaled Disney in artistic style (Harman-Ising) and had characters with their own popular following (Betty Boop, for example, from Max Fleischer), but Walt's mantra of "plussing," constantly striving to improve every aspect of the cartoon medium, kept him at the forefront with audiences, critics, and competitors. Charles Solomon in *The History of Animation* quotes Chuck Jones of Warner Bros. saying, "Of course we stole from Disney then. *Everybody* stole from Disney then." Walt received a special Academy Award for the creation of Mickey Mouse, and that began a sweep throughout the 1930s as he dominated the short subject category: *Flowers and Trees*, 1931/32; *Three Little Pigs*, 1932/33; *The Tortoise and the Hare*, 1934; *Three Little Orphans*, 1935; *The Country Cousin*, 1936; *The Old Mill*, 1937; *Ferdinand the Bull*, 1938; and *The Ugly Duckling*, 1939.

Even though short-subject cartoons were immensely popular, Walt could not recover his costs because he kept reinvesting profits in his films to keep the quality high and advancing. As a huge leap forward in the development of animation, Walt launched his studio into feature film production with the highly successful *Snow White and the Seven Dwarfs* (1937). The film was so profitable that Walt and Roy could afford to move from their studio on Hyperion Avenue to a new studio they

designed in Burbank. With the success of *Snow White*, Walt embarked
on several features, including *Pinocchio* (1940), *Fantasia* (1940), *The
Reluctant Dragon* (1941), *Dumbo* (1941), and *Bambi* (1942). As would be
the case throughout his career, wherever Walt's attention and energy
were focused, that is where the studio shined and that is where Walt's
staff wanted to be. As Don Duckwall said, "For Walt, the feature was *the*
thing. If you were worth your salt, you were going to make it onto that
feature before long." With the exception of a couple of rather weak productions emanating from the Max Fleischer Studio, few other studios
attempted animated feature films at that time, but Walt's competition
continued to develop and expand the field of short subjects.

By 1939, World War II had begun in Europe, and Walt lost his
highly lucrative foreign market, so only *Dumbo* was a success on its
initial release. The studio strike of 1941 was a very bitter experience for
many of those who struck and for those who did not, and decades later
the bitterness was still evident among the survivors. The studio had
grown so quickly in a dozen years that it had lost its intimacy—Walt
could not know his large staff as he had in the early days—and some
dissatisfaction was an inevitable result of that growth. But as Hollywood studios were in the throes of the union movement, some of the
factors that led to unrest at the Disney Studio included a bonus system
that had become dysfunctional as the staff grew very large with feature
productions; a suspension of raises as the studio experienced financial
challenges; a fear of layoffs; and a clash between staff who wanted
unionization, with its promise of better pay and job security, and Walt
and Roy, who wanted to continue to run the studio in a paternalistic
manner as they had ever since the staff was smaller and more manage-
able. The strike led to a lockout and was ultimately settled through arbi-
tration, which left tension and anger in its wake for many. None of the
subjects interviewed in this book went out on strike. Their sympathies
range from strong support for the management position and hostility
toward the strikers (Sharpsteen) to empathy for those on the bottom
rungs of the corporate latter who were paid the least and had little job
security (O'Connor). Most of them vividly recalled the verbal taunting
and threats of physical violence that accompanied their daily arrival at
the studio during the strike.

The attack on Pearl Harbor and America's entry into World War II brought contracts for training films and public-service films to the Disney Studio. These projects became a mainstay of production and financial survival through the war years. A few feature films were made: *Saludos Amigos* (1943), *Victory through Air Power* (1943), and *The Three Caballeros* (1945). In the first years after the war, with the exception of *Song of the South* (1946) and *So Dear to My Heart* (1948)—both of which combine live- action and animation—Walt turned to feature films comprised of short animated sequences: *Make Mine Music* (1946), *Fun and Fancy Free* (1947), *Melody Time* (1948), and *The Adventures of Ichabod and Mr. Toad* (1949).

During the 1930s and 1940s, other studios, focusing on short-subject cartoons, moved away from the Disney style of realism and personality animation and continued to branch out in different directions. Animation studios within Warner Bros. and MGM, started by Disney alumni Hugh Harman and Rudy Ising, were in many ways the most successful rivals to the Disney style, offering wackier, more brash, irreverent, and slapstick humor that became very popular. Bugs Bunny, Elmer Fudd, Daffy Duck, the Roadrunner, and Tom and Jerry challenged Mickey, Donald, Goofy, and Pluto in this later period for audience share. Disney animators enjoyed these films as members of the audience, but many felt that the Disney Studio was striving for something different—more sincerity and sophistication in its short subjects. As Disney interest in short subjects waned with the ascendancy of his feature films, Academy Awards given for short subjects reflected this shift and the emergence of MGM and Warner Bros. as rivals in the field: *The Milky Way* (MGM), 1940; *Lend a Paw* (Disney), 1941; *Der Fuehrer's Face* (Disney), 1942; *The Yankee Doodle Mouse* (MGM), 1943; *Mouse Trouble* (MGM), 1944; *Quiet Please!* (MGM), 1945; *The Cat Concerto* (MGM), 1946; *Tweetie Pie* (Warner Bros.), 1947; *The Little Orphan* (MGM), 1948; *For Scent-imental Reasons* (Warner Bros.), 1949. The 1950s would be the last decade dominated by mainstream studio cartoons; double features and other changes in theatrical programming all but eliminated their market and consequently their profitability.

The 1950s saw a major resurgence and diversity of activity at the Disney Studio. Animated features returned in full force with *Cinderella*

(1950), *Alice in Wonderland* (1951), *Peter Pan* (1953), *Lady and the Tramp* (1955), and *Sleeping Beauty* (1959). Walt also produced live-action films, starting with *Treasure Island* (1950) and a host of films shot in Great Britain, followed by *20,000 Leagues under the Sea* (1954), *The Shaggy Dog* (1959), *Third Man on the Mountain* (1959), and many more. He also moved into the nature and documentary field with the True-Life Adventures and the People and Places series. What Baby Boomer could forget Walt's entrance into the television arena with *Disneyland*, the *Mickey Mouse Club*, and *Zorro*? And, of course, Disneyland opened right in the middle of the decade on July 17, 1955.

The 1960s carried on with more animated and live-action features, culminating in *Mary Poppins*, Disney exhibits at the New York World's Fair, and early work on what would become Walt Disney World in Florida. Much to the sorrow of his family and friends, his staff, and all those whose lives he touched, Walt Disney passed away on December 15, 1966.

Disney was a major icon of the twentieth century and a power-ful force in the world of popular culture. But the stories recalled in this book are also about a man. Disney artist Herb Ryman said, "Walt Disney was a rather unsophisticated, quite simple person. Not a world-renowned philosopher, not a do-gooder, not a religious fanatic, but a very normal, ordinary person with a genius for knowing and caring what people wanted and what they would enjoy." Despite his modest begin-nings, Walt Disney rose to the top of his field. His story is one more manifestation of the American Dream. When we think of the Holly-wood moguls of Walt Disney's era—the Louis B. Mayers, the Harry Cohns, the Samuel Goldwyns, the Warner brothers—we tend to think of businessmen with wealth and power. But when we think of Walt Disney, we think of magic. Sure he had power and wealth later in life, but he was first and always a magician, a showman, and an entertainer. And yet, over the years, he has been an irresistible target for detractors.

For Disney fans and scholars of animation, I believe this book will offer a treasure trove of insight into Walt Disney and the development of the artistic staff that helped him create the magic associated with the name Disney. Herb Ryman said, "He was able to bring out hidden energies. Walt's enthusiasm and his curiosity and his affection for life and for all things were very deep, and he plumbed into the depths of the talents around him, which sometimes I thought were rather ordinary talents. But out of those talents—by encouragement, by stimulation, and sometimes by insult—Walt could bring things out that were phenomenal."

The people I talked with brought years of experience and an intimate perspective to their composite portrait of Walt that I believe is unique. Most of them began their careers in the very early days when the staff was small, and so they had everyday contact with Walt. They could see the complexity of a man driven to succeed in the dog-eat-dog world of Hollywood. Jack Cutting, one of the small group of artists at the studio in the late 1920s, said, "Walt was a paradox: he could be very gracious and charming, but he could be very heavy handed." Don Duckwall, head of the animation department, described him as "charismatic, charming, and hard as nails, all in one guy." Eric Larson, another of Walt's Nine Old Men of Animation, said of his first impression: "Here's a guy that can scowl better than anybody I've ever seen in my life!" But also, "here's excitement." Floyd Gottfredson, longtime Mickey Mouse comic strip artist, never knew which Walt he was going to get. "He was living in his own world all the time and you got wherever he was in his world."

But all of these men were in awe of Walt, and many of them loved him. Leonard Shannon, a publicist for the studio, whom I interviewed in recent years for the Walt Disney Family Foundation, told me, "A lot of guys fell in love with Walt Disney. His secretary, Dolores Voght said to me, 'One thing I want to tell you. Don't fall in love with him.' That was a strange thing to say, except that a lot of the guys did! They couldn't help it. Bill Walsh loved Walt. Peter Ellenshaw loved Walt. God, they loved him, and when they lost Walt, it was just like losing a *mate*! I don't mean in a sexy way. But Walt you could *talk* to." The late Marc Davis, another of the Nine Old Men of Animation, told me in an interview in 1978, "If there is a change in the organization from Walt's time until now, it's this: there is nobody there who could make me feel as good by saying, 'I like that,' as Walt."

As a child, I loved Disney's films, his television shows, and his parks. He was an explorer and adventurer, using the latest technology—whether it was sound or color or the multiplane camera in his films, or embracing television before it was fashionable to do so in Hollywood, or creating theme parks—and along the way, he invited us to join him. He was a magician who could soothe our troubled psyches. As Eric Severeid said on the *CBS Evening News* after Walt's death: "What Walt seemed to know was that while there is very little grown-up in a child, there is a lot of child in every grown-up. To a child, this weary world is brand new, gift wrapped; Disney tried to keep it that way for adults."

Walt Disney was full of curiosity and wonder and he was able to convey those feelings to the world. In essence, he appealed to Lincoln's "better angels of our nature." While he was still alive, I felt that nothing in life could ever become too bad because somehow Walt Disney would find a way to make the world right again. My simple childhood faith in him led to a more mature pursuit of knowledge about him, stimulated by every interview I conducted. Even today, I am still engaged in this unending quest and I have never been disappointed.

In 1997, through Tom Sharpsteen, Ben's son, I was fortunate to meet Diane Disney Miller, Walt's daughter. Our ensuing friendship and professional collaboration led to my involvement with the Walt Disney Family Foundation and its production of a CD-rom, *Walt Disney: An Intimate History of the Man and His Magic*, and the introduction of the disc at a special event at Disneyland. In June 2000, the foundation invited me to participate in a documentary, *Walt: The Man behind the Myth*. During the on-camera interview, I had an opportunity to speak for some of the people I had interviewed who appear in this book. When the documentary was broadcast on ABC in September 2001—the first regularly scheduled program after the tragedy of September 11—I felt that I had come full circle from the six-year-old sitting in front of our black-and-white television set watching *The Mickey Mouse Club* and longing to be part of the Disney world.

Explanation of Terms

SWEATBOX was used as both a noun and a verb by Disney veterans. Originally, the sweatbox was a tiny room about the size of a closet. The closet became a makeshift projection room in the early thirties at the Hyperion studio site. Animators would sweat because of the closeness of the room and/or because of the anxiety of having their work analyzed and scrutinized. Even after the move to the Burbank studio and spacious projection rooms, the term sweatbox was still used. Sweatbox became a verb when someone would sweatbox a work in progress or analyze it to see if it was ready to move on to the next stage of production.

ROTOSCOPE is a technique where live-action frames are projected onto the animator's board so that they can be traced frame by frame to capture realistic action. Max Fleischer patented the technique in 1917 for the Out of the Inkwell films, and Disney refined the process during the 1930s. The key was to use this action analysis tool as a guide, not to literally transfer the live-action image to the animated world.

INBETWEENERS animate the fine gradations of movement in between the extremes made by an animator.

LAYOUT ARTISTS set the stage for animation through selection of camera angles and movement.

BACKGROUND ARTISTS paint the opaque scenes that appear behind the animated cels and are involved with the color styling of the scene.

CLEAN UP ARTISTS refine the animator's rough drawings into a finished drawing that will appear in the film.

INKERS AND PAINTERS transfer the cleanup drawings to transparent celluloid. Inkers trace the drawings on the front of the celluloid or cels, and the painters fill in the color on the reverse side.

Working with Walt

Ben Sharpsteen

Ben Sharpsteen was born in Tacoma, Washington, on November 4, 1895. After graduating from the University Farm (now the University of California at Davis) in 1916 and a stint in the Marine Corps during World War I, Ben began his career in New York working for many of the major animation studios there, including Hearst International, Paramount Studio, Jefferson Films, and the Max Fleischer Studio. He joined the Disney Studio in 1929 as the first of the New York animators and was paid a salary higher than Walt, Roy, and Ub Iwerks—the top Disney animator at that time. Ben animated on ninety-seven shorts, including *When the Cat's Away*, *Traffic Troubles*, *The Birthday Party*, *Touchdown Mickey*, *The Klondike Kid*, *Santa's Workshop*, *Building a Building*, *Lullaby Land*, *Gulliver Mickey*, *The Wise Little Hen*, *Mickey's Follies*, and *The Chain Gang*. He then established a training program for fledgling animators before moving into direction. Ben directed twenty-one shorts, including *Two-Gun Mickey*, *Mickey's Service Station*, *The Cookie Carnival*, *On Ice*, *Cock o' the Walk*, *Broken Toys*, *Moving Day*, *The Worm Turns*, *Clock Cleaners*, and *Mickey's Trailer*, and then served as a sequence director on *Snow White*, a supervising co-director on *Pinocchio*, a supervising director on *Dumbo*, and production supervisor on *Fantasia*, *Cinderella*, and *Alice in Wonderland*. In the late forties, Ben produced *Seal Island*, the first of the True-Life Adventure series. He produced twelve of the thirteen True-Life Adventures (eight of which won Academy Awards) and he produced fifteen of seventeen People and Places series films (three of which won Academy Awards). Ben also appeared on the inaugural *Disneyland* television show. Ben retired from the studio in 1962. He helped create an Antique Tractor Restoration Facility at his alma mater in 1976, and he founded the Sharpsteen Museum in Calistoga, California, in honor of the town's history. Ben passed away in 1980, and he received a posthumous Disney Legend Award in 1998.

Ben Sharpsteen's contributions to the Disney Studio have been underrated by some animation historians, but his memoirs have become an important source of information to others, judging by the number of books that quote from the biographical material that he and I put together that now resides in the Walt Disney Archives. Ben is best remembered for his directorial work—whether for its fast action and slapstick or its simplicity and directness—in the 1930s short subjects. *On Ice, Moving Day,* and *Clock Cleaners* are among a handful of his films that have stood the test of time. In feature animation, his work on *Dumbo* is noteworthy. Ben's continual supervision of animated features in the 1950s and his role as producer on the True-Life Adventures and the People and Places series helped Walt immensely in his quest to diversify his product during that decade.

Ben opened all the doors for me. Ben and I had both attended the University of California at Davis—he graduating in 1916 when it was the University Farm and I graduating in 1972. Through a publication at the university I learned that Ben had worked at the Disney Studio and was retired and living in the town of Calistoga in the Napa Valley. I wrote to him and asked him to sign my copy of Christopher Finch's *The Art of Walt Disney*, because I thought it would be great to meet someone who actually *knew* Walt Disney. It was a serendipitous meeting because Ben was looking for someone to help him write his memoirs. We started working together and continued for about three years. All of our interviews were recorded in Ben's studio before a roaring fire of oak from his surrounding acreage. The room contained collections of early automobile hubcaps and licenses and name plates,

all of which are now in the Sharpsteen Museum in Calistoga. Years
before, Walt and Roy had visited Ben in this very studio and I could
almost hear their voices joining Ben's as he reminisced about his years
at the Walt Disney Studio. Through my association with Ben, I began
interviewing more Disney artists and teaching what I learned, but it all
began with Ben.

The following narrative is based on many interviews I conducted
with Ben Sharpsteen from 1974 to 1977. A good part of this material is
in the Walt Disney Archives.

I first entered the animation business in New York City following my
service in the Marine Corps in World War I. I started as an apprentice
in an animation studio that was owned by Hearst Enterprises [Hearst
International Film Service]. They had a license to handle all of the
characters in the Hearst comic sections. When I first went there, I did
menial things such as erasing pencil marks off of drawings after they
had been inked, filling in places that should be black, and then doing the
actual inking of the drawings after the animators had penciled them. As
the weeks went by, I was gradually given more important work and it
was probably at the end of about six months that I gained the status of
full animator, although I was by no means efficient.

As time went on, I moved from one studio to another in New York
City. In the space of about three or four years, I came to the conclusion
that perhaps I had better have some experience in the art game besides
animation. So I came out and took a job with the Oakland Tribune,
which I held for three or four years. I did a varied type of art work there,
anything the paper needed.

One day I received a letter from Max Fleischer, informing me that
I had been recommended to him as an animator and asking if I would
consider returning to New York, which I did for over two years. Once
again, I was discouraged by what I thought to be the low standards of
the animation field. The attitude in the business was that it did not
matter so much, that the kids would laugh at this, and so forth. It did
not seem to me to be a safe thing with which to cast my future, and
frankly as an artist, I needed developing. So once again I returned to San

Francisco and this time I did freelancing. It was a discouraging job and I could hardly keep body and soul together.

Fortunately, a letter arrived from Walt Disney, who had received a recommendation for me from a mutual friend. He pointed out that he was now embarking on sound pictures, and he inquired if I would be interested in working for him. Walt Disney was hardly more than a name to me; I had never really seen a Disney picture. I only knew that he was engaged in some small-scale enterprise in Los Angeles. I decided to look into this prospect, so I took a train from San Francisco to Los Angeles.

My impressions of the location of Walt Disney's studio were quite unique. When I arrived at the depot in the morning, I called the studio to get instructions. The instructions were rather complicated because the town was strange to me, but it meant taking a trolley car toward Hollywood and then at a certain corner to wait for a bus. I was told the bus ride was a little over a mile. Evidently I messed up on contacts and since it was difficult to find anybody to inquire about the bus and its schedule, I decide to walk the mile, being told that if I just followed a certain street, I would come to the address.

I walked up through what was mainly a residential development, a section of town which had been laid out with streets and curbs, but which had very few homes at that time. It was late March [1929], and the grass and weeds were very tall and they were growing up through the sidewalk in places. It was not a street that was very much used at the time. I thought this was a very strange neighborhood for a cartoon studio, but I finally came to a main intersection as directed and I found the number on a small building next to a service station on the corner. Sure enough, the sign over the door read "Walt Disney Studio."

I soon met Walt and we chatted informally. I found that we could have a conversation which was familiar to both of us. I recognized immediately that he knew the business.

He informed me at that time of a succession of troubles that he had had [climaxing with his loss of the Oswald the Lucky Rabbit series]. Perhaps his biggest problem was that he had lost his release, his outlet to the theaters. The man [Charles Mintz] who had charge of Oswald had decided that he did not need Walt Disney, but he needed Disney's staff, so he persuaded these artists to go to work for him.

Walt had learned a bitter lesson from his experience with the distributors, and he vowed that he would reach the movie-going public in spite of the distributor. If he could establish himself with the public, then he could control his entire business and then the distributors would have to come to him and not he to them. It was an extremely ambitious statement to make. All of my experience in the business prior to that had been that animated cartoons did not amount to much, that producers could not really sell them on their own merits. Distributors would buy them, but they often had to give them away to theaters on the strength of the feature that they were selling to them. It was not a very good position for the producer of cartoons. And I was especially impressed with Walt's statement after walking up that morning through the wild oats and hills of Hollywood and finally locating the studio. It just seemed to me to be an extra ambitious statement. But Walt made a simple statement, "You can lick 'em with product," simply meaning that if you make your product good enough, then they cannot deny it.

During the first day, I had occasion to see a few of the Disney pictures. Walt did not even have a projector at his studio; we had to go down to Los Angeles to a theater. It was in the early afternoon before the doors opened for business, and he got the projectionist to run the pictures for us. My first reaction to them was that they were excellent, that is compared to animation as I knew it. There was something about those Disney pictures that were a cut above those of my experience, and I became concerned about my ability to contribute to them.

I began my first day at the studio with a certain amount of misgivings about my own lack of ability and whether I could satisfy Walt. I was impressed that he held every moment of a scene as being important. He gave me a scene to animate from a picture, *When the Cat's Away* [1929]. I was to animate a scene containing Mickey Mouse, and he showed me the drawings that had been made of Mickey Mouse so that I could follow the character and the style. It was a scene that I would have considered to be of run-of-the-mill importance, but I could see that he did not hold it that way. In Walt's estimation, everything that was done had to be executed with a great deal of thought toward finesse in order to make it better.

Walt struck me as being absolutely sure of himself. There was nothing in his attitude that suggested the approach, "We'll try this to see how it works." He was positive about what he was going to do. He impressed me as being "young"—the fact that he was several years younger than I and had been in the business several years less—and yet his ability to diagnose those requisites for making better pictures impressed me very much.

It is difficult to sum up my impressions of that first day. The size of the operation was not impressive: a small studio about the size of a small grocery store of that day. Frankly, I wondered where he was getting his money. But if the size and setting were not inspiring, their compensation was found in the attitude of Walt Disney. He was not concerned with speed, with the time it took to animate a scene; of paramount importance was the quality of the finished product. As I joined his staff of about ten people, I felt somewhat confused, but I simply went ahead and did the best that I could.

In the early days of animation, we were in the habit of flipping the drawings to get the effect of animation. Walt was not interested in seeing it as such. He wanted to see it on film. I had my first scene photographed and I showed it to Walt. I do not recall just what was his reaction, but I am sure that it was not one of any great optimism. I think he took the attitude of "Well, maybe it will get by." But I was not happy with his reaction. I did not know what he expected.

Walt knew how to take an animator's work, he knew how to feed the animator ideas, and he knew how to put them together and produce a picture. Just that alone was a terrific talent that nobody else in the producing end of the animated cartoon business had. In other words, Walt's ideas were often times more difficult to portray than we would have selected at another studio. We would think up something that could be portrayed before we started to animate it, so we naturally lapsed into a tail-end way of doing something. We wouldn't try something that we didn't think we could get away with. Therefore, the animation possibilities were extremely limited.

Perhaps the most outstanding thing about Walt was his eagerness to talk about the possibilities of a scene or a picture. He would start the idea going on a picture by talking to whomever he ran across in the studio. During my first two or three weeks there, I had gone to a restaurant to have my evening meal, and as I was leaving, Walt and his wife Lilly were coming in to have their dinner at the same lunch counter. I could not leave through the door because Walt stood there.

He wanted to tell me about a picture that we were going to make [*Mickey's Follies* (1929)]. Mickey Mouse is going to give a revue of performances by the barnyard animals with himself as the master of ceremonies. There is going to be a balcony, the roof of a privy [outhouse], and all the kids [cats] will be up there. Walt described each act and the audience response. As each act follows, the applause gets more enthusiastic, and finally when the big act comes, everybody goes crazy with applause and the cats are hooping it up and jumping so much that they all break through the roof of the privy. The sides of the privy fall apart, exposing a hole in the ground where naturally the cats have disappeared and we "iris" right out with "The End." It took a few minutes for Walt to tell this story. We were in a public eating place and I did not know who might be trying to get in or get out, but of course I had to stand there and listen to Walt. I noticed that his wife was standing to one side and that she was not too enthusiastic. When Walt pulled the final punch about the cats all going out of sight, she said, "Humph, I don't think I want to see that picture." Even though her remark was very much to the point, it did not affect Walt the least bit, because we went right ahead and made the picture.

With the misgivings that I held, I was surprised that before long, Walt pushed a new man on my hands as an assistant or an inbetweener. Walt had never heaped praise on me nor was he in the habit of doing so to others. I had a guilt complex that I might be fired if I did not improve my work. So it was only natural that to have an inexperienced assistant shoved on me who could not possibly improve the quality of my work was not easing my state of mind.

You could almost say that here he had hired this man as a finished animator from New York City and he had found him sorely lacking in producing many of the things that he was in quest of. My whole conception was to produce animation that he would respect, that he would like and think higher of me for it, because I felt that he was the only man I had any conception of in the animation business that had that objective.

I was 100 percent for him. If I failed, I felt that it was my fault and not his. I was absorbed in that and naturally when I was given young men of doubtful abilities to use in the performance of my duties, that he thrust upon me, I did not realize that the man had a plan far beyond that of training men for the organization. Diagnosing that I was particularly adept at handling green people sparked him into realizing that there was a place for me in his organization where he could profit from that. Walt was a keen judge of abilities and capacities.

While I was handing out work to beginning animators and Walt was probably giving me a couple of more men, he took the occasion to say, "You know, I don't think that you need to feel you have to do any more animation." Of course I thought that if I was not going to animate, then was I worth keeping on the payroll? He could read my expression and he said, "You can be just as valuable at that as at animation. I don't animate. I found out a long time ago that I could hire much better artists than myself." This was an example of his clear thinking.

In the process of training new talent, there was such an influx of new applicants that a system had to be evolved to properly supervise their operation. There were assistants of various degrees helping animators, but to make animators of them was perhaps putting too great a burden on the director of a picture. The director of a picture had all he could do to carry out and execute the picture as delivered to him by the story department. So in the course of events, there were two of us picked out by Walt to supervise small numbers of beginners. The other man was Dave Hand. We each had small groups of green animators, maybe ten to twelve. By picking up the scenes ourselves from the director, we saved him a great deal of time, because we did all the coaching of these new men. During the course of expansion, Dave Hand was made a director. The sole burden of handling these new men fell upon my shoulders.

There was no hiring hall for animators. You could have picked out the best animators in other studios and plunked them in Disney's, which happened time and time again, and they had to go through a very humble indoctrination: learning how to animate the way we did, learning how to pick your work apart, learning how to diagnose, learning to cooperate with others, learning to accept criticism without getting your feelings hurt, and all those things. We had a saying, "Look, this is Disney Democracy: your business is everybody's business and everybody's business is your business." If you did not have that attitude, you were not going to stay very long.

When Walt assigned me to supervise the work of several novice animators, I was to give them actual animation to draw and not to use them as merely assistants. I picked up the animation from the director and then took care of it in my own way. We used this system for several months and got work out of people who otherwise would not have been too productive or valuable. And we were learning about the capabilities of these young men. That climaxed when he told me about a picture all ready for a director, a Silly Symphony called *The Spider and the Fly* [1931]. He said, "You know, you can pick up over half that picture and you can hand it to this person and that person and so-and-so." There were probably eight to ten young men involved and some of them had very little animation experience. But the assignment was accomplished and the work was quite gratifying.

A director left unexpectedly and his departure created a problem of work for animators. We could not lay people off and then bring them back again if we wanted to develop people, and Walt was eager to develop the organization, to develop these animators. I suggested that I could probably take a picture myself and cover more ground as a director. Walt thought that was a good idea and he said, "I have just the picture in work in the story department. I want you to take a look at it." He told me about a picture that was finally entitled *Two-Gun Mickey* [1934]. I took the picture, broke it down, and planned it out as a director. We had it animated by animators of the second and third rate. It took its place in production with other pictures; it was satisfactory in that respect.

The second picture I directed was *Mickey's Service Station* [1935]. After that film, I directed *Cookie Carnival* [1935], *Mickey's Fire Brigade* [1935], *On Ice* [1935], *Cock o' the Walk* [1935], *Broken Toys* [1935], and others, totaling about twenty.

Walt had long since realized that by himself he could not animate, direct the efforts of other people, take care of the story work, and so forth. He knew he would have to confine his efforts to supervising people and the only way he could accomplish this objective was through a staff. And the only way that he could handle a staff was to have it work under his direction, to do as he would have it done. His forte was in the supervision of his business—every bit of it—and in the feeling that everything that was done, every drawing that was made, was the result of his guidance. In his mind, he was determined to have a team.

One of the outstanding practices of the studio was the preview. As soon as a picture was finished, we would take it to some convenient theater not too far away and we would arrange to have it shown during the peak business hours when they had a full house. After the picture was over, we would usually adjourn to the lobby where we would inevitably meet some of our co-workers. There was a good possibility that Walt would be there, especially if the picture was disappointing in any way and there was some way of putting a finger on the fault.

The director was in a very important spot. If he took the story literally as he received it and tried to put it on the screen just as that was, he could be in for a great deal of trouble in the end result. He had to be alert to the possible failures that the story presented. He had to be alert to bolstering the story, but he also had to refrain from eliminating any good things from the story. You might say that he was walking a tightrope: if the picture was bad, it was pretty sure that they would throw most of the blame onto the director.

As time went on, some of us became directors. The added responsibility focused attention on us if the picture was poor. I remember the story of one director, Dave Hand, who was not at all happy with the way his picture had turned out and he did not like the idea of facing Walt after the preview. He picked an aisle seat in the rear section of the theater so he could easily slip out. The picture was indeed poor, so Dave raced out of the theater and up half a block to the parking lot to make his getaway. He was delayed for a few minutes because some cars were blocking his path. When he finally was ready to drive across the sidewalk and into the street, he almost hit a pedestrian who turned out to be Walt! Walt had come out there looking for him. Even though he was blocking traffic in the parking lot, Walt stood there and let him know how unhappy he was with the picture.

I want to bring up something about Roy Disney and it is appropriate during the discussion of the early pictures. Walt was away on a trip in October 1931 and he may have said something to Roy about keeping his eye on things. But as a rule, Roy never interfered in the production of animation, and we never went to Roy for clarity or for advice of that sort. But he took this occasion to bring up the fact that, after all, he was expected to keep the place in business, that he was watching costs, and that he thought that there was some folly in the planning of a picture we were making about a Christmas party that Mickey and Minnie Mouse planned to give for underprivileged kids. He questioned various animators and anybody who could possibly be held responsible for the production of the picture. One man after another, regardless of his explanation, was bound to conclude that Walt had directed it that way.

After Roy had listened to enough of these explanations, he was exasperated. He said, "What in the hell! Walt—is he some ogre? Is he some tough prizefighter that you are afraid of? Are you a lot of dogs that stick your tails between your legs, because you're scared of Walt?"

One fellow piped up, "Roy, why do you blame us for being scared to death of Walt when you're scared to death of him yourself?"

That speaks volumes. Roy and Walt did not go around with their hands around each other's backs. Walt was a loner. Certainly Roy was no closer to Walt than any of us in production, but they did things together in a business way that we were not even called in on.

Walt lived that business twenty-four hours a day. In the early days when we were making shorts, Walt was driving through town, and he was stopped by a cop who gave him a ticket. He returned to the studio, and he told us about it in a way that he did not think was very funny, but Walt always acted out everything that he said, and he reenacted his conversation with the cop. Each time he told the story, it became funnier and his attitude changed, and before we knew it, we were making a Mickey Mouse cartoon, *Traffic Troubles* [1931].

During the early stages of *Snow White*, Walt was invited to a gathering from San Francisco called the Bohemian Club. They had an annual "high jinks" at the Bohemian Grove at the Russian River. Since it was at night, Walt needed lodgings for the night and he was assigned a tent.

He had a roommate in the tent, and when Walt got around to turning in, his roommate was already asleep and he was snoring. He said, "I couldn't sleep because I kept hearing that guy snore." Walt waxed eloquent on the story and he described all the different ways that this guy snored. It resulted in having the dwarfs in *Snow White* snoring when they went to bed. Walt could take advantage of everything in everyday life.

On Ice was delivered to my room and I began planning its production. Naturally I assumed I would start at the beginning. Walt dropped in unannounced, and he sat down and began looking at the pictures [storyboard]. He said, "This picture as it is is too long." Then he pointed to a section that was pretty far down in the picture. Donald Duck, being mischievous, strapped a pair of ice skates to a sleeping Pluto and then yowled liked a cat. Pluto woke up abruptly and in an agitated state, and as he took off in pursuit of the sound, he hit the ice and skidded around badly and so forth. Walt said, "Here you've got a great situation. It isn't important how we lead up to the situation. This is the best part of the picture. I'm giving you Fergy [Norman Ferguson, one of the top animators of the time] to handle this sequence. Fergy can take this and you can build it." Walt proceeded to describe the various ways that Pluto would try to get up on his feet again, only to flop down. He said, "Now after you get that done and you know how much footage it is, then you can go back and build your opening." It developed into the high spot of the picture. This experience was a revelation to me and a valuable lesson.

Regarding the incentive [bonus] system, Walt decided that people should be paid for what they produced. He did not mean that if a man turned out a lot of animation, then he would get a lot of money. It would have to be good animation. Directors would not only have to turn out good pictures, but they would have to stay within their budgets. He set up quite an accounting system for that purpose. This occurred shortly prior to the making of *Snow White*. At first it was roughly a bonus system where Walt would divide up a sum of money among those people whom he felt were most worthy of it.

A funny story occurred at the time. There were other people who did not get anything. One man came up to Walt and said, "Walt, you overlooked me on that bonus thing."

Walt said, "Oh yes, I did?"

"Yes, I didn't get anything."

Walt said, "Well, I'll tell you what I'll do. I'll look into it and let you know how much you owe us!"

That system developed into an elaborate system that would keep track of not only the hours that one put in on something but also the quality of one's work. Like everything else, it was abused. Nobody liked it really except for a few chiselers who somehow had a way of making it look good for them. This system eventually worked into feature pictures such as *Dumbo* and *Fantasia*.

In relation to other studios, Walt probably paid the best wages, but on some of the lower echelons, the pay was not very good. The reason for that was that he had a system of hiring and then selecting after he had hired. In other words, a person was brought in, and although it was not understood that he was on a trial basis, with Walt he really was. Walt never knew himself whether the person had outlived his usefulness or whether he would ever live up to his usefulness. This often dragged on for years and it was not fair. But he did not follow this pattern with any malice of forethought. Actually, he was so anxious to be sure that a person had something.

Walt was only one man. He was still the head of the business. He was still the prime mover of production. He was still *the* spark plug. The whole movement of the organization was Walt Disney personally. He had to build an organization, but it was his judgment as to who was important in that organization, that exquisite organization of talent of which he could pull the strings and make this man do this and that man do that. He hated to give up on anybody because he hoped that they would come through and be worthwhile.

As a result, he neglected badly the problems of selectivity. He allowed soreheads to stay on who were dissatisfied because they were not receiving recognition and advancement in pay. They feared the possibility of layoffs. So they decided to go to labor organizers in an effort to gain job security, seniority benefits, union benefits, and job classifications with minimum wages. These people never considered who was going to make the pictures good enough so that the public paid the bill so that Walt Disney could pay them. I was involved in the whole problem and you have no idea how important it was to have a selectivity process of personnel in order to produce a superior product. It was very difficult to apply union regulations to such an abstract thing as artistic talent.

We continued to expand after *Snow White*, with *Pinocchio*, *Bambi*, and *Fantasia*. Frankly, Walt Disney was spread as thin as he could possibly be. He never remonstrated because everything was of his own doing. He had his hand on the business, and he knew just about everything that was going on. But he was loathe to let people go until finally it became so bad that he had to begin to cut loose, and that, of course, started a great deal of unrest among people who were not key people. There were some exceptions among this group.

Walt was absolutely on balance all the time. How he went through those turbulent years [1938–40], building a new studio with all the planning and organization that was necessary! First, we had studios in half a dozen different parts of town we were growing so fast. In addition to that, he had to supervise new employees who were plunged into jobs far beyond their depth. Then to have pictures such as *Pinocchio*, *Fantasia*, and *The Reluctant Dragon* perform poorly at the box office. And on top of all that, to have a strike.

We had all that going on plus the fact that we had too many people whom we could not fit into production properly. The people who were being overlooked grew to be soreheads, and they brought on the strike [May 1941]. It was not a majority of people; it was a minority. The quality people whom we wanted to retain were not among the strikers. We went right ahead and continued making those pictures. We finished *Dumbo* during the strike, except for some of the laboratory work. We probably would have won if it had not been for some of the technicians at Technicolor who refused to process the work.

Finally we had a settlement of the strike. We had a terrific ordeal arriving at a formula of retention. The formula had something like an eye-for-an-eye basis: for every striker that we laid off, we had to lay off a non-striker and for every non-striker we retained, we had to re-hire a striker. That was a difficult formula. It meant cutting loose from a lot of people whom we thought very highly of.

The trip to South America [in preparation for *Saludos Amigos* (1943) and *The Three Caballeros* (1945)] took place before the strike was completely settled. They were gone when we had to decide whom we should retain. Walt had no hand in that process, and he even joked about it to his people. He said, "We don't know whether we'll even have jobs when we get back there." He took that philosophically, the strike. He said, "Those men have a right to organize, they have a right to leave. But they don't have all the rights. I have rights, too."

Public opinion was always paramount to personal opinion among the staff at the studio. Walt Disney once said, and this is a famous quote: "We are in this business to enjoy it because we like it. We want to do the things we like to do. But the public pays the bill, and when we do things that the public doesn't accept, then we don't get the money from the public so that we can go on and do the things we like." This is the biggest thing I can think of in Walt's career, and very smart. Quality came first in his opinion; the box office will follow quality.

Walt never wanted to be the guardian of the public. He simply wanted to please the public—that was uppermost in his mind—always to please the public, but do it in a worthwhile manner, do it so that later the public would not find fault with him. He felt a strong responsibility.

He was a great one for making remarks. This is true of Walt's character. He would criticize people to you, criticize members of his staff, because he went under the theory that if the shoe fits, put it on. In other words, now if this applies to you, don't you think that I am just telling you this to run that guy down. He hoped that it would rub off on you. But that seldom did. The people, no matter how important they were, were suckers time and time again to think that it did not apply to them. I hope you follow that. If I were to write something about Walt's basic handling of his employees and the psychology he employed, that would be an important thing.

When I began working for Walt, there were just three animators including Ub Iwerks. If ever there was a right-hand man to Walt, it was Ub. He had been a friend and associate of Walt's since the Kansas City days. I admired Ub greatly for his ability, and on top of that, he was ever so cordial with me, just as friendly as I would ever hope anyone to be.

There was never any standoffishness with me—a new man coming into the studio—and probably I was paid more than he.

Later, [Amadee J.] Van Beuren of Aesop's Fables lured away Carl Stalling [Walt's musical director] and Pat Powers lured away Ub Iwerks. Of course, we at the studio were rather stunned over that. But my reaction to it was why didn't those chumps try to get Walt Disney if they were looking for the right man? They missed the key man. The only remark that Walt made—there was no expression of bitterness anywhere—was kind of an offhand remark, "I sure feel sorry for Ub when he has any personnel problems." Ub was very easygoing. Ub Iwerks was a 100 percent nice fellow; he was a wonderful man, but he was attempting to do something for which he was not qualified. After a few years, it was apparent to Powers that it was not worth keeping the investment up.

Ub started a school of animation. He knew that I was instrumental in that at Disney's, so he called me up on the phone and said that he just wondered if it would not pay the studio to send people to him for instruction; in other words, that we were paying money for instruction. I thought this was belittling, a step down, and as I was very fond of him, I asked him to come over to the studio and have lunch with me. Now I knew of no bitterness between Walt and Ub, so I made the casual remark to Walt that Ub had called me, what he had called about, and that I had asked him to come over and have lunch. Walt just took it casually.

As I suspected, Ub had no real prospects, yet he did not want to go work for some other studio. I said to Ub, "You know, I've thought about you a lot and I can't get it out of my head that you belong here."

"Well," he said, "I suppose there's something to that" or something to that effect.

I said, "There has been an awful lot happen here in the eleven years since you left, things are so absolutely different, and yet I have a suggestion to make. There is a great weakness in our technical set up, especially in our checking department. [Everything that passed from animation to ink-and-painting to camera had to be checked to make sure it was complete and in register.] That's where I feel that I could hire you."

He said that would be all right.

I said, "I don't know what to offer you, but I am telling you that it will be much less than it should be, but I can't do anything about it. It will be $75 a week." That was during the days [1940] when that was a good salary. He accepted.

The next chance I had, I told Walt that I had hired Ub for that amount of money. Walt's attitude with me was "Don't come to me asking who you're going to hire or what you're going to pay him," but I had to be right, I had to be able to justify my actions. So I told him and he said, "Well that's all right." He never held a grudge against Ub. But it was a terribly awkward situation. Walt would have had no occasion to get a hold of Ub and say, "Why don't you come back?" It never occurred to Walt that he needed him back. But Ub needed Walt, and I knew it, and there was a chance without overstepping my bounds.

It was not long after that Walt said to me, "You've got Ub there checking. I think you're wasting the man there."

I thought to myself, "Well at least you're taking an interest." I said, "Yeah, but I didn't know—bringing him in after all these years—where to indoctrinate him."

Walt said, "Yeah, but you know you couldn't go out and ever hope to hire a man who is as well schooled in optics as Ub. He's a genius. I'm developing that [optical] printer and we're getting it all set up, and I'm going to put Ub in charge of that printer."

Ub found exactly what he wanted to do, and up to the time of his death, he made many valuable contributions. His two sons have continued on in a like capacity at the studio.

Walt, in being vigilant at all times in order to keep his staff functioning properly and to prevent any individuals from dominating others, had constant confrontations with his employees. One man who was directing a sequence in *Bambi* had gone entirely too "arty" on it. He did not particularly understand comedy situations or entertainment, but he was inclined to think mostly of the artistic impacts. As a result his sequence had grown far too long. A great deal of expense had gone into such a sequence, and in desperation, Walt sat in the projection room with him and others in an effort to cut the sequence down, to cut loose from too much material that did not relate closely to the story line. In going through the sequence, Walt would say, "Now you can cut here . . . now you ought to cut something out of this . . . now cut here."

After a little bit, the director complained, "Well I think that I would be losing something if we cut that out." Then he repeated again, "Walt I think I would lose something if I cut this out."

Walt was exasperated. He said, "You're telling me what you'd be losing. Here I am losing my shirt and you're telling me what *you'd* be losing!" That was so typical of Walt's retorts to his people.

Walt was not inclined to theorize on what he did. He never seemed to have any formula for what he was doing. This is one of the reasons why it was difficult to keep up with Walt as you worked with him. But in some uncanny way, he knew all of the elements that were so vital in the making of a screenplay or anything creative of that sort.

Walt had an extremely captivating personality, especially towards those who had just met him. Strangers meeting him for the first time found him very engaging and very delightful. He was very easy to talk to. He could disarm people by using the word "we" instead of "I." Obviously everything was based on what Walt Disney did, what he wanted to do, and what he expected to do, but he would invariably say "we." This was disarming to a novice, because when he used the word "we," they somehow construed it as meaning between the two of them.

Though we had a highly trained staff of specialists, as time went on, we realized that we could do better in the area of music and lyrics by hiring outside people who knew very little about the problems of animated cartoons. They were brought in purely on the strength of their own reputation and abilities, but they were also exposed to some of the production that went on.

During the production of *Dumbo*, we had considerable problems between the story and the direction, and as a result, it became necessary to have some new songs written that applied themselves better to the picture. When it came to recording these songs, one particular lyric writer wanted to be present.

This writer had written the lyrics to a song sung by the crows, which was an outstanding sequence in *Dumbo*. The singers suggested a change in the lyrics that seemed to be in character and to fit what we were trying to do, so we improvised the change. The lyric writer was greatly upset. One of our musicians said, "Now take it easy. This isn't as serious as you think it is. You've got to realize how we do things here at Disney's. Everybody has his opportunity to say something. In other words, everybody chips in ten cents and somehow it all seems to add up to a dollar." This man had completely forgotten that Disney had made great pictures and had a great reputation of his own. His pride in his own pet lyrics was more important than our judgment of the picture. This is an outstanding example of the outcropping of ego amongst our various contributors.

The question often asked is "What kind of a person was Walt personally?" or "What was he like outside of hours?" To which I must reply that there was no such thing as "out of hours" with Walt. Every hour of the twenty-four in the day was a part of his routine. He never had his work off his mind; he never had time set aside for play. I know that he had to set aside time for sleep at night, and I wondered how he ever managed to get any sleep with all the problems that absorbed him. But evidently he did because he always came to the studio prepared to put in his day's work. To be at leisure with Walt outside of the studio was not to be at leisure. He was always preoccupied with the studio; it was his life.

On one trip aboard the *Super Chief* for Chicago, I shared a drawing room with Walt and naturally I had plenty of opportunities to chat with him during the so-called "out of hours." But he was not a man to relax and invariably problems of some sort related to production would come up. I never could separate him from his work at the studio; he was always either talking about the business or he was silent because he was preoccupied with problems.

We were always eager to keep up a pace with Walt—what he was trying to achieve and how he was thinking. But many of his courses he kept to himself. We would learn of it far later and often to our chagrin, since we had once again pursued the path of the old course. We used to say that Walt was a hound dog. He was hot on the trail and we would follow him, but as he led us on, he would lose himself far ahead of us. We would plunge on blindly and find ourselves hanging on to the old trail, or as we put it, the end of a trend.

Walt always stressed organization at the studio. He persisted peri-
odically in complaining that we had no plan for management and that
we had to organize ourselves. But all the time he meant that he had
to organize himself. There was a note of comedy to Walt's attempt at
organization. During the war, propaganda was issued which stressed efficiency. One firm came out with a work entitled *The Importance of Good
Management*. To simplify their point, they briefly stated the "ten com-
mandments of good management." But we laughed at that because Walt
consistently broke every one of them.

Once when we were concluding a meeting in Nelson Rockefeller's
office [the Coordinator of Inter-American Affairs in Franklin Roosevelt's State Department], Walt said to me, "I want you to be there to
keep me from giving the studio away." It was a good experience for me
to see the way Walt conducted himself. He was extremely conciliatory
in his attitude. He did not brag of what he could do; he took it in all
sincerity. He presented himself as someone who would like to apply
himself to the effort and do a good job. He was concerned that money
was a factor in doing a good job and that they had to keep the studio
on an even keel. When the question of money came up, I was perhaps
influential in setting forth the approximate amounts that we could make
these pictures for.

We recognized immediately that *Gulliver's Travels* [Max Fleischer's
1939 feature-length film] was a production that was made by men certainly not superior to our shorts animators. So it wasn't that we thought
that *Gulliver's Travels* was a howling success; it was that we just thought
there was a market for feature cartoons that weren't up in class with
Snow White. So our shorts story men developed *Mickey and the Beanstalk*
[eventually part of the feature, *Fun and Fancy Free*]. That progressed
up to just about Pearl Harbor. When things became so upset, work was
stopped on it. Then after the war, it was also based on the premise of
accumulating shorts in feature length.

At the transition period [from war to peacetime] in 1947, Walt spoke
to me about doing something about Alaska. It was a new thought to me.
I had not known that that was on his mind. "What are we doing about
it?"

I said, "Nothing that I know of."

"Well," he said, "we should look into it. We should look into the possibilities and probably send somebody up there or, anyhow, we should look into the possibilities first."

In my mind what seemed most appropriate was the story of the fur seals and perhaps something on the life of the Eskimos. We ended up sending a man and his wife [the Milottes] up there to do photography, and out of that came a lot of film that we did not know exactly what to do with. Walt had never designated what kind of picture would be made. I had no idea what he was thinking. The film had been edited into categories and grouped, but that was all that we had done with it.

After a long time, Walt came up with the idea that we could segregate all the film about the seals, but only the footage that was about the seals in their natural habitat. He said, "I don't want any evidence of man in any of the scenes of habitation. I don't care how long the picture runs, but any footage that could be in the environs of the seals, we want it in there." It turned out to be twenty-eight minutes long, and he said, "That's all right, that's a three-reeler." He liked it and the people at the studio liked it and we gave it the usual audience test and everything was fine.

But our distributing agent, RKO, said, "Never mind if anybody likes it or not; it's an impossible length. It's too long for a short subject and theaters won't run that with a double feature because it makes the program too long. It's no good; you're going to lose your money on it." In typical "Walt manner," he completely ignored RKO's attitude. He knew what the public wanted and he was willing to gamble on it.

Independent of RKO, we had the picture run for a week at the end of the year in Pasadena. We let the theater have the picture for a week in return for the privilege of passing out postcards in the lobby and asking for reactions. The audience was asked a very pointed question, besides the usual one, "Did you enjoy the movie?" They were asked, "If you enjoyed this picture, would you accept it in lieu of a second feature?" The response was almost unanimously affirmative.

We entered it in its class for the Academy Awards. It won the Academy Award in 1949. I attended the ceremonies, and I accepted the

Oscar for the studio. Walt wanted to send Roy to RKO with the Oscar so he could hit those fellows who had predicted that nothing would come from *Seal Island* over the head with it. Now RKO could advertise it as an Academy Award winner, and they were happy to take it. [This was the beginning of the highly successful True-Life Adventures series.]

In addition to the film shot of the seals in Alaska, our photographers also shot some footage of the Eskimos. We used that footage to make a picture about the Eskimos, and it inaugurated our People and Places series. The film about the Eskimos also received an Academy Award.

In 1952, the studio became interested in some sixteen-millimeter footage of Tibetan rituals and pageants. The photographer had previously exhibited the film, and it had become scratched. He had taken his pictures at silent speed—sixteen frames per second—and we had to work with twenty-four frames per second. The photographer and his agent showed the film, and Walt called some of us in, including Ub Iwerks.

This story is typical of my relations with Walt. He liked the film, and when it was through, he said to Ub, "There are some bad scratches on this stuff, but that new cleaning process we have practically eliminates them, doesn't it?" Ub, I think, wanted to get out the easy way, and he did not want to say no to Walt. Walt continued, "Now on sixteen per second, on the [optical] printer we can adjust to twenty-four, can't we?" Once again, I don't think that Ub wanted to say no. But I knew that I did not want to see that footage purchased.

Walt excused himself, started out of the room and motioned—I could always tell by the way he looked at me—that he wanted me to follow. We got out in the hall and he said, "That man has some pretty good stuff. I think you ought to make a deal with him."

My relations with Walt were such that I could not ask him how much he thought it was worth. He would not have liked it, and I would not dare bring up those scratches or the different speed. I did not know what to do, and I had to do something right then as the session was over. So I asked the two men to come up to my office, and we talked a bit. They had heard Walt ask those questions about the scratches and the speed so I could not bring that up. Those two men thought they could get a good price for their film from Lowell Thomas, a popular lecturer who had made a similar trip to Tibet.

I said, "I don't feel that I can offer you as much as you want." I made an offer. They did not react, but were polite and said that there were lots they had to consider.

It was not long after that that Walt came upon me and he asked, "By the way, did you buy that footage of Tibet?"

I said, "No, I don't think so. I don't think they were satisfied with my offer." I thought I was going to catch hell.

He said, "How much did you offer them?" I said $8,000. Walt said, "$8,000—I think that was a very fair price. And they didn't take it? To hell with them!" What a relief!

I want to talk about Walt and the lawyers and the bankers. I was in a situation once where the legality of the matter might be involved. I was talking with Walt, and I said as I was leaving his office, "Walt, I'll check with the legal department." I could see by his expression that I had said something wrong. I stopped.

He said, "No, we don't check with the legal department. We know right from wrong, and when we are right we go ahead. We don't get an O.K. from the legal department."

The head man, the man who started as his full-time legal counsel, said to me more than once, "If Walt would only tell me these things he's doing, we wouldn't get into all of this trouble." It was not trouble to Walt. It was right. He was defending. "Let them sue, we'll go to court." And invariably he was right.

Once Walt agreed to meet with a couple of the Bank of America's men. They came into his office, introductions were made, and then Walt turned to our man in charge of finance. He said, "We're in wrong with the Bank of America? What's the matter?" Then he turned to the bank's men and he said, "Something wrong? Haven't we been paying our interest?"

"Oh, no, Mr. Disney, it isn't that," and they started to explain.

Walt said, "Well, I don't get it. Here I always thought the banks were in business to loan money. They have depositors to whom they pay interest. Where do they get the money to pay the interest? They have to loan it, don't they?"

"Yes, Mr. Disney."

"Well I always thought you *wanted* to make loans so that you could get more interest." Walt had no reverence for bankers.

Another time, the squeeze was on and it was decided not only to lay some unnecessary people off, but maybe to reduce some salaries. However Walt said, "I want a raise for certain men, for my top animators." Somebody remonstrated that it was not on the books. Walt said, "You know, I can't make pictures without those people. I can't hire bookkeepers to draw pictures for me."

One time an invitation was issued to Walt by the foreign correspondents of the motion picture industry. They had chosen at one of their regular luncheon meetings to honor Walt and the work he had done on the True-Life Adventures. So Walt had a small group of us accompany him. Walt made his remarks to the people there, and then he introduced the various people he had brought along. In introducing me, Walt somehow stumbled as to what sort of a title to give me, and he said, "Maybe I don't know what you do there, Ben," or something to that effect. He said, "Perhaps you ought to address these people here and tell them what you do on these pictures." It was an embarrassing situation for me—at least I took it that way—so I told them a few of the duties that I performed. Then I got on to the subject of title.

"My title is Associate Producer. The story goes around Hollywood that the question was asked of someone, 'Who is an associate producer and what does he do?' The answer was that an associate producer is just what it says: an associate of the producer. But it usually means that he is a relative." So I chuckled and I said, "But in my case, I can assure you that I'm not a relation of Walt Disney's, although I'll admit that at times he treats me like one—a poor one that is!" Walt got a big kick out of it and he laughed.

I think that maybe a grand climax to his treatment of me, as far as pushing me on to greater things, occurred during the early days of the True-Life Adventure series when I produced *Water Birds* [1952]. We had completed two or three of the shorter versions (thirty-minute subjects), and we had accumulated a great deal of fairly good material on birds, mostly shore birds or birds whose life cycle was connected with a body of water even if it was only a small stream. He wanted to keep the wheels of his studio going, so he said to me, "I am going to be gone for six weeks [on an extended trip to Europe], and I want you to get all that footage we have on birds, and I want you to get something up that we can get hold of, something that we can judge. We've got to find out what we have and what we might possibly build onto." He said it in such a way that he wanted to see this upon his return, or if not, why perhaps I had better go looking for another job. Now he did not use those words, but I knew Walt well enough to know that that could have been on his mind. It certainly spurred me on and fortunately I was able to grab hold of a well-known piece of music, Liszt's "Hungarian Rhapsody." It fit the situation beautifully, and it gave the structure for a good picture.

But I couldn't expect to live on that indefinitely. On a career at Disney's, I knew that it meant digging in all the time and looking for every insignificant little advantage to make yourself more valuable.

He bruised lots of feelings, but it was only in the pursuit of running a business. He was trying to forge a team. He was trying to forge everybody, bringing out the best talents and contributions of everybody into a well-working machine. You can call it a cog if you want, just like an assembly line. You could liken some of the inbetween work and the inking and painting to the assembly line work. And is a guy a villain just because he uses those techniques?

When I went there, there were a dozen people, less than half of them animators, people in a position to do creative work. And out of that, he developed one specialty after another after another after another and worked them all together. The one thing he slipped up on was in direction, and he ran afoul of a lot of grief because there was that one person—the director—who had the opportunity to change and shape that picture. Walt either had to take it or leave it. If it turned out to be too bad, why maybe he'd rip it all to pieces and make part of it over again, but the chances were he'd let it go and wrote it off as experience. He finally triumphed over the whole thing by working out his story department so completely, to develop it to such a high state that the whole of production was pretty well ordained when it left there, but that took years to do.

Roy Disney was a very loyal and respected man in the organization, and Walt respected him too. Unfortunately, Roy would be caught by surprise at some of Walt's schemes and undertakings, especially involving large investments, and he would not respond enthusiastically. I think that that would annoy Walt somewhat. However, Walt knew perfectly well that he could dominate that situation at any time he wished and that Roy could not do anything about it. On the other hand, Walt *wanted* Roy to raise objections if he felt like it. He was only too glad to have Roy differ with him because it gave Walt a chance to tell Roy more explicitly about it, and it forced Walt to be more articulate in his thoughts. It often ended up with a situation being greatly improved, so Walt would have resented it if Roy had not questioned him. At no time was Roy the guiding genius.

Roy never felt any loyalty to bankers as opposed to Walt. He always stretched himself 99 percent of the way to go along with Walt. It is true that he did oppose Walt on some of the ventures, but he had made his start with Walt and as far as he was concerned, Walt's judgment was final. I know this so well because my experience with Walt was exactly the same in many ways as Roy's.

As far as going ahead is concerned, that was part of Walt's policy: you went ahead on your own, you did not ask Walt's permission for every little thing you did. You learned to know the things that you should speak to him about and get his okay on. On the other things, you went ahead, and you just had to wait until Walt discovered whether they were suitable and workable or whether they should be modified or thrown out completely. That was the lot you played. I had always had a great deal of sympathy with Roy, because his problem with Walt was so similar to mine, and I always felt that Roy was very sympathetic to me for the same reason.

Just think of Walt as a young man coming up, trying to achieve fame, trying to achieve satisfaction as a showman. He is a storyteller. As a kid, he put on amateur shows with other kids. It was just something in him. And that is behind *everything* he did. Now he employed Dali. The whole thing was outlandish, very hard to reconcile to the animation medium, but that did not make a bit of difference to Walt. He saw it as something different. "Here's something shocking. Here's something I can wrest attention with. Now maybe I, Walt Disney, can create that something that will make this palatable, make it understandable to an audience." But he failed; the whole thing faded out and was forgotten.

It was a thrilling experience from first to last. Walt was not easy to get along with simply because his whole plans were in his head. He was a man who was always alert to better opportunities. Now in the case of Ub Iwerks, when I first went there, he would never say, "There's the hallmark of animation; do it like that. Find out from Ub how he does it. Do it his way. That's the way I want it." He never had a thought in his mind like that. He had an object of making a picture that the people would demand that the theaters run. But how was he going to do it? He no more thought of resting on Ub Iwerks's level. "How can we do it better? How can we get better animation? How can we think of better ideas?" Always right in the middle there; he was the whole thing.

The fact that Walt had to change his mind from time to time meant that he could not be as kind to people as he might. He was awful abrupt with people. He would give you authority and then take it away from you. I never could blame him. I never could hold it against him, because I was always overawed by the terrific problem he had and how much he accomplished.

He was always on guard to keep that organization status quo. I do not mean by that that he would not replace people whenever he saw fit, but it had to be a unit, a well-oiled machine. He said many times that this was a team effort, and we cannot have prima donnas getting out of line. Now there were exceptions to that, and I would say that the greatest exception to it were the musicians. They had something that Disney never gave them. Of course, the artists too could say that, but the artists were a product of the organization. The success of the pictures they worked on depended upon the talents of many other people. He could not allow any of them to get out of line.

The big story of Walt and his success is that he was determined to make a superior product; he was determined to give the public more for their money than they thought they had paid for. He could not do that without demanding the utmost in effort from his people. To do that, he

had to have a well-balanced organization. He could not have prima donnas who thought the place was made for them.

Walt very seldom terminated employment personally with anybody. He either did it through various people who were in charge of the
person's efforts, or he would do it through the personnel director, which
was an impersonal way of doing it. But it was always a ticklish thing
to carry out because you never knew but that man might have recourse
with Walt and talk himself back into the organization again, and then
you are in the embarrassing position of having fired a man and then have
him hired all over again. That happened in a number of instances and I
learned to be extremely wary of it.

I had plenty of evidence in my own case to know that he was very
true and very loyal and very appreciative of my participation over the
years. But I also knew that he did not have any place for me outside of
his organization, and how I adapted myself to that organization, and
that if I refused or was not willing to adapt myself, that he would not
tolerate me around the place for very long. Now that may be a cold way
of putting it, but I think that it was quite true.

Oftentimes, I would pick up the phone and get a quick reaction
from him, and I found him very helpful. But I will say that I had to
be careful that the question was a valid one and worthwhile and that *I
had a recommendation to make.* That was the thing to do. Never dump a
problem in his lap; always figure out a solution. It might not be right;
sometimes you found out you were wrong. But he did not like to have
problems dumped in his lap that required thought and solutions. He appreciated it when you figured them out.

You never got slapped down by him if you approached him properly
about the right thing and did not give him a burden. When we had to
offer jobs to people sometimes or spend money or something, it was not
the thing to do to get his advice. It was just to think it over thoroughly,
go ahead and do it, and if you made a mistake, why that was all part of
the game, because that was the way that he considered it. He considered
his time and his capacity as being limited, and it was far too valuable to
be taken up with petty things that you, his underlings, might take care
of yourselves.

He was a man of many moods. He might hardly notice you as he went by or he might stop and cheerfully discuss something with you, just depending on the mood he was in. He was abrupt and rude at times. No pat on the back. But sometimes he would grin and you knew that he was pleased.

Walt went around with so much on his mind that you never knew when to talk about things or not. He was pretty consistent: if you had some logical reason to talk to him, he was always receptive. If you were talking to him and just wasting a lot of his time, he could be very rude. If you asked him to solve problems that you should be solving yourself, he could be very rude. We people in the first echelon had to know how to do that.

Walt was actually very human and very understanding. He had a keen insight into your personal affairs and problems without ever getting paternalistic. He was probably the most unpaternalistic employer of any note that you would ever know about. Walt had a keen sense of values and he never got petty; he never allowed petty things to involve him. Because he had an objective of making great pictures and the objective demanded this exquisite organization, everything had to be the organization. If you did your part in the organization, then you were on your right track. But if you disrupted that organization in any way, then you were detracting from a means of his achieving that goal. But he always was very straight and to the point, and he could detect in a person's casual speech whether they had some ulterior motive that they were trying to put across.

Walt's greatest weapon was his ability to build this marvelous staff and manipulate it and perpetuate it. As people did not prove their worth or were dissident and got out, he could replace them. He was always able to replace them, because he was not looking for men who could do the job for him; he was always looking for the innovations that he could put in and then the men on his staff who could turn the trick for him. Or if it was possible, he would hire people from the outside. In later years, there were quite a few people who were well experienced in many other fields of motion picture art that came into the studio and made a place for themselves. They did not have to be apprenticed.

He did not want yes men around him, but he did not want people to throw cold water on his enthusiasm.

In summing up, you can say that the success of Walt Disney, right up until his death, was his ability to develop a highly specialized staff of artists and artisans and to develop himself in the adroitness and keenness with which to manipulate the staff. To manipulate it required a great deal of understanding of human nature. It required a great deal of planning and thinking on his part. It required that he insist that the staff should not get "top heavy," that it should not be dominated by any one faction or any one individual.

My personal reaction to Walt was that I never took him for granted. I never considered myself to be a sure thing at the studio. I always figured that what happened to others could happen to me. If I did not prove myself useful, I could be on the way out. And so in the process of terminating my long career of thirty years with him, I was rather amazed and pleased that his attitude toward me was as nice as it was.

Though Walt was very kind to me, there was never anybody who was indispensable at the studio. I once made the remark about indispensable people by saying that if I had never come to the Walt Disney Studio, I knew one thing for certain: I would not have known what my fortunes would have been. But I knew for certain that the Walt Disney Studio would not be one bit different. And that would apply to anybody.

After my retirement, I began to visit the studio about twice annually. On this occasion, I thought it might be a good time to pay my respects to Walt himself. As I walked in to his office, Walt was seated there and he looked greatly emaciated. I had noticed over the years a slight aging in Walt, but he was the sort of man whom I had somehow subconsciously thought would never grow old. When I saw him this time, I was shocked.

He looked up and said, "This is my first time back in the studio. I have been out for three weeks in the hospital for an operation." He intimated that part of a lung or perhaps a whole lung had been removed. We exchanged some brief conversation, but sensing that I should not tire him, I excused myself. He said, "Why don't we have lunch together." So I picked up my wife and we joined him for lunch.

It was perhaps the best conversation that I had ever had with him in all the years that I had known him. He brought many things to conclusion and into focus, many of his problems and how he had solved them [concerning a personnel matter and the ending for *The Jungle Book*]. As the meal progressed, I felt that he was gaining strength and feeling like his old self again.

We were seated at a table in the corner of the Coral Room, and I noticed that many of his top men had filed in to have their lunch and they were seated close by. I could not help but be impressed with their attitude at seeing Walt. Some of them would have liked to have shaken hands with him and to have talked about his absence and so forth while others wanted to talk about business problems, but they all refrained from any overtures such as that, and they quietly sat at the table.

At the conclusion of the luncheon, it was a good time for us to leave and I noticed that Walt had turned toward this group of his men as if to say, "Now what's on your mind?" They all rose and came toward the table, and they started to engage him in conversation. I could not help but feel that this was a very good sign, that this was a very happy climax, and that he was feeling himself again.

Later that day, I was walking through the main building and I saw Walt talking to another group of men about production problems. I was more convinced than ever that Walt was back in the groove. Naturally to hear only a couple of weeks later that he had died suddenly was a terrific shock to me.

I was very much gratified overall in working for Disney, whereas it was a very difficult job as compared to most studios, where only perfection was lauded or considered. That was always uppermost in my mind. However, as I've said before, it was like playing on a winning ball club. You found out the public was always interested in what Disney was doing. So my whole career there was primarily based on striving to put in a performance that fit in with the Disney scheme of excellence. I never had a possessive attitude toward something I felt was all my own, because, in truth, everything done was participated in by many other people.

Dick Huemer

Dick Huemer was an animation pioneer, joining the Raoul Barre Cartoon Studio in New York City in 1916. Born January 2, 1898, and raised in New York City, he attended art classes at the National Academy of Design, the Beaux-Arts Institute of Design, and the Art Students League. After Barre, Dick became the animation director at the Max Fleischer Studio and the Charles Mintz Studio.

Dick joined the Walt Disney Studio in 1933 as an animator, contributing to twenty-five cartoons, including *Lullaby Land*, *The Pied Piper*, *The China Shop*, *Grasshopper and the Ants*, *The Wise Little Hen* (in which he animated Donald Duck in his first screen appearance), *Peculiar Penguins*, *The Goddess of Spring*, *The Tortoise and the Hare*, *The Band Concert*, *Music Land*, *Broken Toys*, *Mickey's Polo Team*, *Alpine Climbers*, *Lonesome Ghosts*, and *Wynken, Blynken, and Nod*. Dick directed two classic cartoons, *The Whalers* and *Goofy and Wilbur*. Dick progressed to feature films as a story director on *Fantasia*, and story on *Dumbo*, *Saludos Amigos*, *Make Mine Music*, and *Alice in Wonderland*. Dick left Disney's from 1948 to 1951 to freelance on a comic strip, *Buck O'Rue* and returned in story and early television work from 1951 to 1955. From 1955 until his retirement in 1973, Dick wrote the True-Life Adventures comic strip. Dick received the Annie Award in 1978, presented by the Hollywood Chapter of ASIFA [The International Animated Film Society] in

recognition of his continued excellence and distinguished contributions
to the art of animation. He passed away in 1979.

Dick Huemer is highly regarded by the animation community,
not only for the quality of his work, but for the breadth of his career,
spanning the whole spectrum of animation history, from the early
fledgling years through the Golden Age of Animation and beyond.
His early Disney animation is appreciated, but he truly left his mark
with his story work on *Fantasia* and *Dumbo*.

I visited him several times after our first interview in 1976,
because I thoroughly enjoyed being with Dick and his wife, Polly, who
participated in our discussions. Dick had a great sense of humor—or
is that heumer?—he loved history, and he had a bemused attitude
toward life. Our interviews were conducted in a little den off the living
room, surrounded by books and memorabilia from Dick's career. Once
I asked him to do a sketch for me of Mickey Mouse shaking hands
with Koko the Clown since Dick had been a prominent figure at both
studios, and the finished drawing—so typical of Dick's wry wit—has
the two figures shaking hands, with Koko, behind his back, holding a
balloon featuring Dick's caricature and Mickey, behind his back, holding a long sharp pin.

The following conversations with Dick and Polly took place on
March 26, 1976; January 12, 1977; and February 17, 1978.

DP: Tell me about your first meeting with Walt Disney. I read that you
said he seemed to be brooding. How would you characterize him at that
point?

DH: Preoccupied. I figured he must be in some kind of trouble and he was,
as you know. [Charlie Mintz had recently hired most of Walt's artists.]

DP: He asked you to come to work for him.

DH: I agreed I would, because I was about to leave Fleischer's [Max
Fleischer]. But something interposed in between. Mintz got a hold of
me. He offered me a proposition which was a participation in the company as well as directorship, which incidentally he never honored. I never
got anything other than my salary. So then I was faced with the problem

of telling Walt that I was *not* coming to work for him. I told him that I had changed my mind; I had gotten an offer I liked better. There was a silence at the other end. Walt said, "You'll be sorry," and, of course, I was.

DP: This was after Mintz took control of Oswald the Lucky Rabbit away from Walt?

DH: Yeah. I don't know much about that, because I was so busy with the Fleischers.

DP: After coming to Disney, was there any stigma attached to the fact that you had worked with Mintz?

DH: Well, he didn't admire me for it! As a matter of fact, Walt had to go to New York animators because they were all there were who were experienced. But it turned out that he was, in general, a little let down by them. I mean his best animators came from the new men, like Freddy Moore. But we filled a gap and did what you see.

DP: I'm sure it was a growing experience, too, because the newer people learned from all the things you had learned.

DH: Oh, of course. But we learned a lot from Walt, too. In the sweat boxes, for instance, I learned little things like this: Walt said as he watched the film, "You know, you got this fat guy walking. He doesn't walk straight. He leans back, he's compensating for his weight. He's got a big belly." I thought, "My God, that's right!" Little things like that. Walt taught us animation. He said, "When a man does something, he anticipates it. He doesn't go straight out in two drawings, *swish*, to what he is doing. He gets set. If he puts his hand in his pocket, he comes back first, then he puts his hand in his pocket. He doesn't *swish* and it's in his pocket." That's what we used to do. We didn't bother. After all, we figured it wasn't worth the trouble in the sense that it wasn't worth the money. We worked on very small budgets. On *Mutt and Jeff*, we made a whole picture for $1,500.

DP: I'm interested in your impressions of *Gulliver's Travels* when it came out. I have just read one account that thought the Fleischers were cashing in on the success of *Snow White* since it followed so quickly.

DH: Obviously they were, but none of us liked it. You can't compare it to *Snow White*. It's not in the same league.

DP: From what I've gathered, emotions really ran high during the studio strike. What were your experiences at that time?
DH: I didn't go out on strike. People like Ben and myself—directors and people like that—were exempt. We didn't belong to their group. We wouldn't have been allowed to join as people who were in overseeing capacities. So I didn't go out. I know they hooted at me.

PH: But the strike was a terrible thing. Dick always thought that people got paid for what they did—
DH: He was very fair about it.

PH: —and this business of paying everybody the same salary because everybody's got a title: you're an animator, therefore you must get what the others do. Some animators did a hell of a lot better work and were worth more to Disney—
DH: And he evened it up by having bonuses, which was great—who else did that? Nobody did that.

PH: —and he wanted to reward the people who did the best work, I mean who were most valuable to him.
DH: He was very grateful to those people who did it. In a sense, he loved them.

PH: The strike changed everything at the studio. Not the same after that.
DH: He was very paternalistic with all the things that he did, and this was a slap in the face.

PH: And a needless one. It wasn't a factory. That was one place that didn't need to be organized.
DH: No, of all places.

PH : He was being ground down. I don't understand why Art Babbitt did it.
DH: He was a born troublemaker. I like the guy a little, you know. I have nothing against him, but that was his nature. He used to go around

suing department stores on account of sales tax and stuff like that. Of all places, it was the least one that you'd think would be struck.

PH: It was really like an art studio.
DH: Like when we struck Mintz, there was a reason, a damn good one.

PH: You did strike Mintz.
DH: That's why I left. And I just kept going.

DP: Was the strike as bad as a lot of articles have made it sound? Was it the end of the good feeling from the Hyperion studio?
DH: That's hard to answer. I'm sure Walt would have resented it, because, as I said, he had a great paternalistic feeling toward the studio. Whether that's an arbitrary bad term or not, I don't know. But he did. He generally wanted to help people and he generally liked his staff. He instituted things like bonuses and a loan society with no interest. Just great! "You'll have the money for that. You can build a house." He was thinking of the people. He gave vacations which damn few studios gave. Once as he came around the corner, he saw a bunch of guys jump into their places and get to work. He balled them out. He was as mad as hell. He said, "Don't let me catch you doing that again. If you feel restless, if you feel like getting up and walking, go out in the patio, walk around, and then come back. But don't you ever let me catch you doing that. I don't want you guys to be afraid of me." That's a wonderful thing, you know.

DP: I get the impression that a lot of people were afraid of him even if he said that.
DH: Well, I admit to being a little afraid of him myself. In the presence of such power and such genius, you can't help but feel a little—it's not fear exactly—

DP: Maybe awe?
DH: Doubtless, oh yes. But the minute he came in the room, there was electricity in the room with this guy.

DP: I wish I had seen him sometime in my life.

DH: It's too bad. He was not pleasant to be with socially. I don't mean unpleasant. He wasn't restful. You couldn't relax. At least I couldn't ever, even socially.

DP: That's the impression I've gotten.

DH: Oh yeah, that's absolutely true. In the early days, we went to each other's house. We knew each other socially. But even then, you had the feeling that he wasn't with you. He was working—still working at what was left back at the studio. And he would pick up things in conversation that would set him up, you know. Something that he could use maybe in what was bothering him.

DP: How would you characterize the Golden Age of Animation? What was it like to be there in the thirties?

DH: Well, we were dedicated, there's no question about that. You can compare it to Rubens. Rubens had a staff of about fifteen guys who were working on his paintings and they were dedicated people. They were artists, they loved doing it, and that's why they were there. And they knew that they were doing the right thing.

I didn't work on *Snow White* much. I had gone into directing then. I directed some shorts. Before that, I worked on a couple of scenes on *Snow White*. It was always my luck to work on things that were cut out. I worked on the bed-building scene and the soup scene. [Both scenes featured the dwarfs.] Walt would do that. He would buckshot around and he would try things. He didn't hesitate to spend money. And, *bing*, big chunks came out. Like the start of *Pinocchio*, I was the first director on that, coming from the shorts. It didn't open the way it does now. It opened with Spencer Charters as Gepetto and not the guy they finally used [Christian Rub]. Spencer Charters was a fat guy, bald like me a little bit. He was mooning around the shop, talking about how lonesome he was, which was kind of pedestrian now that I look back on it. And then he looks at his watch and says, or the watch ticks, "Three o'clock. They'll be coming by soon." He runs to the window and a mob of kids run by. That was the part I worked on. Suddenly that was changed. Walt went to the singing of the song, which was a wonderful beginning.

DP: There are a lot of things in *Pinocchio* that I find most appealing.
DH: I think it's a fantastic picture. I think it's probably, to me, technically the best. Just beautiful. Well, anyway, that's what happened there. When they stopped that sequence, Walt and Dave Hand took me to lunch at the Tam O'Shanter. They said, "We're starting a new project. We're going to make a musical. We're going to make a concert feature." From then on, it was called the *Concert Feature*, almost to the last month. So that's how I got off *Pinocchio* and onto *Fantasia*.

DP: Did you think in the thirties and forties and early fifties, that while some of the other cartoon studios started to maybe pass Disney on some of the shorts, or at least their focus was more on that—
DH: I don't think we ever thought that they passed us.

DP: Well, when Bugs Bunny and some of those characters came out—
DH: No, as far as I'm concerned, I always thought ours were better. I liked them very much. They were great. Fine. I always thought somehow ours had more style. Is that the wrong word? More class. More polish. More finish. Better thought out. Not as wild.

DP: How about Popeye?
DH: No, that was third rate to us, I'm sure. In their way, mind you, they were fine. They're in a different league. I'd hate to think that there would be no Popeye. They were fun, funny.

DP: Was the relationship between most studios amiable or was there competition? If you saw somebody from another studio, would there be a good feeling? There wasn't a cutthroat feeling?
DH: Oh, no. There was no feud.

DP: How about with UPA, because I understand that some people who left during the strike were involved later with UPA.
DH: Actually, I think we admired UPA more than anybody. Of course, we thought they were being sort of avant garde.

DP: Do you think Walt did? Do you think he resented those of his staff who—

DH: No, I don't think Walt paid any attention to anybody else. I daresay he didn't even care at all.

I did the story on *Toot, Whistle, Plunk, and Boom*, and I turned it over to Ward Kimball, who amplified what I gave him. It was Ward Kimball's baby then. He greatly admired all that modern approach. Everybody concurred. I know Walt liked it very much.

DP: I grew up with the image of Walt Disney as the host of the television show. If you could characterize him for someone like me who never met him, aside from this restlessness—

DH: Walt had opinions on everything, really everything, even politics. He was against Upton Sinclair because he was very socialistic. Walt was very square that way. And Walt was a very moral man. A great husband and a very fine family man. I mean an old-fashioned guy, like you don't see anymore. So in short, he was a good man. Not like some people I know.

DP: Someone criticized him for his tendency to chew people out in front of other people.

DH: Yes, and that's unfortunate. He did that. In fact, he did it once at a table where there was Roy, his brother, and Roy's son, Roy, and myself and Walt. It was at the studio. And he chewed him out unmercifully.

DP: Which one?

DH: He chewed out Roy, his brother. I was so embarrassed I wanted to sink under the table. I don't know why he did those things. Walt, I think, was a genius in many ways. Walt could have been a great *anything*, because his opinions on things, whether he was right or wrong, they were very strong. And he did have opinions on almost everything. Of course, in running his place, it was generally his idea that would dominate.

DP: His image from television, did that side of him exist as well? He came across as very kindly, somebody you feel like you'd be very comfortable with right off the bat.

DH: No, absolutely not.

DP: He wasn't that way at times?

DH: He was acting. Walt could have been a great actor. Don't forget that ever about Walt.

DP: I've heard that he could pantomime as well as Charlie Chaplin.

DH: Sure. At the story meetings, he could knock you on the floor. He could sell even a bad thing, I think, by just acting it out so funny.

DP: Some people who are critical of Walt say that his staff didn't get credit for what they did because so many products only had Walt Disney's name on it. Floyd Gottfredson and Carl Barks have become unsung heroes who were never known until recently for all the comic book work they did. In your own case, did it bother you that so many things went out under his name? Did it seem like he should have given more credit to people than he did?

DH: No, it never bothered me, and I was in the same boat with the True-Life Adventures [comic strip] for the newspapers. It didn't bother us, believe me. I know it didn't bother Floyd or [Al] Taliaferro or George Wheeler, the guy who drew my piece. No, you see we loved the place. We loved Walt in our own way, figuring it was quite true that without him we wouldn't have the jobs.

DP: I understand that on *Fantasia*, you were involved with helping to select the music.

DH: Oh, that was the job. I was picked for that. I was in on all that. The meetings were generally Walt, myself, Joe Grant, [Leopold] Stokowski, and Deems Taylor. Incidentally, if you pronounced *Stokowski* as "Sto-cow-ski" instead of "Sto-kof-ski," he would say, "I don't see any cows around here." We were going to do a piece of music, *Cydalise*, which is a French operetta. It is obscure, but a nice thing. There was a part called *The Entrance of the Little Fawns*, which was a fine thing. But we couldn't make it work. It just went along on an even keel. It gave no pauses or high spots, low spots, or changes of mood. So Joe and I one day got together and decided to look for a new piece. We picked out [Beethoven's] *The Pastorale*. That's how it happened. When we told Stokowski, he said, "Absolutely not. No, Beethoven didn't mean that." This is a pastoral thing and people are going into the country. But Walt said, "No, let's do it." He overruled him.

DP: What was your opinion of *Fantasia* when it was completed?
DH: I loved it. I thought we had done a wonderful job, except in one instance: I didn't think then and I still don't care much for the *Toccata and Fugue*. I think somehow if we were to do it today that it would be an entirely different thing pictorially.

DP: When it came out and didn't do as well in the beginning, was it a shock that the public hadn't accepted it? Did you feel you were ahead of the time?
DH: That's right. That's very true. Actually we blamed the public. I did, anyway. What the hell's the matter with them! This is a fine thing that will never be done again. It never was. It never will. It can't be. You couldn't afford to do it.

DP: How about *Dumbo*?
DH: That was a happy picture. You know how it originated don't you? It was a little give-away gimmick of some sort, almost in the form of a comic strip. You know this, don't you?

DP: No.
DH: By two people, a man and a woman [Harold Perl and Helen Aberson]. That's all. Walt bought that. I don't know who showed it to him or how he found it, but that's what he had. That's all he had. In it, maybe there were four or five frames like a comic strip with the story of the elephant with the big ears. They were making fun of him and then kicked him around and then at the end, he's flying and they're all cheering. That's all there was. But

this was the nut of the whole thing. I didn't work on it at first. Neither did Joe Grant. Then it was put aside for some reason. Walt wasn't satisfied with it. Joe Grant and I decided we would do something. You could do things like that in those days. You could make up things and try to goose Walt along. He loved it. He wanted you to do that, like we did with *Baby Weems* [from *The Reluctant Dragon*]. That didn't exist until we gave it to him. So Joe Grant and I would talk it over and then I would sit down—I fancied myself a writer—and I would write up the story as it went along and do maybe two or three pages a day, and then at night give it to Walt. All of a sudden it sort of pricked his interest. He said, "This is fine. Why don't you go ahead and keep doing this." In that way, we worked out most of the things that were in it—about the pink elephants and the crows, which weren't in it at the time. The train was in it—the Casey Jones was in it—so we carried that along. Naturally, the basic story was held.

DP: You were involved with *Saludos Amigos* [the cartoon sequence of Pedro the little Airmail plane in Chile], weren't you?

DH: There again, Joe and I worked it up and brought it in to Walt, and he bought it. He paid us extra like we had done it on the outside. The same with *Baby Weems*. I wrote that on the chair in there [gesturing to living room] just one Sunday afternoon, just the basic story. Joe took it in and showed it to Walt. He said, "Good! We'll buy it." So that's how it happened.

DP: Do you have a feature that is your favorite?

DH: It would be between *Pinocchio* and *Snow White*, very definitely. At all odds. I mean nothing comes close, not even *Dumbo*.

DP: How about the Disney shorts?

DH: There's one called *The Whalers* and then there's another one called *Goofy and Wilbur*. And you know why they are great? Because I directed them! I should have stayed with directing shorts, but Walt put me on *Pinocchio*. One of my scenes was when Pinocchio puts a rock on his tail and he goes into the water looking for Monstro. And then I was taken off that to work on *Fantasia*. But I wish I had stayed on shorts.

DP: In *Funnyworld* [a seminal magazine on animation], you said that it was exciting to be a director, to come in and get a story that Walt had helped to prepare and then to translate it, put it together to go on the screen. In some of my interviews with Ben, he said that when you got the story, you couldn't take it the way it was okayed by Walt and translate it to the screen, that there were things in the story that might be weak points that even Walt didn't realize.

DH: That's very true.

DP: And that you had to review the story and strengthen it. He also said that Walt wasn't a good director. With *The Golden Touch*, Walt got caught up and missed things. So you really had to bolster the story throughout.

DH: That's very true. That's one thing a director did. Of course, *Three Little Pigs* is still the greatest. There's no question about it.

DP: I like *The Band Concert*, too.

DH: That's very good. Was that the first time I did the Duck in that? No, the first time the Duck was used was in *The Wise Little Hen*. I animated that, too.

DP: On *Lonesome Ghosts*, Ben said that Walt assigned Bert Gillett to direct it and assigned you as an animator. Ben said that you and Gillett had had some differences prior to that and that this was an example of Walt putting two antagonists together. He was talking about Walt's sleight of hand.

DH: Walt liked sparks to fly between people. He did that deliberately. He thought that was creative. It made friction and then stuff would come out of that.

DP: Over the years as you moved from animation to directing and story work, did you enjoy the changes or was there some resistance or reluctance that you were leaving your area?

DH: No. I'll tell you how I felt. I had gotten heartily sick of animating, having animated since 1916. It didn't please me, what I was doing. I saw other guys doing so much better, and I knew I couldn't cope with that, although I was getting by all right. But all the time I had been in the business, I had always been aware of one thing and that is that the play is the thing. If you don't have a good story, you've got nothing. In other words, I emphasized in my mind the importance of story work. And I liked it. You know, in the old days, we were our own story men on *Mutt and Jeff* and at Fleischer's.

DP: You were everything.

DH: Well we didn't photograph it nor did we paint in the blacks [on the cels], but we were it. We directed what we did on paper. We were little directors and we were little story men as well as being the animators of it. So naturally I was aware of how important it was. Not only that, but you were judged how good an animator you were by how good a story man you were, because *you* put the gags in there. You could animate like hell, but if it wasn't funny or wasn't good, you were ergo a bum animator. So I always liked story. And I always liked directing, because that's what I did at Mintz's. So when [Bert] Gillett quit there, I went to Walt and told him I would like to go into directing. He instantly said fine. And that's when I got into doing those two keen things I told you about.

DP: So for you, it was a happy move?

DH: Oh very happy. Every move was happy. I consider it a privilege to have worked and been a pioneer in the goddamned thing.

DP: I have gotten the impression that some people felt they were being pushed out and they were being passed by.

DH: No. No. Gee, I asked for it. To this day I think, you can take your Milt Kahls and you can take all these fantastic animators, what good are they if you haven't got a hell of a story? So I always felt this is the very root, this is where it starts. You can have not the greatest animation in the world as we had in *Dumbo*—not the greatest—but it had a good story. It was a solid absolutely rock-bottom thing, which actually to this day, I don't think can be improved on. Neither can *Pinocchio*. Neither can *Snow White*.

DP: What was the first studio you worked for?

DH: I walked up a flight of stairs in the Bronx, opposite Fordham University, in 1916 and I walked into the animation business. At the top of the stairs, there was an office and there was Mister Raoul Barre, the little chubby Frenchman with a happy smile. I said, "I'm a cartoonist. I would like to have a job."

He said, "Ah so, well, you just step into the next room and they will put you to work."

And I was in the animation business. That simple. Of course, I had been to art school, the Art Students League, and studied under the famous Bridgeman. I also went to the National Academy of Design. I wanted to be a painter. I wanted to be an illustrator. Who didn't? That was what you did in those days. There was a vague thought, "Maybe you can have a comic strip. That would be nice." So when I didn't make it as a painter or a fine artist, I started thinking about cartoons, which I used to do for myself. I thought they were great. Of course they were lousy. But then when I saw the sign on the door, "Raoul Barre, Artist/Cartoonist," I walked upstairs.

DP: Those were the days before portfolios.

DH: I didn't need any samples. They didn't put me to work animating. I had to wait two weeks until I did that. At first, they put me on something called tracing, which is like inking.

DP: Where did you go next?

DH: In those days, it was a very precarious business. At contract time in the spring, when the studios signed up for another series, there was a frightening period where you didn't know whether it was going to be renewed or not. There were sometimes lapses of a few months at which you would do other things. Once I decorated parchment lamp shades with scenes. Fashion drawing I did at one time for *Pictorial Review*. Finally, the thing really exploded around 1921; no more *Mutt and Jeff*. So I went to Fleischer's, who were only doing the clown back then. He [Koko the Clown] didn't even have a name then.

DP: Was *Mutt and Jeff* through Barre?
DH: He had the rights to do it, but he didn't own anything on it.

DP: So then you went to Fleischer's.
DH: Then I went to Fleischer's. They were doing the clown then and they did him until about 1926 when they got into some kind of trouble with somebody else who had put money into the company. But we did something else called Song Cartoons. I can't express how fantastically these went over, with the bouncing ball. Max [Fleischer] invented the bouncing ball.

DP: At Fleischer's, I understand that Max asked you to use an inbetweener, so you could produce more work.
DH: That's very true.

DP: Was that the beginning of inbetweeners?
DH: That was the very beginning of inbetweening. I had the first inbetweener, Art Davis. I was surprised at how it worked out.

DP: Did that lead to other studios—
DH: Yeah, at first that led to other guys in the studio doing it. That was the origin of it. That's the only thing I got in on the origin of.

DP: Was it hard at first to accept someone else doing part of your work?
DH: We took a lot of pride in our little pen-and-ink drawings. You didn't think they could do it as well as you. You didn't want your stuff spoiled. That was really what it amounted to.

DP: I want to ask you about the comic strip, *Good Time Guy*. Did this run for a while?
DH: Oh, yeah. That ran for a couple of years.

DP: This was after you left Fleischer's?
DH: Yeah. I left Fleischer's a few times.

DP: Were you freelancing?
DH: No, I got a job. I had been recommended by a friend in a syndicate. Did you ever hear of a cartoonist called Feg Murray?

DP: No.
DH: He was a sports cartoonist. He recommended me. I drew it. I didn't write it. Did you ever hear of *Ella Cinders*?

DP: No.
DH: God, it's astonishing, the gap between people! Gee whiz! That was a big cartoon strip in its day. He wrote that and then he wrote this, too, and I drew it. This was a big job. It was a good job until it petered out.

DP: That's interesting that you drew this strip and then later, you would be writing strips.
DH: Then I did one where I wrote and somebody else drew. It was called *Buck O' Rue*. Well you see all us animators had one goal and that was to become a cartoon strip creator. Animation didn't measure up to that. That was the goal. Later, I wrote the True-Life Adventures strip for Disney.

DP: I've been reading about some of these other people, like Paul Terry and Walter Lantz. What did you think of their product?
DH: When they first came out, we thought they were great. They were better than anything being done. They put more money into them, because Terry had the foresight to let RKO buy into his company. RKO was then obligated to run these things in all their theaters. Every cartoon was assured of being run and being well paid for. Another guy who did very well was [Pat] Sullivan.

DP: Felix the Cat?
DH: Not that it was so great, which it wasn't—none of these were really great by our modern standards—but it made a lot of money, because he did something that Walt subsequently did: he had licensees selling little

things, handkerchiefs or whatever else, imprinted with the goddamn cat. With that, he did very well.

DP: Some critics want to debunk Disney or attack him.

DH: Well, don't you believe it. Walt was a wonderful guy. I mean for a boss, he was just out of the ordinary. Nobody like him as a boss.

DP: It sounds like he had a charismatic way about him from what I've read and heard.

DH: You bet he did. He was fair, very fair. Of course, he was unkind at times like we were saying before. You know, he would ball people out in front of other people, and he had no patience with bumbling or hesitancy. He was impatient, but he had a right to be, because his mind raced on ahead of everybody's. Walt would come into a problem and he would go right to the nut—*bing*—right there. We were wrangling over something and worrying. He'd come in and sit down and—*bing*! Fantastic! That's what I call genius. We were in the presence of great genius.

Clarence Nash

Clarence "Ducky" Nash, born in Watinga, Oklahoma, in 1904, toured on the Chautauqua and Lyceum vaudeville circuits before arriving in Los Angeles in the early 1930s. While entertaining school children for the Adohr Milk Company and appearing on local radio, Clarence came to the attention of the Walt Disney Studio where he became the voice of Donald Duck. Donald vented through Clarence in 150 shorts, including *The Wise Little Hen*, *Orphan's Benefit*, and *Der Fuehrer's Face*, and five features, including *Saludos Amigos*, *The Three Caballeros*, *Fun and Fancy Free*, and *Melody Time*. Foreign audiences heard Ducky's inimitable Donald in their native tongues. Clarence also provided voices for Huey, Dewey, Louie, and Daisy Duck, as well as those for a bullfrog in *Bambi*, dogs in *101 Dalmatians*, and some of the birds in Disneyland's Enchanted Tiki Room. With his Donald Duck ventriloquist doll, Clarence frequented school assemblies, hospitals, and orphanages. Clarence passed away in 1985 after a triumphant year celebrating Donald Duck's fiftieth birthday. He received a posthumous Disney Legend Award in 1993.

Clarence Nash played an invaluable role in creating the persona of Donald Duck by voicing the character. That is his mark on Disney and animation history.

Clarence was interested in everything and everybody. When I wanted to do a sound check, he responded in Donald Duck's voice so I knew we were off to a good start. We recorded our interview in the living room of his Glendale house. The *New Yorker* had featured an article about him some time before my interview, and it was so thorough, that I recognized everything as soon as I walked in. At the end of our interview, Clarence sang "Happy Birthday" á la Donald for my nephew who was about to turn four. We kept up a correspondence for a while after our interview, and I continued to admire his zest for life.

The following interview was conducted on January 11, 1977.

DP: I understand that you knew Harry Truman when you were a boy.
CN: Yes. He was a very fine fellow. I believe and many people believe this, too, that he will really go down in history as one of the great presidents. He was a very principled person. When I knew him, I was a boy working in a grocery store, and he would come in and visit one of his army buddies whose father-in-law owned the store.

DP: You also had a paper route.
CN: Yes. I threw the same paper [the *Kansas City Star*] as Walt Disney one time, too, but I also threw a paper called the *Kansas City Journal*. Then later on, it became the *Journal-Post*. There used to be a streetcar line out there, and we had paper bags that we hung on a post so that people could buy the papers on their way to work and they'd put the coin in the bag. Many a time I'd find an empty bag and the money gone, too. I never had to make up [the loss]. The papers were really good to me. They paid me better than my working in the grocery store.

DP: I have read different accounts of how you happened to go to work at the Disney Studio.
CN: I'll give you quite a story on that if you'd like to hear it. When I first met my wife, I was doing what my folks wanted me to do; they wanted me to get married, settle down. I had traveled in show business before that, Chautauqua Lyceum and some vaudeville. After I finished a tour with the Canadian Chautauqua in '28, I went back to a little lumber

town in northern California where I worked and where I met my future wife. Later, we got married in San Francisco where I worked for the Postal Telegraph.

I was entertaining once at a Kawanian luncheon and a gentlemen sitting next to me, Jay Dutter, said, "If you are ever in Los Angeles, I'd like to have you look me up." A month after my wife and I got married, I was out of a job. The Depression was beginning to set in up there. So I decided to come on down to Los Angeles. We took the cheapest transportation, a freighter. I contacted Jay Dutter, who was with the California Dairy Council. He arranged for me to appear on a radio program on KHJ and then he asked me to entertain at the Dairyman's Association picnic. Jay picked me up and he picked up another fellow who happened to be the vice president of a milk company. He hired me because I could entertain. I could not get a job unless I could entertain. I am a fairly religious person. I do believe that this is what the Good Lord meant for me to be. At one time I was going to study medicine. I became the biggest quack in the country instead!

About two years later, some friends wrote to me from San Francisco. They said, "We haven't heard you on the radio lately." So I went down to that same program and offered to go on without pay. That was the night that Walt Disney heard me. I didn't know it, of course.

In the meantime, I would entertain through the courtesy of Adohr Milk Company. I would drive a miniature milk wagon around with a team of miniature horses. Peter Pan horses they were called. On New Year's Day 1931, I drove that little miniature milk wagon in the Rose Parade following a big Adohr float. I entertained at schools and school assemblies. I'd imitate birds for the kids. The teachers didn't seem to mind. I'd give them little puzzles and things with advertising.

Sometimes people would say, "You ought to meet Walt Disney." Well I'd never even heard of Mickey Mouse. I couldn't afford to go to shows. Two days after that free radio program appearance, I was driving along Hyperion Boulevard [Avenue], and I passed this building with a billboard-size picture of Mickey Mouse on it: "Walt Disney Studios. Home of Mickey Mouse." I pulled over to the curb and went in wearing my Adohr uniform. It was a little organization then. The switchboard operator was the receptionist. I gave her a little circular advertising my work with the milk company. A couple of days later, Wilfred Jackson called me. He wanted some bird sounds for a Silly Symphony. I gave him some imitations of various birds.

"Anything else you can do?"

I said, "Yeah, I'll give you what I used to do on stage." I imitated baby chickens, baby turkeys, baby ducks, a pet canary singing. I also had a duck reciting "Mary Had a Little Lamb." Wilfred Jackson reached over on his desk and flipped a lever that sent the sound to Walt's office. Walt was down there right now. I hadn't completed "Mary Had a Little Lamb" [when] he turned to Jackson and he said, "That's our talking duck." I didn't know what he meant.

On my way out of the studio, I met Ted Osborne who was the producer of that radio show *The Merry Makers*. He said, "Hey, Walt heard you that night. He was going to look you up." We just had to meet, that's all! I always called this little character Mary because I recited "Mary Had a Little Lamb" when I was in the Chautauqua and Lyceum work.

DP: I understand that when you were in Chautauqua, you learned how to manipulate your hands so you could play "Who's Afraid of the Big Bad Wolf."

CN: Oh, yeah. One day early in the morning, Walt and I just happened to meet. I said, "Hey Walt, I've got a new sound."

He said, "Well, let's hear it." I did it and he said, "Someday, we're going to find a place for that." And he did. He remembered. He had me do it in the TV production, *A Day in the Life of Donald Duck*.

DP: When you recited "Mary Had a Little Lamb," was that the same version that is in *The Orphan's Benefit*?

CN: Yeah. It sounded more like—you see, Donald's voice developed more than Mary's voice did. Now I can't even see Mary anymore. It's Donald.

DP: I've never seen *The Wise Little Hen*, but I guess that was the first picture—

CN: That was the first picture he appeared in. He just had a small part. So did Peter Pig. I did his voice, too.

DP: What were your impressions of Cliff Edwards, Pinto Colvig, and Jim McDonald?
CN: Jimmy McDonald was a very good sound effects man. He did Mickey's voice, but not for film, only for records. Now Walt was the original Mickey. When Walt was away on trips, I did about nine pictures, doing Mickey's voice.

DP: Oh, you did Mickey's voice, too? I didn't realize that.
CN: Yes.

DP: What did you think of Pinto Colvig? I've read stories about him being in a circus and so on.
CN: One story I heard about him was that he ran away from home and joined a circus. He could play the clarinet real well.

DP: That always sounded like the quintessential American story.
CN: Years later he was playing in his hometown there in Medford, Oregon, marching along with the band. His mother saw him out there and she pulled him out of the band. Every time the circus would come to town here when Pinto was living, he'd take his clarinet and go down and play with the band. Wally Beery would come down and pet the elephants. He used to be an elephant trainer in a circus. I knew Wally, too. I went to school with some of his cousins back in Missouri.

DP: Did you do other work at the studio besides voice work?
CN: They didn't seem to want me to do much around here, but just be on call for sound stage. I'd take various guests through the studio. I've taken a few sultans through the studio in the old days there. Opera and ballet stars, too.

DP: You used to visit hospitals, too, didn't you?
CN: Oh, yes, I entertained in a lot of hospitals.

DP: A while back, I was listening to a broadcast of some radio shows from the forties and they played an excerpt of an Edgar Bergen and Charlie McCarthy show with Walt Disney and Donald Duck.
CN: I was on Bergen's show two times. We had *Mickey Mouse on the Air*, sponsored by Lever Brothers. I can remember, though, when we did radio work, he [Walt] had a little bit of false courage in his hip pocket!

DP: When you work on radio, is it easier to work before a live audience?
CN: I always enjoy audiences. That's why I liked Chautauqua and all—I enjoyed it more than working in front of a microphone when you're recording.

DP: How would you characterize Walt Disney?
CN: Walt could be very friendly at times. I had one little argument with him one time, and usually when you had an argument there, you were not there anymore. But when I left his office, I was whistling. A couple of weeks later, I got a raise in pay. He was good to me. They had a policy in those days that we voices were not supposed to get any publicity, and somehow or other, my name leaked out. I had nothing to do with it, but he was giving me—he could chew you out. He could do that real well. He can make you feel mighty darn small.

DP: It sounded like he could also be the other way and build people up.
CN: Yeah. I think he was a very fair man, but if somebody crossed him, it took a long time [to get over it]. Now even with Pinto Colvig, he had a problem one time. Later on, that was all forgotten. Same way with Ub Iwerks.

DP: Do you think that the image of Walt Disney that was on TV when he would host the show, do you think he was that way, too, kind of a fatherly figure?
CN: I liked him on that show. I think he was really himself on it. I thought he did very well with it. He was a genius. I certainly was very fortunate to meet him.

DP: Did you do a voice for *The Song of the South*?
CN: No, no voice, but the bluebird. "Mr. Bluebird's on my shoulder."

Wilfred Jackson

Wilfred Jackson, born in Chicago on January 24, 1906, was fresh out of
Otis Art Institute, when he joined the Disney Studio in 1928 during
the transition from Oswald the Lucky Rabbit to the Mickey Mouse
cartoon series. He played an instrumental part (no pun intended)
in developing a system for synchronizing sound and picture using a
metronome. His discovery set the standard for sound synchroniza-
tion. Although he worked as an animator, he quickly became one of
Disney's early directors, widely respected for his work on thirty shorts
including Academy Award winners *The Tortoise and the Hare*, *The
Country Cousin*, and *The Old Mill*, as well as the classic Mickey short,
The Band Concert. Jaxon (as he was known around the studio) moved
from shorts to animated features, directing *Snow White*, *Pinocchio*, *Fantasia*, *Dumbo*, *Saludos Amigos*, *Melody Time*, *Cinderella*, *Alice in Wonderland*, *Peter Pan*, and *Lady and the Tramp*. For *Song of the South*, he
directed all the cartoon and combination live-action footage. During
the 1950s, he turned his talent to television, where he directed thirteen
shows, including *The Story of the Animated Drawing*, before retiring in
1961. Wilfred passed away in 1988, the same year that he received a Disney
Legend Award.

   Animation historians consider Wilfred Jackson to be the best
of the Disney directors from the 1930s. Wilfred produced shorts of the

highest quality, and many, including *The Band Concert*, *The Old Mill*, and *Music Land* are considered classics today. A master of integrating music and action, he brought his skills to feature films such as *Snow White* and the animated sequences in *Song of the South*.

When I interviewed Wilfred at his home on Balboa Island, I found him considerate and generous with his time. Only afterwards did I come to understand how much the studio meant to him and how emotional it was for him to talk about it. It was a privilege and an honor to meet him.

The following interview was conducted on January 12, 1977.

DP: How did you happen to go to work for Walt Disney?

WJ: I can't remember when I didn't desperately want to be involved with animated cartoons. I was very young when that became an obsession with me. From high school, I worked a year to get some money, and then I went to Otis Art Institute. I despaired of ever getting to work in animation, because all animation as far as I knew was done in New York and I didn't have the carfare. Then I discovered that there was a man in Hollywood who made animated cartoons named Walt Disney. So through a friend, I found out where he was, what his phone number was, and I called him up. Much to my amazement, Walt answered the phone. He consented to talk to me if I would come out and see him, which I quickly did. Walt wasn't the least bit impressed with the samples that I brought and said very candidly that I needed to have a little bit more training before I would be able to go ahead. I was simply not a good enough draftsman. So I said, "Fine, Walt, I'll study whatever you tell me to study. I'm not taking a regular course. I want to get into cartooning, so I am just taking subjects I think will suit me to get into cartooning. Now if you'll tell me what to study to learn how to do animated cartoons, I'll study those things and come back and see you later on."

He said, "There's no place you can learn to do animation except in an animation studio."

I said, "Well then, how would it be if I just came and worked for nothing here and learned how here?"

And he said, "We couldn't do that."

So I said, "I'd be willing to pay you tuition just like I do to go to school if you'd teach me."

He said, "Oh, hell! I'll hire you for a week to see if you can do anything worthwhile." That was how I got in. And it turned out that Walt's appraisal was right. I did need a better background as a draftsman to do anything very good with animation.

Walt made one statement that I thought was funny. He said, "I'll hire you for a week and we'll see if you can do anything useful. After a week, I don't know if there's going to be a studio here." I thought, "Gee, that's a funny way for a guy to talk. Something must be going on." Anyway, I was tickled to death so I came. I got a job helping the janitor sort out old celluloids that were too scratched to be used again from the ones that were to be saved and used again. Before the week was out, they let me start painting black spots on the characters [already traced on to celluloid], which was as far down the ladder as you could go with the cartoons.

All during that week, there was so much laughing and clowning and noises of people horsing around there that I had an idea this was a real strange place to work, because it didn't sound as though anybody was doing much work. I couldn't figure out how a business could be run with people who would be having that big a picnic.

At the end of the first week—we worked on Saturdays half a day until 1:00—I didn't want to be the first one out. Nobody told me if I was going to come back next week or not, so I was kind of interested to see. I pretended to be busy and hung around, and I observed that most of the fellows who came out of the room next to the animators' compartment were carrying all their personal belongings, even the pads that they sat on. I thought, "This is awful funny. These guys don't trust each other. They have all this fun during this week, and then they take all their personal belongings home with them, things you wouldn't use at home, and they'll have to bring them back on Monday. This is a real screwy place to work." It wasn't until later on that I found out the significance of Walt's remark. This happened to be the last week that the fellows who were leaving Walt were going to work there.

DP: They were going to work for Charlie Mintz?

WJ: Yes. Walt and Roy had lost the copyright to the Oswald [the Lucky Rabbit] character. They had lost their release. They had nothing. And, of course, you know the story: [cartoon distributor Charlie] Mintz and [Margaret] Winkler had found out that Walt didn't make any of the drawings, and they thought, "Well the guy doesn't do anything. We are just carrying him. We'll hire the people who draw the pictures and cut out his profit and we'll make that much more." This happened to him again later on. There was an individual named [Pat] Powers who thought the same thing. Each one of them found out to their dismay that Walt *did* contribute something.

DP: Ben Sharpsteen once said that he thought if they were smart, they would have tried to hire Walt Disney and forget about everybody else.

WJ: Forget everybody else because what Walt did could be done with Walt and quite a few other people. You could leave any of *us* out of it and it would have been the same, but you leave him out and it wouldn't.

Let me go just one step farther and wind up the thing I got into with myself. I waited until everybody was gone and then finally the bosses were going and I figured I'd get locked in, so I'd better leave. They hadn't told me to come back and I wasn't pushing my luck by asking, so since they didn't say "Don't," I didn't say anything but goodbye. They paid me for the week. I got, if I remember correctly, either $16 or $18. In 1928, that was very satisfactory. So since they didn't say to not come back, I came back the next week. It went on that way for quite a long time. It was a long time before anybody indicated that it was all right for me to work there. Of course, they were busy with a lot more important things than whether some new kid was there or not.

DP: Yes, but for you it would be—

WJ: For me it was life or death practically because I desperately wanted to work on animated cartoons.

Can I step farther with a thing that's of personal interest to me and might be of interest to you? My desire to work in cartoons and finding Walt when I did and as I did and his being willing to hire me in spite of my shortcomings and to hang onto me in spite of my continued shortcomings, explains one difference that you may find in the attitude I will express to you about the studio from that of some others that you may talk to. My relationship to Walt and Roy was a different one from almost everyone else there. Almost all of the others were working for a man who was their boss. It was a job; they knew how to do it; they liked to do it; they did it well; they enjoyed their work; and they had whatever relationship they did with Walt. Mine was different. Walt was the person who knew how to do the thing that I desperately needed to find out how to do, which was how to make animated cartoons, and he was good enough to be showing me how to do it. Not only that, he was paying me while I was learning. So Walt was my guru. He was like a second father to me. So you may find if you ask about things that I'll express a slightly different point of view than some others.

DP: It seems that everybody came to work there in a slightly different way.

WJ: Oh, yes. Ben Sharpsteen, for instance, came in as a man who was, I think, a little older than Walt. Certainly more experienced in a worldly way. Ben had a college education. Walt didn't, which Walt as well as I felt the lack of. Ben was an experienced animator. Walt was not an artist; he didn't animate any more. He had the ideas all right. Walt and Roy were learning how to be businessmen. Ben already knew how to be a business man. Ben came in in a way that he could contribute something that us raw kids, who just came there fresh out of school, couldn't do. So there again, it's a completely different relationship. Ben still had all the same loyalty to Walt that I had and I'm sure the same affection for Walt and Roy that I had, but it was a completely different relationship.

DP: I think that Ben [Sharpsteen] felt under pressure, being hired as an experienced "New York Animator," to produce something that Walt would like. I guess it was a different kind of pressure than you might have experienced.

WJ: Yes. It was pressure on all of us. We were led; we weren't pushed. Walt was never somebody who got behind and shoved and said, "You go there." Walt always said, "Come on, this is where we're going." You followed him and worked awful hard to keep up.

DP: That is what I've gathered, that you went into a lot of areas that you might never have thought of attempting on your own.
WJ: Yes.

DP: When you went to work there, how many employees were there that first week?
WJ: I was number 13. That's my lucky number, I guess. The second week, I was closer to the top. Of course, that was my great good fortune. So when it came to more people coming to the studio, there was plenty of room at the top, and as far up as I could go, it was open. I eventually went a step beyond where I belonged and felt a little uncomfortable there. My ambition was to become an animator, but Walt was right. I didn't have the ability as a draftsman to compete with the good artists who came later on. I did animate for a few years, and when I simply couldn't keep up with the competition, Walt did the thing that was so characteristic of him: instead of kicking me out, he kicked me upstairs and made a director out of me. I had absolutely no qualifications to be a director, but Walt pointed his finger at me and said I was a director, so I had to try to be one. And I tried desperately to be one for years.

DP: Were you and Dave Hand the first directors after Walt? I assume that Walt directed the first films.
WJ: At first, Walt did everything. Yes, that's right. He really saw to it that the stories were shaped up. Ub did the layout at first, such as they were. They were just a bunch of thumbnail sketches. The animators made their own background drawings from Ub's sketches. Walt, of course, directed them. At first, the pictures were silent. Then things got quite a bit more complicated when sound came in, but Walt still did the directing until Bert Gillett came out from the East. And Bert Gillett, I don't think, moved right away into directing. It is my recollection that he did a little bit of animation first, but he seemed to be more often in there at first helping Walt with story, helping him to shape things up.

I am not sure, but he may have made a few of the thumbnail sketches, too, along with Ub. Everybody just did whatever needed to be done in those days.

But it was not too long until there were two series of cartoons—the Silly Symphonies and the Mickey Mouse cartoons. Ub Iwerks was in charge of the Sillies and Bert Gillett of the Mickeys. They weren't called directors. Walt regarded them as story men. He still called me a story man for a long time after I was actually a director, but I was doing all the things that they later said directors were doing. So really, if you accept the term *director* for the one who did what was more like an associate producer for Walt, then Bert Gillett and Ub Iwerks were first. Then Walt kicked me upstairs into directing next, and I think Dave Hand may have stepped in briefly when Ub left to finish handing out a picture that Ub had started. But then I think he went back into animation. I became a director after Ub left, and for a while there were two directors, Bert Gillett and myself. And after Bert left, I am not sure whether it was Ben or Dave who picked up directing next. They were not too far apart.

DP: I think it might have been Dave, because Ben has said that he was doing some kind of sub-directing at times for you and Dave.
WJ: Yes, Ben did have a department of younger apprentices. Ben would pick up a scene or a whole series of scenes from a director and then he would farm these out to these apprentices, and he would oversee what they did and help them learn how to be animators. He did that for a while before he began to direct, and I guess probably Dave began to direct during that time. Dick Huemer had a turn at directing for two pictures.

DP: Were they *Goofy and Wilbur* and *The Whalers*?
WJ: Yeah.

DP: He always mentions those two. He kids that those two were the best shorts because he directed them. It has become a standard joke when I talk to him.

WJ: I'll tell you one on Dick Huemer. Dick Huemer used to come out of the sweat box mumbling, "These doggone directors! You do a nice job of animation and they want the thing changed. You go into the sweat box and you can't win. You just can't win." Then Dick got to direct two pictures and I heard Dick saying as he came out of the sweat box, "These lousy animators! You hand a good scene to them and they turn in some other thing and then they don't want to fix it up. You can't win."

DP: Going back to the early days again, I read an account of the evening when you, Walt, Ub, and Roy put on a sound performance of a portion of *Steamboat Willie* for your wives and girlfriends. Would you describe that experience?

WJ: How long an answer do you want?

DP: As long as you would like.

WJ: When sound pictures first came in, they played a record that ran in sync with the film. This was fine except for one thing: when the film would break, the projectionist wouldn't replace the frames that were gone with blank frames. He would just splice the two good frames together. So the longer a picture was run, the longer one print was used in the theater, the shorter it got. Consequently, the later you got into the picture, the farther it was out of sync. Naturally, sound was not a very great thing, not until they found a way to put sound on film.

Now at the studio in those days, when Walt would start on a new picture, we would always have a gag meeting, usually at his house or Roy's house. Usually Walt would have a basic idea for the picture: a locale, an incident, a something or other. Sometimes not. Sometimes it would be, "What ideas have you got about what it would be good to make a picture about?" In any event, we'd either begin to gag Walt's synopsis or determine something or other the picture would be about. We would all just come out with all the ideas we had.

Well at one of these gag meetings, Walt said, "I've just heard that they've invented a way to put sound on film." He said, "Now that they can get sound on film, they're not going to have the trouble that they had with these discs. If the film breaks and gets patched wrong, it'll still fit, because the sound will be right on the same piece of film with the picture. Before long, there are not going to be any more silent films. Before long, everything will be sound. I wonder if there's a way that we could put sound with cartoons. I know how fast the film is going to go. The film is going to go ninety feet a minute. But how in hell do you tell how fast the music is going to go? How do you know how fast the sound is going to go?"

Nobody at the studio was a musician and that included me, too. But my mother did teach piano lessons. I was too obstinate when I was a kid to take them, but I did learn a few things, and among other things I learned what a metronome was and how it worked. So I told Walt, "I can show you how fast music will go." The next day, I brought my mother's metronome down to the studio and I could set it so it would "tick" every eight frames, every twelve frames, etc. It was just mathematics. I could also play a few tunes on a mouth organ, so I could set the thing ticking and play my mouth organ and Walt could see how fast the music would go. It was on that basis that *Steamboat Willie* was planned. That was the third Mickey Mouse cartoon. He made two silent ones.

DP: *Plane Crazy* and—

WJ: *Gallopin' Gaucho*. But *Steamboat Willie* was planned to have sound, and it was planned to have sounds that would happen at certain exact places in the picture, so that the score could be made separately from the picture and the two would still fit later on.

Now the business of trying out the first little part of it. I've read about this a whole lot of times and there's a point that I think is very important that I don't hear ever brought out. In the sound pictures that they made at that time, they would photograph the action and record the sound simultaneously, so that if somebody spoke a line, the dialogue would be recorded. Just a matter of mechanically putting it in sync and it looked like it was the person up there talking to you. Somebody would come into a room and slam the door and they would record the sound of the door getting slammed. It would seem to you as though you heard the door close when you saw the picture in the theater. Now when you see a cartoon, the drawings don't make any noise, so we had to work out

a different way of recording them. But in addition, there was another
thing that Walt had enough sense to realize that the rest of us didn't
think of. People are used to seeing people make noises, sounds, speak
and say words. They are used to hearing a noise if some object drops.
People are not used to hearing drawings make a noise. Walt's point was:
will the people believe that the sound is coming from the drawing or
will they just think there's somebody up there behind the screen talking
while the picture is running? Will this be effective? Will they believe the
cartoons?

This, of course, was a terribly important thing as to whether the
cartoons would be believable, something Walt went after that other
cartoon studios didn't. This was what made his Mickey Mouse and other
pictures so terribly popular. Walt wanted people to believe his characters
were actual things, not just drawings jumping around on the screen, and
that they were real, individual beings with minds of their own and individual personalities of their own. He had a great drive in that direction,
and this was the difference in really getting across to an audience. Most
of the rest of us didn't have a real appreciation of that until years later.
We just did what Walt wanted us to do.

In any event, Walt needed to know before he invested an awful lot
of money, which he didn't have much of, whether the sound cartoon
would be an effective thing. So after a few scenes had been animated,
and while the rest of the picture was being worked on, Walt had those
scenes inked and painted and had backgrounds made. They were the
scene of the steamboat coming around the bend and the scene of the
captain, Pegleg Pete, and Mickey, doing whatever he was doing and
then bumping into the captain. I forget what it was, some little incident that got him in trouble with the captain. Walt had these scenes
photographed, developed, printed, and sent back from the laboratory so
he could project them and we could make sounds and judge whether it
seemed like they were coming from the characters and from the action
on the screen.

He didn't have a projection room. He had a projector that made an
awful lot of noise when it ran, a real clatter. So that projector was set
up outside the studio at one end of a long room, so the picture could

be projected in through a window. Roy Disney stood out there in the
dark and ran the projector. In this way, the clatter of the projector didn't
interfere with the sound. Walt's office opened into the other end of this
long room, and it had a door with a glass window, so we were able to
close the door, stand there in a little group, huddled together, and look
through the window and see out into the room. A bed sheet was hung
up across the room, so the projector projected the image on one side and
we could see the reverse image through the bed sheet on the other side
when the lights were turned out. Walt made the little sounds for Mickey.
Nobody else seemed to be able to get a little falsetto voice quite as well
as Walt, so he made Mickey's little sounds and he also made the sounds
that Pegleg Pete made, whatever they were. I don't think there were any
words. Somebody, I don't remember who, did the whistling. We had
various things; we had cigar boxes that we could hit with pencils, we had
something that we could hit that made a sound like a gong for a bell.
Somebody made a sound like a boat whistle, and Johnny Cannon was
real good at making funny noises with his mouth. He could imitate all
kinds of sounds vocally and he made a pretty good chug-chug sound for
the steamboat. I had my mouth organ and I played the *Steamboat Bill*
tune. So the group of us supplied the music, dialogue, and sound effects.

Roy's instructions were to run it, rethread it, run it, and rethread
it until further notice. Ub Iwerks had constructed a speaker out of a
radio, and he took a telephone apart and somehow or other constructed
a microphone out of that, which you're not supposed to do, but he did
anyway. In any event, we had something that worked for a microphone
in Walt's office by the door where we were looking through the glass.
Behind the screen, Ub had positioned this speaker from the radio set.
For an audience, we brought our wives and girlfriends. Janie, my wife
now, was my girlfriend then. Walt's wife, Roy's wife, and Ub's wife were
also there and Walt's sister-in-law, Hazel. I believe that was the audience. We ran the thing several times, then rehearsed it, and got pretty
good at hitting these things off right in sync with the picture. After we
had gone through it and done it pretty well, Walt went out to find out
what had happened. I guess we probably had had quite a few not very
good rehearsals; nobody out there was very impressed. They were just

talking about things and hadn't really been paying much attention. Walt had the rest of us go through it while he looked. And then we took turns and everybody went out and had a look at it. Somebody ran the projector for Roy so he could come in and look at it. When I went out, there wasn't any music. When Walt went out, the Mickey sounds and the dialogue weren't too good, and so on. But we all had a turn looking at it to see if it was believable and the consensus was that it did seem as though the sounds came from the characters when they were synched well enough and that it was a worthwhile thing to go ahead with.

DP: Did you have any idea that it might catch on like it did or were you all surprised?

WJ: Well, I didn't. I was just so thrilled with the idea of having sound with pictures. Anything to do with animation was a terrific thing with me. The idea of animation with sound—I could hardly sleep that first night after that gag meeting. I was so excited about being allowed to work on a thing like this that I didn't have really any thought about the business end of it—the audience, that sort of thing. I wasn't doing what I was doing for an audience so as to make money. I was doing it for the love of doing it. I'm sure of one thing though: all of us during all those years—especially during the thirties—had no idea at all that this many years later, anybody would be interested in what we were doing then. Had I had any idea, I would have kept a diary. How I wish I had! And I'm sure if the studio had had any idea of all this interest later on, they would have kept better records of what was done. They don't even know who directed some of the shorts. They have a "guess-timate" that they go on. So to answer your question, I don't know who may have foreseen that the thing would be very successful. I certainly didn't. Success to me at that time was a matter of Walt still continuing to have a studio where I could help make cartoons.

DP: I want to ask you about Ub Iwerks. I have read different accounts of his departure from the studio and then his return. One account indicated that there were some hard feelings. How do you think Walt accepted his leaving and then his return? Were they friendly after Ub came back? It seems to me that things must not have been too bad if Ub stayed on as long as he did.

WJ: I did not ever hear or see any indication of any bad feeling between Walt and Ub, either immediately before or after he left, and especially not after he came back. When Ub came back, he was very quickly put in complete charge of the Special Effects Department, which was the sort of thing that Ub really loved to do. That was right up his alley. It's hard for me to believe that Walt would have put him in a spot like that right away if there had been any reluctance to take him back at all. As a matter of fact, there was no reason why Walt should have let him come back if he didn't want to. I never saw any evidence. I heard nothing of any sort of hard feelings. I don't know that there weren't. I don't know that there was not some unpleasantness, but I don't know that there was.

DP: From the different people I've talked to, I have heard that Walt could be very kind, but he could also be rough with people.

WJ: Oh, yes, Walt could be rough. My own personal experience with Walt was that he was unbelievably kind and generous with me, that he put up with things from me that he shouldn't have, that he went along with me way beyond what a man should have in helping me to fill a position that I wasn't really, *wasn't really*, well qualified to fill. I was like a plough horse in a stable of race horses. I could whip myself up and I could get to the finish line all right, if it didn't matter who got there first, but I did what I did by working harder and longer than the other fellows, envying the guys who could write the stuff out and have a wonderful time while they were doing it.

DP: I am sure that your dedication was something he appreciated.

WJ: Walt appreciated loyalty and you can see why, with his early experiences of people walking out on him one after another. As long as you'd try hard, Walt would work with you. I saw him do this with other people besides myself. I saw him take people who weren't making it in one position—they weren't worth their salt—and try them in another place and then try them in another place. He would find places for them to work in his studio to see if maybe they could cut the mustard there. He was very reluctant to kick anybody out who worked hard for him and was loyal to him and was really trying hard to help him make his pictures.

But on the other hand, Walt could be awfully rough. He could make you feel bad when he wanted to. Of course, it was easy to make me feel bad, because I wanted more than anything else to please Walt. As I say, he was not just a boss to me; there was more than that involved. So I always felt really terrible when I didn't come across with something that he wanted.

There was another thing about Walt. When he would get an idea for a cartoon, he would picture it in his mind so thoroughly and so completely that when the thing came out, if some part of it wasn't quite the way he thought it was going to be, then it had shortcomings for him. Consequently, it was seldom, I think, that a picture came out that wasn't a little bit of a letdown to Walt from what he had expected and thought and hoped it would be. As a result of that and maybe other things, Walt was sparing with praise. He didn't usually come around and say, "You've done a great job." That was a pretty unusual thing. I think there were maybe three or four times that he came right out and said, "Jack, that was a good picture." And, of course, after that, I didn't touch the ground for days. Usually the first thing that happened was that he would go over every shortcoming in the picture. Once in a while, it would happen that he didn't find much fault with it and I always figured I'd done a hell of a good job when he didn't pick it to pieces.

DP: Ben told me that sometimes at the preview, if a picture didn't go over very well, you would hear about it from Walt right there in the lobby.
WJ: Yes. The first picture that Walt had me direct was *The Castaway* [1931], a Mickey Mouse short subject. I got to be a director by a mis-understanding. I had wanted to animate a whole picture, but I used the wrong word. I didn't realize that I was not a very good animator. I caught Walt in a good mood one time and I said, "Walt, if it should ever work out this way, I'd like it if you would let me handle a whole picture myself."

He said, "Yeah, yeah, I'll think about that, Jack."

I thought, "Well, I've muffed that one." I didn't realize it at the time, but I had given him the wrong idea. When I said "handle," I meant "animate." But it meant "direct" to Walt, and we never did get this misunderstanding cleared up.

Later on, he called me into his office one day and said, "Jack, you told me you wanted to do a picture yourself." He said, "I've hired a new musician. I don't know if he's any good. I'd like you to work with him and see if he can do anything for us." This was Frank Churchill ["Who's Afraid of the Big Bad Wolf," *Snow White, Dumbo, Bambi*]. He turned out to be any good! Walt said, "I've got a lot of pieces that I've cut out of pictures. I'm behind schedule, and if we can salvage some of these and get a picture out where we don't have to do very much animation, I won't sink a lot of money in it and I can try this musician to see if he can do anything." Walt was trying me out, but he didn't put it that way. He said, "I won't have a big investment in it. You take these trims from these pictures, run them, and see what you can come up with in a story where you can tie them together and use as many of them as you can and just animate the hookups with new animation." With the diversity that was there, the only idea I could come up with was to have Mickey on a boat like Robinson Crusoe that was shipwrecked on a desert island and a lot of stuff from the ship washed ashore. That might account for the fact that he had a grand piano, that he had some adventures with a lion and with a monkey, and I forget what else. It was a hodgepodge of stuff. That was the only way that I could see to tie it together. So Walt okayed that and we put it through.

Partly because I was so inexperienced, partly because the different pieces of material weren't tied together very convincingly into a story, and partly because they were also the stuff that had been culled out of all the other pictures—for some reason or other they were a drag to the pictures or they didn't measure up to expectations—the result was not anything that overwhelmed the audience. When the picture was done, we all went to the preview. I could tell that the picture was not going over real well. So I went out in the lobby and there was Walt over in one corner. He had his overcoat all up around his ears, his hat clear down over his eyes, and his hands in his pockets with his shoulders up around his ears. Roy was talking to him. There was a little crowd of animators around him and I walked unobtrusively past. I didn't stop, but on the way by, I could hear Roy saying, "But Walt, it doesn't look like a Disney picture. I don't know if we ought to release it."

Walt said, "We've got to release it to meet our schedule, Roy."

And Roy was saying, "But Walt—" I got out of earshot then!

But Walt was very nice about it; he didn't scold me. This was something else about Walt, as far as Walt's relationship with me was concerned. There were many times when I goofed in a way that cost Walt a lot of money. I made some very serious miscalculations in judgment. Walt was always very kind about them. He pointed them out but he wasn't rough. These were real boo-boos that I had pulled. On the other hand, all the things that weren't important, that I knew weren't really a matter of life or death, he didn't miss a one in pointing them out, and he was plenty rough about it sometimes. When he was through, you weren't going to make that mistake again if you could help it. He could be rough, but when it came to things that really mattered, my experience with him was that he was unbelievably generous and understanding.

DP: It sounds like he shared the affection for you that you had for him.

WJ: I don't know why he should have.

DP: When you did make the move from animation to direction, aside from the apprehension of moving into that area, were you disappointed that you were leaving animation?

WJ: Right off, of course, I didn't know I was leaving animation. I thought I was going to animate the whole picture. After Frank and I had worked out the timing of it and the score for it, I took the first scene of hookups to be animated back to my room and I started to animate it. Walt came by, after I'd been there a day or two, and he said, "What are you doing, Jack?"

I said, "I'm animating my picture, Walt."

He said, "Oh—oh, yeah. Hey, Rudy Zamora is going to be out of work pretty soon. Would you mind giving him a scene?"

I said, "No, no, I'll do that."

This thing kept up and all I got to do was one scene on the picture. After I had it all handed out, I was back in my room animating on the scene when he came by. He looked in the door and said, "Jack, what are you doing?"

I said, "I'm animating that scene I've got left in my picture, Walt."

He said, "Oh, yeah. Have you thought any more about your next story? You know, you're going to have a lot of men out of work. You're going to have to hand out some scenes to them." That's how I discovered that I had become a director. So after that, I was so busy trying to keep scenes coming out to the animators that I didn't have much time for anything else.

But the answer is yes, I had many, many regrets that I did not make it as an animator. It didn't take me long to realize that there was such a difference between what I was doing as an animator and what these better artists and more experienced animators were able to do that I could clearly understand what Walt had done. But I didn't understand it right away. I had many regrets about leaving animation, but I was lucky that I was able to do it, because I was able to continue to be associated with making animated cartoons. But I always felt myself to be at a terrific disadvantage in directing the efforts of these men who were capable of doing what I couldn't do.

DP: But they probably couldn't do what you were doing. I'm sure that not all animators can become directors.

WJ: Maybe they could, maybe they couldn't. That is neither here nor there. If I could do both, I wouldn't have been directing. But in order to coordinate the efforts of the different men, it was necessary sometimes to tell them what they had to change. Also, there were many times when I didn't feel that they were getting the thing in their scene that Walt was looking for, and in those cases, I had to talk them into making changes. It was difficult controlling the collective efforts of such a very talented and often opinionated group of artists.

DP: I am sure that it would be difficult to direct a group of creative people. They would be inclined to be more temperamental and concerned about what they were creating.

WJ: Well, if you had a bunch of bookkeepers there working with arithmetic, if it's two and two, it comes out four, and if it doesn't come out four, then they haven't done it correctly. With anything creative, it's quite a different thing. A creative thing is a very personal thing and I was always aware of the fact that it was the animators who made the pictures that you saw on the screen. I was *always* aware of the fact that all the work that all the rest of us did—in story, in direction, in music, in everything else—should be slanted toward trying to help the animator get the best result he could on the screen, and that it was *his* result on the screen. So I had tremendous respect for all these men I worked with, and as you say, it was a little difficult sometimes to know how to control them.

I think that my experience in this respect was quite different from that of the other directors. Ben was a good artist and a good animator and he knew the business. When he was directing another animator, it was "me talking to you—I'm on an equal basis, you can't do something I can't do, and I'm telling you how to do it anyway." Dave Hand likewise. Bert Gillett likewise. Name the directors, they knew how to do it. I didn't. I think that this gave me an understanding of Walt and his situation with the studio that a lot of others may not have had. Walt also was not a very good artist. Walt also was not a good animator. Walt did not have the education that a lot of these people had who were working for him. Walt did not have a lot of the things that they could bring in. There were some excellent excellent artists who came to work for Walt later on. There were musicians working for Walt and Walt didn't know anything about music, and yet Walt was the boss. They were his pictures. He was responsible for them. They went out under his name and he wanted them a certain way. Can you imagine? I thought *I* had trouble in the sweatbox with the animators. Can you imagine the position of being Walt and having to be in charge of all this? These were temperamental guys, and a lot of them didn't have the feeling for Walt that I had. Some of them even had hostility and still Walt had to control all this. Now you hear a lot about Walt being rough with people. Try to imagine how you would handle all that and get those people to work together and not be a little rough now and then. So Walt had to use the spurs on us sometimes. I had an appreciation of that that a lot of others didn't. I had a little bit of the difficulty that Walt must have had a great deal of.

DP: I guess there was also a problem of keeping people from dominating a picture, a particular animator or musician or someone, from—
WJ: —from taking over and dominating the situation. And, of course, they were Walt Disney pictures. He didn't want me to make Wilfred Jackson pictures. And I'll tell you another thing: Walt was *the* boss, he was *the* head man there, and I think he handled it wonderfully well.

DP: Following up on our discussion of his relations with his staff, what were your reactions to the studio strike in the early 1940s? Did it seem to break down the "Hyperion Days" feeling [the atmosphere that existed at the studio located on Hyperion Avenue from 1926–1940], or was that already disappearing? In many accounts, people talk about how they felt during the making of *Snow White* and prior to that, during the making of the short subjects. The excitement and almost family feeling of those times are contrasted to the period after the move to Burbank. In many of these accounts, people see the strike as breaking up or at least adversely affecting a paternalistic feeling that had existed at the studio.
WJ: That is a big subject. It's hard to give you a concise answer. I've given you the background on myself. You can understand that I was a company man; I was not a union man. I was more than a company man. I didn't ever feel that I was working for Walt Disney Productions. I always felt that I was working for Walt Disney personally, that I was trying to accomplish whatever he set me to do. I had this feeling for him that was different from what most of them had, so I didn't really have a very normal reaction to the strike at all. As far as I was concerned, people who were working for Walt should be trying to do what he wanted them to do. If they didn't want to do it or didn't like what he paid, then they ought to find something else to do. And I had no patience with people who wanted to make any trouble or be an impediment to what Walt wanted to do. So as far as I was concerned, the strike was wrong and it shouldn't have happened. This was my—I'll say childlike—reaction to it.

On the other hand, a lot of my very best friends were out there walking the picket line. I had a lot of respect for some of the people who were out there and I realized that they weren't just a bunch of darn fools, just a bunch of mischief-makers, so there must be something to it, but I felt that they were wrong and that they should not be doing it. I also had a very definite feeling that the strike was being instigated by forces from outside the studio more than it was from forces within the studio. There were some willing accomplices within. I may be completely wrong; that was just my personal feeling.

DP: I think that a lot of people have said some of the same things.

WJ: Now as to the feeling within the studio and how it changed after that. Of course, the strike was a very traumatic thing, not only for us as individuals, but for the business itself. The business was hit by the strike at a time when it was on the verge of being in trouble anyway, and the strike didn't help. It was a terribly disruptive thing, because when the strike was settled, the studio was required to accept a quota of strikers in relation to non-strikers, so that they were taken back not for what they could contribute, but arbitrarily by numbers. They had to keep people or fire people or they had to hire back or not hire back people by numbers, not as individuals. Now, when you're working with a bunch of creative artists, they are not just a bunch of numbers. So this thing played havoc with some of the crews. In my own case, I lost my head layout man and my two assistant layout men. I've never been sure why my crew was decimated more than some others. Maybe I didn't go in and make enough fuss about it; maybe I didn't know what was going on until it was too late. I'm pretty dumb about things. I can always tell afterwards what was going on, but at the time, I'm just a babe in the woods. However, this didn't only happen to me. Crews that had been working well together were broken up. The schedule of pictures was disrupted terribly.

Now there is another thing about the old Hyperion Street spirit. When the place was very small and growing, everybody had close personal contact with each other. The studio was not big. Walt was the kind of person who did not want you to just slavishly work. He wanted you to work creatively. He didn't care, in my own case, whether I sat in my chair eight hours each day or whether I was in my chair less time. He didn't care if I roamed around the studio talking to my friends. The point was: did I get my work done and did I do it well? And that was how he judged all the rest of them. As a result, there was not a strict discipline—far from it. We were rather encouraged to go around and talk with each other and to contribute our ideas to what the other fellows were doing and to seek out their ideas on what we were doing. We were all working together selflessly, trying to make a good product. And this, of course, made it a thrilling place to work and knit us together into a tight brotherhood, so that we—all of us—felt very close to each other like members of a family.

As the studio grew, there got to be more and more people. First of all, there were so many people there that we could not visit each other as often. We could not be as close to what each other was doing. People became specialized; they started working in different departments. It became necessary for a director to work with the head of a department and to work through him with his people and not have the same contact as before with the people who were actually doing the work. To the extent that I was able to, I always liked to personally contact the individual who did the work. It seemed so much better, but you simply couldn't do that. When there got to be thousands instead of hundreds of people there, this in itself—strike or no strike—was going to mean that you couldn't have the same tightly knit feeling. It is like the difference between a squad of soldiers who get in and out of a pickle together in a war—you come out and boy, you've got a brotherhood there!—and the whole company. You feel a sameness with them and you're all fighting together in the same war, but when you come out, you don't feel as close. So this had a lot to do with it. The strike happened to come at a time when this was going to happen anyway.

Another thing that happened when we moved from the Hyperion Street studio to the Burbank studio was that we moved from a very inefficiently designed studio into a very efficiently designed studio. The Burbank studio was one where you could do what you did with much greater facility. The Hyperion Street studio was something that grew in an organic manner. It started with a little place and things were added on. As you needed room for somebody else, a little room was added on. It is possible to be comfortable and to function in a place like that in a way that you can't in an efficiently built factory. So we, in a way, moved from our home on Hyperion Street into a mouse factory.

All these things were involved, but as I have said, the strike came right at the time when it was going to happen anyway and it precipitated the thing. The old family feeling—whether it was really there or not—was carried on anyway even though we weren't functioning that way. You don't realize—it changes so gradually—you don't know it's gone. Then suddenly there is a strike and half the people don't come back. As far as you're concerned, the wrong half is there anyway. The ones who were out must have felt about the ins the way the ones that were in felt about the outs. So all of a sudden, this is brought into sharp focus.

At the same time, the studio gets into financial trouble. We were going along before that fat, dumb, and happy. *Snow White* was a wonderful success. It looked like you made a cartoon feature and, oh boy! you can spend the money on it, so we were lavishly working on *Bambi* and *Fantasia*. It turned out that *Pinocchio* didn't do quite as well. The reality of the situation was beginning to come before us. All of a sudden, we had to be more businesslike. I had to stick closer to my budget. Up to that point, if I did what Walt wanted, nobody scolded me too much; it didn't matter how far I went over budget if I didn't go too far over schedule and get them into too much trouble with release dates, I could make the changes that Walt wanted. I now found that I had to watch out that I didn't do everything Walt wanted me to do if it was not in the best interests of coming reasonably close to my budget, reasonably close to my deadline. All of a sudden, I had to grow up. Everything changed at the same time. You can pinpoint the strike and say, "This is when it happened," but I don't think the strike did it all.

DP: It must have been difficult to not do everything that Walt wanted in order to stay within your budget and schedule.

WJ: It was a long time before I really adjusted and found out what it was that I was supposed to do. In the meantime, I floundered around and did everything wrong. People didn't come out and lay this down on the line. It all just happened a little at a time.

DP: You directed some of the sequences in *Snow White*, didn't you?
WJ: I did.

DP: Which ones?
WJ: Without running the picture, I am not going to be able to remember all of them. The one that comes to mind first is what we called the entertainment sequence, after the dwarfs discover Snow White in their little cottage. Then there was the sequence with the witch, a kind of heavy sequence where she was making her brew and the plot was thickening. As a matter of relief, we came back to the dwarfs' cottage that night and they were entertaining Snow White with the singing and dancing of *The Silly Song*. That part, beginning with the dwarfs' cottage at night with Sneezy blowing the place apart with his sneeze and breaking up the party and on into the part where the dwarfs went to sleep that night, up through the snoring sequence—that whole sequence was mine. The ending of the picture was mine, from the time after the witch has been killed, when we come back to the dwarfs all together there grieving, to the end of the picture.

DP: That is one of the most moving scenes in the picture. It still retains its emotional impact.
WJ: In spite of the terrible animation at the end, of the Prince and the girl as they go away, in spite of that, it is a moving thing. It had heart in it. Again, look how wonderfully Walt handled this whole thing with Snow White. You couldn't, with our animation techniques then—you probably still can't now—take a young girl and with animated drawings put across a really sympathetic character in a way that could compete with a good actress well supported in a live-action picture. There is no way that it could be done. As good as animators are today, I still don't think you could do it. See how Walt overcame that with those little dwarfs. The audience could care about them. Whether they cared what happened to the girl or not, they could care how the dwarfs felt about it.

And through the dwarfs, Walt turned their sympathy on at the end of the picture. It was a masterful thing.

DP: In contrast to *Snow White*, when *Fantasia* came out and didn't do as well as the studio had hoped, was there a feeling that the public didn't appreciate what was in the picture?

WJ: I felt that we were victims of circumstances on that, because when the picture was run with *Fantasound* at the Cathay Circle Theater and we came down to the finish of the thing, you couldn't have asked for a more tremendous, overwhelming audience reaction than we had. Walt had more planned for the *Fantasound* system than ever came out. On the way through production, money caught up with us. He had planned parts in the picture where the three speakers behind the screen would move the sound, carry it back and forth across the screen to work with the action. This is old stuff now. But in those days, it had not happened. You didn't experience sounds around you unless you were immersed in a real thing. To have a picture do that was something else, and I tell you, the audience loved it. However, we couldn't afford to equip many theaters with the *Fantasound*, and the theaters couldn't afford to equip themselves. Motion pictures were falling upon hard times very suddenly, and for the most part, the people who saw *Fantasia* just saw it flat. I think that is one big reason why it didn't go over too well.

There were other factors, too. The times were changing, what was going on in the world when *Fantasia* came out. It's like what happened to *Bambi*. *Bambi* came out when we were involved in a war. Nobody got excited about somebody shooting a deer when their own brother was over there getting shot at. Later on when *Bambi* came out again, it wowed them.

There were darn few people who had the ability that Walt had, to be able to guess what people would want to see by the time you could get a feature-length cartoon made. It takes quite a while to make all those drawings. To decide now what will go big enough with an audience to pay off in a year or two or three is something else.

DP: Bob Thomas wrote that there were some problems involved with the transition from live action to animation in *The Song of the South*. Was that something you were involved with?

WJ: I did all the animation and combination animation and live-action sequences, so whatever he was talking about, I did.

DP: He was talking about the transitional problems in moving from the live-action footage where Uncle Remus says something like, "This is a Zip a Dee-Doo-Dah Day," to the animated footage. Apparently there was some problem with rear projection.

WJ: Let me tell you my version of what happened there. We had planned to have a rear projection scene behind Uncle Remus as he sat there and began to tell the story to the boy. This rear projection scene had a live-action background on it, the same background that was behind him in scenes before when he had sat down in his cabin. We cross dissolved—we had a lab dissolve made from that to a cartoon background—and this was to happen as he was talking. I can't remember the exact words, but it was where he was leading into the first "Zip" in the song: "in dem days the creatures was closer to the folks, the folks was closer to the creatures, and 'twas better all 'round," and something about "It happened on one of them zip-a-dee-doo-dah days. Zip—" and he went away into the song. During the last line of dialogue, it was our intention to have the background change to a background of a springtime blue sky with some blossoms in it, and from that, we were going to cut back to the live-action set where Uncle Remus was to walk forward. As we cut back, we were to cut and the camera was to be dollying on the cut and he was to be getting up and starting to walk forward following the camera as it trucked back and we would then disclose this cartoon setup that he was in with the butterflies coming in, a bird on each shoulder, and whatever other creatures were around.

My sequence, due to scheduling, got delayed and delayed, and the opening of this sequence finally was put off, due to live-action retakes until the very last week of shooting. This scene had had all kinds of difficulties in getting photographed, but we finally had gotten a print

that was all right and we had our rear projection set up. We got down
to the next to the last day and we shot the scene. Late that night, the
word came that there was difficulty, that Technicolor wasn't able to get a
satisfactory result with what we had shot.

Walt didn't come to the set very often. This day Walt came. We had
to be able to get from the live-action picture into the cartoon somehow.
So Walt called all of us together, and we sat around in those canvas
chairs, and Walt said, "The rear projection isn't working. Jack, what ideas
have you got? What alternative did you have?"

Well I hadn't been sleeping the night before, but I still didn't come
up with any ideas that I thought were a good way of doing it. I said,
"Walt, I can't think of a satisfactory way. I don't know any other way to
do it than just cut back from Uncle Remus, from a live-action scene to a
cartoon scene. We will lose a good connection, but I can't think of a way
to connect into it that will do more than just be a scene cut."

He said, "Okay."

Now this is an example of how he treated you when you goofed. I
had him in a spot, so he said, "Anybody else got any ideas?"

Perce [Pearce, associate producer] was there, the camera man and
live-action director were there, the assistant director—they were all
around and nobody had any ideas. Walt said, "Well look Gregg,"—to Gregg
Toland, the head cameraman—"would it be possible to take this scene
where Remus is talking to the boy and gradually turn down the lights so
that the whole background just becomes black, but Remus is lighted?"

Gregg said, "Oh, that can easily be done."

Walt said, "Would it be possible to do the reverse, but on signal to
suddenly have the background and everything light up?"

Gregg said, "Yes, we can do that if we can coordinate some of the gaf-
fers to suddenly remove a mask—a piece of pasteboard or board—that we
have put in front of the lights. Then the lights would suddenly go on. You
can't do it by throwing a switch, but you could do it that way."

So Walt said, "Well, then why don't we do this, since you can't think
of anything better, Jack," like I was running the thing. Walt said, "Jack,
why don't we retake that scene where Remus is talking to the boy, just
before your cartoon scene and just gradually turn the lights out on the

background, so we just have the light on his face in the dark there. Then why don't we cut in a scene of the boy listening and then why don't we cut back to Remus with the same exact lighting, except that he is in front of your cartoon background that you were going to come to after the rear projection shot. When we come back there, as he sings the first 'Zip,' why don't we have them take the covers away from the lights and just light up the set."

So that is what was done and it was a thousand percent more effective than the thing that we had been slavishly working on all the time that didn't work. This was Walt Disney working. This is my version of what happened. It was a tremendously effective thing, yet a very simple thing, but it took a creative mind that was better than mine to come up with it.

DP: After the war when *Cinderella* was released, Roy Disney referred to that year [1950] as "our Cinderella year," when the fortunes of the studio started climbing again as they would continue to do. Was the making of that film more reminiscent of the feeling that surrounded the making of *Snow White* than anything that had been done in the interim period? My impression has been that this was a happy time at the studio. Was it that way for you?

WJ: Not for me personally. I think that the happiest time I ever had working on any picture, after the first few early years, was on *The Song of the South*. That was a wonderful experience for me. I'll tell you why it was a wonderful experience: Walt was again very closely, personally involved with what we were doing. This was his first venture into live-action features, and he was quite interested in the outcome. This meant that Walt was working closely with us and this always made a thing really exciting. During the years, it had gotten so that he was trusting us to do more; he was spreading himself a little thinner and he wasn't in as often. In the early days when it was so much fun, hardly a day went by that Walt didn't drop into the office to see what you were doing and to talk things over. You could bounce your ideas off of him and tap that great mind of his and you could make your picture great by using Walt Disney. We had Walt working for *us* in those days. Later on, we were doing more of it ourselves.

Now on *The Song of the South*, I was again in very close association with Walt. Also, since this was an important thing to him, he had the cream of the animation crew on it. He had this wonderful story team, Bill Wright and Bill Peet, working together, and we had Perce Pearce as an associate producer. They were a wonderful bunch of creative guys. Ken Anderson was my head layout man. Ken and I didn't get to work together very much through the years, but that was one time we did. All of this, I think, made it the most exciting and interesting and wonderful thing I worked on.

When we got to *Cinderella*, we were much further along the path of Walt having handed more of the responsibility to us and carrying less of the full load himself. By this time, Walt was already involved in beginning his first or maybe his second live-action picture in England, and he was over there part of the time. Also he had a lot of things going here in Burbank, so he was spread thin. It was getting to the point where it was hard to get Walt in on decisions that he needed to be in on. So when it came to *Cinderella* in a way, there was much more of a challenge for we directors who had come to Walt as raw kids who knew nothing and had kind of grown up in the business. Now we had to become better executives, we had to become better businessmen, we had to use much more of our own judgment on matters that would really pay off or not pay off in the pictures. So this was not a happy thing like you say.

Now the business end of the studio was something that, as far as I was concerned, Roy Disney and his office took care of, and I'd get in trouble with his end of it if I spent too much money or took too long to get a picture out. Roy knew how to run things and with his end of it working the way he worked it, I always got my paycheck and that was great. But I didn't have to worry about that end of it, except when things got really tight. Then I'd be apprehensive that maybe the studio would close down and there wouldn't be a chance to help Walt make pictures anymore. So as to whether times got better for pictures and that sort of thing, for Roy Disney it was one thing, for me it was quite a different thing. For Roy Disney, it may have been a big sigh of relief that finally we weren't going completely into the red. For me, I didn't have the excitement of working closely with Walt Disney anymore.

Marcellite Garner

Marcellite Garner, born July 3, 1910, in Redlands, California, applied for a job at the Disney Studio in late 1929 and began work in February 1930, joining a studio staff of about thirty-five people. She was in the fledgling Ink and Paint Department but is best known for being the first voice of Minnie Mouse. Marcellite recalled that her first film as Minnie's voice was *The Cactus Kid* in 1930 (although the web site IMDB credits her with Minnie's voice back to 1928). Marcellite and Minnie were a duo in over forty cartoons, including *The Birthday Party*, *Traffic Troubles*, *Mickey Steps Out*, *The Barnyard Broadcast*, *Mickey's Revue*, *The Klondike Kid*, *Ye Olden Days*, *Mickey's Gala Premier*, *Two-Gun Mickey*, *On Ice*, *Hawaiian Holiday*, *Brave Little Tailor*, and *Mickey's Surprise Party*. She left the studio in 1941 and worked occasionally at other animation studios. She passed away in 1993.

Marcellite Garner, like Clarence Nash, served an important early role in defining the screen character she voiced. She had a cute voice—just right for Minnie—and represents a conception of voice selection for the early films and features that contrasted heavily with the casting of well-known voices in later films.

I interviewed Marcellite twice at her home in the Gold Rush community of Grass Valley. She was a delightful person to talk to and fun to be with. After our sessions, she loaned me a home movie she had taken of the studio strike in 1941. I was amazed to see color footage, up close and personal, of the picket line. The strike had become more vivid to me as I started to hear first-hand accounts from those who had experienced it, and now the live-action footage of people milling about with their well-drawn (what would you expect!) signs of protest sharpened my perception of it even more. Nothing in the footage was sinister or violent or showed the highly emotional response that developed on both sides of the strike. It just showed a group of people demonstrating in front of the Burbank studio. Some of this footage later appeared in the documentary, *Walt: The Man Behind the Myth*.

The following interview was conducted on February 12, 1977.

MG: We all started out as painters and after you learned that, then if you could ink, you went into inking, but inking was something you really had to learn to do. Not many years ago, I visited a friend, and her brother brought out the first inking I ever made of Mickey Mouse on a piece of celluloid. I couldn't believe it. Learning to control the pen on the celluloid was hard to do, and Walt demanded shaded lines in his inking which made it even harder.

DP: How did you happen to go to work there? Were you interested in art?
MG: Yes. I was going to night school at Polytechnic High School in Los Angeles. One of my classmates, Carlos Manriquez, used to say to me all the time, "You ought to come out to the studio and get a job." So one day, I decided to try it. I took some of my drawings out. It was pouring rain, I remember, and when I got in the studio, my hair was hanging down and I was a mess. I still think that's why they gave me the job, because I came out in all that horrible weather.

DP: What year would that have been?
MG: It must have been the latter part of 1929, because I think I actually started working at the studio in February of 1930.

DP: How many people worked there then?

MG: I would guess about thirty-five people including the janitor. There were just a handful of girls and a handful of animators and two or three directors.

DP: Was it still one room or had they expanded?
MG: It was the one room, and in fact, a lot of the animators were just on the other side of a partial partition from the inkers and painters. The partition was open underneath and up above. When we used to work nights and the bosses were gone, we'd shoot olive pits back and forth at each other. We were just kids. Most of us were nineteen, twenty, twenty-one, something like that. We used to have a lot of fun.

DP: Were you interviewed by Walt?
MG: No, just Hazel [Sewell, Lillian Disney's sister].

DP: What was she like?
MG: She kind of scared me a little bit, but she was nice as far as that goes. But you know, I still dream about her. I still dream about being late to work.

DP: Did she demand a lot?
MG: Not really, but I suppose I was just young and it was my first job really of any consequence. I was probably more scared of everything in general. Sometimes she could get a little bit fussy when she used to call me and say, "You didn't turn out enough drawings today. How come?"

DP: What would they expect you to turn out once you were trained?
MG: There was no numerical amount, but I guess they figured according to certain scenes that you should be able to do approximately so much. Some of the girls were much faster than others naturally. I worked into specializing in very fine inking of some of the little tiny characters that had to be done in real fine lines. For some reason, I could do it, and, of course, sometimes it took longer.

DP: Was there much turnover in Inking and Painting?

MG: Not really as I recall. A few came and went, but most of the girls stayed. We all enjoyed it, and I'll have to say that we were treated very, very well. It almost seemed to me that when the union came in, it spoiled everything. Up to that point, we used to go to the cafeteria and visit. We didn't have to pay for our coffee cake or anything, and if we were a little bit later than we were supposed to be on our breaks, nobody said anything. But after they became unionized, then we had to buy our own coffee cake, buy our own coffee, and be back at such-and-such a time.

DP: That's what I have heard, that there was the loss of a certain feeling—

MG: To be friends with someone one day and then the next day having them call you names because you go through a picket line to go to work was a bitter experience. When the union got in and these people came back to work in the studio, there wasn't the same feeling anymore. I think it destroyed something. And they said such terrible things as you went through.

DP: What did they say?

MG: I'm a lady, I can't tell you! You know, SOB and so forth—just really pretty rough talk.

DP: I take it that you were sympathetic to the studio as far as the strike is concerned.

MG: Yes I was. I couldn't see that we were not being treated fairly. People weren't so union oriented then I guess.

DP: Someone I talked to said that whether or not Walt was paternalistic, you had all the conveniences.

MG: We were just like one big family. We could take time to play around a little bit and everyone knew everyone else and there was a real good feeling. But after the union came in, it just changed, and, of course, it would have changed anyway probably, because the studio had become so much larger then and you didn't see everyone and you wouldn't have known them anyway. It went from thirty-five, more or less, up to about twenty-five hundred.

DP: How did you happen to film the strike?
MG: We had a home movie camera and I had half a roll that hadn't been used. It was a big event, so I took the camera and took pictures of it.

DP: Do you know Art Babbitt?
MG: Yes. We always felt like he was the one that got everything started. Now whether he actually participated in all the rabble rousing, I don't know. After he came to work at the studio, things were never the same. He was a pretty rough element, and we'd never had anything like that before.

DP: How long did you work at the studio?
MG: Off and on, I suppose twelve to thirteen years, but I also worked in a couple of other studios during that time.

DP: I'm sure this is a question that everybody asks you, but how did you happen to do the voice of Minnie Mouse?
MG: Well, it's so unexciting, I hate to tell it. Bert Gillett [an early director of shorts] came through the inking department one day and wanted to know if anybody could speak Spanish. I said, "Well I can't speak it but I can read it." Marge Ralston said she could too, so they took us both over to the sound stage which at that time was on Melrose. When we got there, they said they were sorry, but they had hired a Mexican woman to do it, because in that picture Minnie's really kind of cussing him out and they wanted somebody who could do it with feeling. But they said they wanted Minnie to sing and would either of us like to try out for the singing part. We were both scared to death, but I said sure I would. Marge said she wouldn't and that's all there was to it. Evidently it worked out that my voice fit the character.

DP: Did you sing *Minnie's Yoo Hoo*?
MG: I can't remember. It was back so long ago.

DP: Did anybody else do her voice?

MG: As far as I know, no. In *Steamboat Willie*, they had some girl do some screaming, and then they told me that after that, I was the only one that spoke for Minnie. When I left the studio in 1941, they did try someone else, but it's pretty hard to have two voices sound the same and it just didn't work out. So then they dropped Minnie.

DP: Do you remember the first cartoon in which you did her voice?

MG: It must have been *The Cactus Kid*.

DP: I have heard from different people that when Walt would do the Mickey Mouse voice, he wasn't the happiest person doing that.

MG: I recorded with him lots of times.

DP: Did he seem to enjoy it or seem to be annoyed at having to do it?

MG: I always thought he enjoyed it.

DP: A couple of people said that he was hard to get over there to do it.

MG: Well, now that might be. Maybe he didn't want to stop what he was doing or something, but once he got over there, he seemed to enjoy it. Of course he was great to work with. In order to set the stage for me to get the spirit of whatever Minnie was doing, he'd tell me the story and he'd *be* each character as he'd tell it. As he described that character and what it was doing, he'd just become that character. He was a wonderful actor when it comes right down to it. But he never told you if you did anything well. He would say, "You're supposed to do it well. If you do it well, there's no reason for me to say anything. If you don't, I'll tell you." But it used to be discouraging sometimes, because you'd wonder if it was all right. When I went to work at the studio, he was just like one of the kids. After all, he was only probably five or six years older than I was.

DP: Do you remember your first impressions of him?

MG: I was just scared of him. He was the big boss even if he was just a kid, but he was a lot of fun as I remember him. He used to get out on the lunch hour and play baseball with the boys. I remember one time when they were playing. Somebody hit a foul ball, and Walt said it wasn't or something. Anyway, Johnny Cannon sat on the ball. He and Walt were just going round and round like a couple of kids. But I always used to think that was wonderful, because we'd get out in a vacant lot like a bunch of kids and play. I enjoyed him, but of course, there was always that little feeling.

DP: During that time you were there, did he seem to change as the studio became more prosperous?

MG: I didn't see him as much after we moved to the new studio, just in recording sessions, but he seemed the same.

DP: When you worked in Ink and Paint, did it bother the women that women were only employed there and not in animation?

MG: No. Oh, I think there was some little feeling that there were no women in animation at that time. And they used to say that there never would be any women animators, because men couldn't be as free in the gag meetings. But when I went to work for Walter Lantz, they had a woman animator and she didn't seem to create any problems.

DP: I have read about the rules—I guess they were at the Burbank studio—that men were not supposed to be in the Ink and Paint Building and women were not supposed to be in the Animation Building.

MG: That's true.

DP: They were strict on that?

MG: Yeah, we were pretty well separated. I think the only time I ever got over there was a couple of times when I had to go over and talk to Walt about something.

DP: When the films switched to color, did that have a big impact on your work?

MG: No, except that Walt was so meticulous about the way it was done. For instance, on *Fantasia* there is a scene where the hot bubbles in the mud are breaking. Each one of the bubbles was inked in five or six different colors.

And it never showed in the picture, but you'd have maybe five shades of pink on one bubble, highlights and shaded lines and so forth. But Walt always said, "They don't notice it while it's there, but if it wasn't there, they'd notice that it was different." I suppose that's one of the things that made his cartoons better than others; he paid so much attention to details.

One thing they used in the Disney cartoons that the other studios didn't was shaded lines in inking.

DP: How does that work?
MG: Instead of being just a heavy line like most of them used, you had to make a more artistic line. For instance, if you are going around a curve, part of it would be heavy and part of it would taper out to a thin line. It was left pretty much to the inker's judgment, but you almost naturally would do it on a curved part. They wouldn't let anything go through that wasn't like that. We had little scrapers and once in a while if a line was too thick, we'd take our scraper and scrape it until it was right.

DP: That's interesting. I hadn't heard about that.
MG: I hadn't thought about it until just now. That was something that we had to learn to do.

DP: Did you feel that Disney was more concerned about quality than some of the other studios?
MG: Yes, very much so.

DP: Was it more lax at the other studios?
MG: Yes, a lot more. They weren't too concerned about how the lines looked as long as they were thick enough. But they were pretty fussy at Disney's, and it all showed up in the finished product.

DP: Were the thirties, with the success of the shorts and the acclaim that followed, an exciting time for you at the studio?
MG: It didn't feel that much to us, because we still just inked and inked! Many is the time we used to ink straight around the clock to keep the

wolf away from the door, you know. We'd go to work at eight in the morning and work until eight the next morning sometimes.

DP: Were there practical jokes or anything to break the tedium?
MG: Not particularly. Not too much. That was more in animation, because they're just a different breed of people, and when you worked with them, you started to look at life like they do. More situations seem so hilarious to someone that's been connected with the cartoon business, and to someone else, it doesn't seem funny at all.

I can tell you a little story that I think was kind of cute that happened to me. I hadn't been in the studio too long and we were working at night, when all of a sudden, I heard this terrible squealing and couldn't imagine what it was. I finally looked down under my drawing board and I'd caught a mouse by the tail. I let it go. After all, it was my close cousin! We all thought that was so funny. When you lean on the boards to ink, it pressed them down on the table. The poor little mouse thought he was in the right place, but he wasn't.

DP: Did you do any other voices when you were there?
MG: None other than maybe meowing for cats or barking for dogs or screaming in crowds and so forth, but primarily Minnie.

DP: When you went to work at other studios, how did they compare with Disney's?
MG: The others were nice for a change. I got kind of tired of working at Disney's. It's the same old story. Anything you do all the time gets tiresome. The sound work was always fun—that I enjoyed—but inking got pretty monotonous. The only time I ever really got a vacation was when I had a baby. So after a baby, I'd go to work at another studio for a while for a change of pace.

DP: Would you come back and do Minnie's voice if they needed her while you were at the other studios?
MG: I didn't work at the other studios long enough. They didn't use Minnie in every picture and sometimes there would be three or four pictures

when they wouldn't use her. I did go back once after I quit to have the last baby and did a recording. Then we moved to Los Gatos [Northern California]. It was from then on that they didn't have Minnie any more.

DP: Was it hard to go to another studio and then come back?
MG: No, not at all. Hazel was always very nice and let me come back whenever I felt like coming back. Maybe I worked better and enjoyed it more for having worked some place else for a while.

DP: Among the inkers and painters, was there a certain distinction to the fact that you were Minnie Mouse's voice?
MG: No, I don't think so as I look back. Just one of the gang.

DP: Can you recount the celebration of Walt Disney's daughter's birth?
MG: We were having a dinner celebration and I don't remember what the occasion was, whether it was a Mickey Mouse birthday or what it was. It was at the studio on a sound stage. I sang a few solos. I guess it was while I was still at the microphone that someone called up and announced that the little girl had been born. We all drank a toast with water, so she had a good beginning—pure!

Ken O'Connor

Ken O'Connor, born in Perth, Australia in 1908, immigrated to the United States in 1930 and joined the Disney Studio in 1935. He began his career in animation and later gravitated to story work and then layout and art direction. He worked on thirteen features and one hundred shorts. He is best known for his layout of the "Dance of the Hours" from *Fantasia* and "The Pink Elephants on Parade" sequence from *Dumbo*. After working on war-related films such as *Food Will Win the War* and *Education for Death*, Ken returned to features and created the Fairy Godmother's coach for *Cinderella*, the marching cards for *Alice in Wonderland*, and Skull Rock for *Peter Pan*. Ken's other feature credits include *Snow White, Pinocchio, Make Mine Music, Melody Time,* and *Lady and the Tramp*. In the 1950s, he worked with Ward Kimball on the three Tomorrowland television specials: *Man in Space, Man and the Moon,* and *Mars and Beyond*. He also worked on the celebrated short *Toot, Whistle, Plunk and Boom*. Ken retired in 1973 but continued to consult on Disney projects and taught layout and art direction at the California Institute of the Arts (CalArts).

Animation historians regard him as a good to great layout artist for his contributions to Disney films. He left his mark on a number of films, most notably *Fantasia* and *Dumbo*. Ken received a Disney Legend Award in 1992 and passed away in 1998.

Ken O'Connor contributed some of the stunning art work to the Sharpsteen Museum in Calistoga, California. While working on that project, he stayed in a guest house at Ben Sharpsteen's residence. It is there that we conducted our interview. I had stayed in that guest house many times, so it was a familiar setting, with its wood-burning stove, old fashion refrigerator, and gramophone. Ken was very easy to talk with and very candid.

This interview was conducted in June 1977.

KO: I'm glad to hear that you are stressing the fact that Walt Disney should be taken more seriously, because I feel that I was lucky enough to be there in the Golden Age of Animation. I don't expect to see it repeated in my lifetime, although I would like to. Through constant winnowing, I feel that he collected the finest stable of artists who were able to work together—which is a rather remarkable fact—since Rubens, who had a bunch of apprentices to start or finish the picture. It really was a remarkable galaxy of talent and I feel privileged to have been a part of it. He'd have busloads come out from New York to try out just for inbetween [an entry-level animation position]. The rest of us had to also, and it was rather a baptism by fire. It was tough, particularly for those like myself who didn't know what an inbetween was. It's a wonder I lasted.

DP: It's interesting that you mention Rubens, because when I talked to Dick Huemer, I asked him what it was like to work there in the thirties and he compared it to Rubens.
KO: Did he?

DP: He thought that the kind of dedication the Disney artists had during that time was similar to the dedication of Rubens's artists.
KO: Well, it wasn't just the dedication I was thinking of. Part of that, you must admit, was brought on by economic fear. The Depression was not far away. It was practically on our heels. But it was the sheer accumulation of talent—some of whom could practically be classed as geniuses—

that is very, very rare. I had a ten-year mini-career in various fields of art before I went to Disney's. I worked on newspapers and magazines. I did caricatures, sporting cartoons, theatrical cartoons, political cartoons, drawings for the real estate page, and whatever was necessary. I went into commercial art. I worked for a poster company in San Francisco that was a silkscreen company. We did twenty-four sheets and also window displays. I had studied fine art in Australia and in San Francisco. I never saw such an accumulation of talent in one place as Disney had achieved by constant and perhaps rather ruthless winnowing. He would have Black Fridays that were not very funny when people would be thrown out. But it did have an ultimate, remarkable effect of raising the standard of art in the pictures. Some of the stuff I understand is hanging in the Metropolitan Museum in New York, including the witch chase in *Snow White* where the vultures circled and the lightening split the rock and all that, which I laid out. But I laid it out under the strong influence of other artists who were good. Gustaf Tenggren was active then, and we had remarkable artists who set styles for us like Albert Hurter, so we couldn't take full credit for having laid something out on paper. Tenggren, I'm sure, was the inspiration on that one. I liked the result of the winnowing, even though I didn't enjoy it as it went on, because it was rather fearsome. I think Walt had to be rather ruthless in order to step up the caliber of the men. He was always pushing. He was the needle behind us that made us reach further than we could. Sometimes we succeeded in reaching that far and other times we fell on our face, but that idea of *plussing* [improving] was his major driving contribution. Everyone all down the line questioned everything and tried to plus it. And they were supposed to. Nobody minused anything without hearing about it. So you got that habit. In the story department, the director and the layout man, who worked together, would question story, and the animator would question the layouts, and so on all down the line. The background man, in his mind, would question the finished layouts and ideas on color mood and so forth given by the layout man. Sometimes he could plus it and sometimes he couldn't. But we always tended to question, because Walt expected constant improvement.

DP: Was there ever a feeling of resentment when someone would change something that you had done, something that you liked?

KO: I wouldn't be human if there wasn't some resentment, but I'd say the resentment for a layout man probably came from animators switching things apparently without good reason. As far as background men switching, they usually didn't, because the layout man had to okay the finished painted backgrounds, so we had control over that. Anything the background man could do to plus the layout was most acceptable. But we did not have control of animation. The director had that. But I'd say there was a minimum of resentment and a maximum of teamwork. This really surprised me, because a lot of these chaps were and are very creative, but we could all work to model sheets, so that you could pick up half a dozen drawings of Mickey from a specific picture and you wouldn't know who the devil did them.

DP: That has always amazed me.

KO: That is an amazing thing. I don't think Rubens had that problem. Every picture he did was new, and as long as you put the halo in the right place, it was okay. But we had to be so exact on all the models of all the characters, once the model sheets were out. We had to sit down and learn them. We traced them and copied them. We did them in different poses for ourselves, so we understood them in three dimensions, all the way around. It wasn't a flat decorative art, as you know, with Walt. He always had a hankering for third dimension. But that was a great achievement: to make these individual characters do the same thing and do it over and over again throughout the picture. There were some who didn't conform to that. But most of us had to be regimented and we were.

DP: I have read articles in which Mickey Mouse in *Fantasia* is referred to as Freddy Moore's Mickey Mouse or somebody else's Mickey Mouse. When you saw Mickey on the screen, could you tell if Freddy Moore had animated him or if somebody else had animated him?

KO: I could in his case probably, because he was one of the early Mickey animators, but he set out to evolve Mickey into something more drawable. Mickey started out with the rubber hose legs and arms, and they are not very alluring to an artist. But I think Freddy wanted to give him more than that, and so in a couple of pictures he slicked him up. He made him a city slicker with all sorts of slick gestures and slick clothing. He added eyebrows and he added whites around his eyes with black pupils. He made him more of a complete character with more drawing in it. Freddy was a genius if anyone was there and he did well. Mickey, I guess, never really went over as a slick character.

DP: That probably ties in with the fact that the Mickey Mouse which is reproduced on T-shirts and other things is the old Mickey who seems a little more colorful.

KO: Yes, they've gone back to the more primitive Mickey. It had strength like all primitive art. It had a native strength partly due, I feel, to the enthusiasm of the early animators like Ub Iwerks, coupled with a certain amount of ignorance—anatomical and other—which primitive art has and which helps out as far as strength goes. It doesn't have the finesse and sophistication, but it has a certain strength. This is the era we're in now where it seems to be the thing to do to look backwards. When I was young, the whole drive was to be progressive and look forward. We were looking for breakthroughs.

DP: There are certain values that are in Disney stories and films and in Disneyland that touch people subconsciously. They seem to be part of the whole myth of American life or maybe life in general.

KO: I'm not really sure it's a myth. They represent longings and wishes— some of them hopeless, some of them hopeful. He was a one-man combination of a whole family or at least all the men in the street, you know, intuitively. And I'm sure he couldn't really tell you how he arrived at a lot of his decisions. *He* was the average man rolled up in one bundle, and if he liked something, the average man, woman, and child would tend to like it and the reverse. So if he didn't like it, we would change the story. [At Disneyland] you were in a boyhood dream that Walt had and finally brought to fruition late in life. I guess we all have boyhood dreams. I did a little work on the park, and it was irritating to some of us who worked our insides out making all sorts of great exhibits, that when people would go and see them and we'd ask, "What did you think?" they'd say, "Boy! It was clean!" In other words, the damn street sweeper got more credit than we did. But Walt was smart. He knew people would respond to cleanliness, which most amusement parks can't claim. He was a fanatic on that and he was right again. It was just part of his showmanship, I guess.

DP: Going a little farther back, when did you first go to work at Disney's?

KO: In 1935 I went there, and I was there continuously, aside from the strike and the lockout that followed, until 1973. I was there thirty-eight and a half years, so I got practically into a rut, I guess, but it was a pleasant rut. I'd had ten years of other art and this was the first place I could bring it all together. Everything I knew, I needed, and maybe more. After a short stretch in inbetween and on the rotoscope, which was slightly horrific, and in story sketch, I got into layout which was my line.

DP: What did you rotoscope?

KO: It was a scene that Norm Ferguson wanted. I was horrified when I saw the image. The image was about half an inch square on my light board. It was a long shot of a judge beating on a stump, and every time he beat, there was a book that flew up and the pages opened. I didn't know what scene it was going to be used for. Then later, he was down the end of a long line of characters in *Who Killed Cock Robin?* This thing was minute, and they wanted me to reduce the drawings to literally about half an inch square or screen size, which isn't exactly square. I thought, "Oh god, this is frightful!" But I had decided, "Well, I'll show them how good I am," because I was new in the business and wanted to make an impression.

So I got a 9H pencil, which is as hard as you can go, and a long thin point which I kept sharpening on fine emery cloth. I fixed up a magnifying glass so that I could see what I was doing. I worked on that and I made tracings throughout the cycle. It had been animated a lot bigger and then shot smaller, because it was easier to animate that way.

Within this half-inch drawing, I drew it so that the stump was about a quarter of an inch high and the judge was the rest of the way. The little book was about an eighth of an inch wide and when it jumped up, the pages—you can imagine the size—flopped open and then went back. And I drew every damn page, because I had a magnifying glass. I couldn't have done it otherwise. I did a steel engraving of it, and when you flipped it, it all worked. Norm Ferguson flipped it and he couldn't believe it. He'd never seen anything like that. He thought I was a genius at it. I was actually an ass at it. I shouldn't have done that. I should have done it badly. "My god! This guy's a natural at rotoscoping!" They didn't know that I had used a 9H pencil and a magnifying glass, because they were put away. They thought I had extraordinary eyes and an amazing mode of skill. It was really a bad move because they said, "He's so good; give him all the rotoscoping to do."

So then I sat in a black room for six months by myself all day, eight hours a day, and I made tracings. An animator might animate Mickey skating and then I'd put a truck [camera movement] in it by moving the projector back and making it bigger so that Mickey would come toward you. On *Snow White*, I did a lot of tracings of Snow White live action. I felt sorry for myself, because I thought, "God, this isn't very creative. I'm stuck by myself in the dark all day, every day." Until one day, Walt came in. He said, "Boy, you're lucky."

I was about to tell him how lucky I thought I was, because I was slightly teed off at this. I couldn't think how to get out of it. I'd been an art director in a poster company where I had ten guys under me and here I was tracing. I said, "Yeah, I guess I am, if you say so Walt. Whatever you say. I'm lucky. Okay."

He said, "Yeah, this is your big chance to do action analysis. Here Snow White is moving her hands. You see how it goes blurred on this frame? You see how it sharpens up as she comes into the hold. It shows you just how human animation moves. That's the most difficult form and here's your big chance. You can study it all day long. I have to send the guys to a class to learn it."

Not being a character animator, I hadn't been to class. But, god, by the time he went out, I was all enthusiastic. That darn guy could sell iceboxes to Eskimos! And he was really right. I began to say, "My god, instead of sitting here suffering, I should be trying to analyze what the hell I'm doing." I did about two hundred tracings that day and I kept it up. I really did study how when you are going to move your fingers, your shoulder moves, then your elbow, then your wrist, and the last things to move are your fingers, and that's follow through. I learned about that, and he sold me on that terrible job. So I didn't mind it and I really did learn quite a bit.

DP: How did you finally break away from rotoscoping?

KO: At that time, we were paid $4 an idea for submitting gags. I started at $15 a week at Disney's. That was $5 more than some of them did. I felt in the upper class. I couldn't live on it, but thank god I had a family and I had saved some money from my other job. I set about trying to get out of rotoscoping—even though I was so "brilliant" at it—by submitting gags. I would think up something humorous or appropriate, I thought, and then render them much better than they needed to be done, because I was trying to impress somebody that I could draw and that I could render. I don't remember whether I sold any or many, it was so long ago. But somebody saw the drawings and said, "Say maybe this guy would be good at story sketch." So they hooked me out finally from the rotoscope when they had a need for story sketch. I did story sketches satisfactorily because I was used to visualizing through the various other fields I'd been in. I found ultimately, as an overview, that fine art, commercial art, newspaper and magazine and animation layout all have similar problems— selling problems. In animation, you're selling acting. You've got to know the scene, what the point of the acting is, and so on. So I did all right at story sketch and I liked it. Then Ben Sharpsteen needed a layout man. He had one, Leo Thiele, but he needed another, because he had to supply more animators with work than he was able to. So they gave me the story I was on and me to Ben.

DP: What was the story?

KO: *Mickey's Circus*, something that has been forgotten by millions.

DP: Mickey's the ringmaster?

KO: That's right. Ben had been the chap who interviewed me in the first place and gave me the tryout at Disney's. He was a director then, and I worked for Ben from then on, first under Leo Thiele. He held my hand on the first picture, and then I was slapped into production. It was rather sudden, because I wasn't too up on layout then. Layout is very technological as well as artistic. You've got to know the camera and all: what it can do and what it can't do.

DP: When you said that you made these little drawings and then you would truck in, would the camera truck in or would the animation be drawn successively bigger? Could they move the camera or did you have to draw the character bigger?

KO: Say they had an ice rink on a [frozen] river and there was a crack in the ice that got bigger as it came forward. Now they wanted Mickey to start in the distance and skate toward the camera, straddling the crack. Mickey gets bigger, but the background doesn't get bigger, so you can't do that with the camera. Not on one pass, and they weren't about to matte him in—that was too expensive. They would just draw the skating cycle and then I would put the truck in in successive drawings by pushing the projector away. I would bring him up, but the background had to remain static.

DP: But what if you wanted to zoom in on Mickey. Could they move the camera and photograph him or would he have to be drawn?

KO: They would truck in with the camera, provided it was okay to go in on the background too, because the camera goes in on everything.

DP: Okay. Can you recall how you first met Walt Disney? What were your first impressions of him?

KO: Actually, we of the lower echelon saw him around a good deal without talking to him. I didn't talk to him for quite a long time. He was busy with Dave Hand and the other guys up on top. So I formed opinions at a distance and also by his actions. My impression was fairly unvarying of him. He was always a gentleman to me. I'm not sure why, because he was not always to other people. He would wear what they called his "wounded bear suit," and everyone hid under the table when he was mad about something. But he was always nice to me. He was always reasonable, even when he turned down my ideas, which was fairly frequent. But he was a mercurial man. I gather he could be exceptionally fierce. But he could also be absolutely charming to anybody.

I thought of him most of the time as a great showman, because to me he was like Barnum of Barnum & Bailey. He had an intuitive, instinctive feeling for entertainment, and in his case, he thought all the time of entertaining the whole family—not children as he is generally credited with. The fact that he succeeded is brought out at Disneyland where I understand that four adults to one child attend. That was his objective, to entertain the whole family. I felt his education had been limited in an academic way, judging by his language, even making allowance for the fact that I'm British and he's American and therefore he would speak differently anyway. But he had tremendous natural abilities that I couldn't but stand in awe of.

The main thing was his story ability. We'd have a storyboard meeting and we would be a bit bogged down on it, not knowing where to go. He was very annoying to show a storyboard to, because you would start pointing along and you would look at him and he was down near the bottom. He was quick. But you would have to go through it anyway, and he would let you. Then by the time you got done, he would say, "Now take that part out. Develop this part. Now put this part up here." And then he would go out and you'd say, "Why the devil didn't I think of that?" This was his intuition and judgment that worked all the time marvelously. As I said, my main impression was that he was a great story man. Many times I felt he had made serious mistakes in judgment and showmanship, but in view of the fact that about nine times out of ten they turned into gold mines, after a while I quit feeling that way.

DP: At least you suspended judgment until you could see what happened.

KO: That's right. I was wrong more often than not. He was a little ahead of me on showmanship.

DP: Did you feel he had charisma?

KO: Yes. He's been compared in *Time* to a Midwest hardware store owner in his general appearance. But actually, he was a natural born leader. I think had he been in another line, he would have led there, too. He was the sort of man who could and would and wanted to lead, and many people wanted to follow. That's pretty darn rare in itself.

When I went over to the studio on Hyperion, there was a very paternalistic feeling on his part. It was his family, sort of, and he could spank you if you went wrong. Half the time he'd say, if he spanked you, "Well if you weren't worth anything, I wouldn't bother spanking you, so that means you're worth something. Therefore I'm telling you you did it all wrong." So you'd take it. He used to cut up a melon, as they said, and give those he felt had most contributed to the pictures quite generous bonuses. I got in on about one of them, because I wasn't there at the right time or early enough or I didn't amount to enough at the time, at least in his eyes.

This went on until the strike. And that changed the whole attitude. He was shocked and horrified by the strike and hardened up. He put in time clocks and six-minutes-late-and-you-get-docked-a-tenth-of-an-hour and all that. It spoiled the atmosphere forever. He really had no understanding of the union movement. I see the union as a very necessary thing, numbers being the only force that the worker has to impose his will on the guy who's got the money. When I went there, the girls were getting $18 a week. I didn't see how they stayed decent, but it was because he didn't have to pay them more. When the union came in, that changed. Even though I objected strongly to the way the first union got in, the union that got in later was fairly reasonable and did a lot for the workers. They would always be enemies of Walt's because he felt it was infringing on his private control of his business. So that changed the whole atmosphere in relation to the employees, although to some of us who had been there a good while and demonstrated some sort of loyalty over the years, he still maintained a somewhat paternalistic point of view.

DP: Did you feel a certain closeness with him for the rest of his life?

KO: As close as you could get. Walt was not a guy that anyone—perhaps his family's an exception—got very close to. A lot of guys tried to avoid it. It was something like the moth and the flame. But he was not an ordinary man. They said he hated anyone to touch him. I don't know whether that's true or not, but I never saw anyone touch him. He was standoffish. And I don't hold it against him for a minute. I'm sort of standoffish myself, I guess due to a British background. But you didn't really get close to Walt as a rule. He could come in and be very friendly, but you knew at the end of the conference it would shut off. Bang! And he's gone and you're working and that's it. He got to be so damn busy with the diversification of his empire that he was running like hell all the time. Even during vacations, he'd read scripts by the dozen. But he had the bull by the tail, and he couldn't let go. I don't think he wanted to let go. But the result was a terrific constant strain on him, after the thing grew very large. It was a strain all the time, but he was not without a sense of humor. He had a damn good sense of humor. And he was a good actor, too. He could act out in story meetings a keen way of doing things. He would get up, take off his coat, and act like the devil, and pour out ideas. He was marvelous. But I think it must have taken it out of him, because any sort of creative effort is a strain. It can wear you out quicker than ditch digging.

He was an unusual man. I don't think I ever fully understood him. Very few people did. Ham Luske, a director for whom I worked for ten years or so, was a very nice man and a very able animator and director. He taught me not to listen to what Walt said, but to read between the lines. He was an expert at it. I'd say, "Well, Walt said—" and he'd say, "Oh, I know what he said, but what he means was this," and he'd explain, because he was used to picking up the inferences between Walt's lines. I had the devil of a time, because I'm a literal, straightforward person, and I take what they say as being what they mean. You couldn't always do that with Walt. He sometimes was throwing out lines and sometimes just fishing. He couldn't express it perhaps or he expected you to do some detective work. So he wasn't an ordinary sort of a guy to deal with at all. He could be down to earth and just as regular a fellow as the next guy when he wanted to be. Half the time, he was forced by his position onto a pedestal, you know, "The Great Walt," with everyone bowing and kowtowing and saying, "Yes, Walt." I don't think he always enjoyed that either. I think maybe he would have liked to have been more one of the fellows, but I don't think he knew how. He had a different approach to life.

DP: Do you have one layout or one particular film that you worked on that you are the proudest of or the happiest with? In Christopher Finch's *The Art of Walt Disney*, he gives special mention to your work on the "Dance of the Hours". I, too, think it is beautifully done.
KO: Well, that's nice of you to say, because there were two pictures out of a hundred and fifty or so that I liked what I did. But the "Dance of the Hours" was one of them and the other was *Dumbo*. I could explain the "Dance of the Hours" if you haven't heard it.

DP: Sure.
KO: I got the idea—I think it was my original idea, although we discussed a lot of things and it might have been a community idea, but I subscribed to it and I carried it out—that the music seemed to divide into about four parts, just like a symphony. I saw it that way in graphic motifs. The first movement was very quiet, morning music and there I adopted a very quiet motif, verticals and horizontals which are quite static. I used it in the windows behind the ostriches, the horizontals across the steps, and so on, wherever I could. We were helped in each of these cases, by the shape of the characters. An ostrich is horizontals and verticals. It has a vertical neck, a horizontal body, and two vertical legs luckily. They did mostly quiet things up to where they got hold of the grapes and ran into the colonnade. So that was Motif One.

With Motif Two in the colonnade, I got a little more active. I got into the ellipse as the motif: an elliptical pool, an elliptical colonnade. When the hippo—fat ellipses all over—came up, she pirouetted, which is an elliptical move.

In the next sequence, we had an idea of a serpentine motif. We thought it was appropriate for elephants, the trunks and the moves and so forth. The serpentine is more active than the ellipse, so we got through that.

Then I went to the most active lines in art: diagonals and zigzags. I used that on the crocodiles. I started, for instance, with an upshot of the corner of the architecture. There's a point, a zigzag, in the upshot of the column, and then the guys and their steps were at an angle. The guys were angularly drawn: head, body, tail. They were supposed to move like this, too, and they did, I believe, in part. Angular, because they were the big menaces. For the guy who slid down the pole, I invented a type of column that was drawn thin, thick, thin, so you get a long shot, close up, long shot, down shot, in one vertical camera move. I was very pleased with that one. Then at the bottom, we were looking down at the steps which were zigged and zagged, because it was a down shot on stairs that angled around the column and so on.

We got these four movements—pictorial motifs—in as much as we could. Then there was a big ruckus at the end where we tried to recapture all of them, because everything went to hell and it was a big flurry and the whole thing finished in ruins as the music got sort of tempestuous. So I liked the fact that that seemed to me to have worked overall, with the exception of the serpentine thing.

DP: When I see that movie, audiences respond to most to that particular sequence and a couple of others, but particularly that sequence. You can tell people are really enjoying it.

KO: Well, I guess they must like satire. We were scared of it at the time because we were poking fun at the music. I don't know what the composer would have said.

DP: And your other favorite sequence was in *Dumbo*.

KO: I did the sequence where Dumbo and Timothy Mouse wander outside and drink out of a tub of water which also contains a bottle of booze. They got drunk. I did that sequence and the Pink Elephants Parade. In that, I was able to get some effects such as we hadn't got before. For instance, I did a graded background—pink to white—and then the characters were actually just black cels with holes in them that displayed part of the background, so it looked like the character. Also, we invented—I think I invented it—the first real black. This sounds minor, but it wasn't.

We could never get a decent black in the cartoons, because they used black paper on the stand and it picks up all sorts of little motes and dust that light up when lit very powerfully with cross lighting. So we put this on the multiplane camera. We'd have a lit level of glass with the cels on, and way down at the bottom, on the floor, I put black velvet and we didn't light it. It didn't matter if it got dust on it, because there was no light on it. There is nothing blacker than a piece of black velvet with no light on it. So that worked behind the characters and was satisfying. There were a lot of things that I really liked, aside from it being really nutty and wild and having plaid elephants and spotted elephants and all sorts of crazy things we worked out pictorially as well as Ollie Wallace's music that I thought was keen.

DP: When you are doing layout work, do you have a certain amount of freedom or is that relative to the director that you are working with? Over the years, would some directors allow you more freedom in your layouts or would some of them limit what you could do?

KO: That, of course, depended greatly on who the layout man was and who the director was. Some brilliant layout men, some not so brilliant directors, and vice versa. Undoubtedly, there were varying degrees of freedom. In my case, I had a great deal of freedom. The last director I worked with was Les Clark on the educational films. He was originally an animator but then he got into direction and we worked for a decade on educationals before both of us left at the same time. By that time, he had confidence in my ability. This is partly what determines whether the director will let you have freedom or not. Also, whether he's any damn good at layout himself, which a lot of them were not. He gave me almost total freedom.

There were a few outstanding directors; one with whom I worked very slightly was Wilfred Jackson, who did *The Band Concert* and some really excellent things. He had heart trouble and had to ease off. He had a reputation of figuring out every frame before he gave it out. When he gave what they call an animation handout, you knew exactly how to do it, which didn't mean the animator couldn't plus it again if he had a better way of doing it. But he was very thorough. Most directors were less thorough. I didn't find him a restriction in layout. He seemed to go along with most of the ideas I had at the time I worked with him.

DP: Was Ben a restriction at all?
KO: Ben was a very strict disciplinarian as to office procedure, behaving yourself, and doing everything just as you were supposed to do. Within that limitation, I'd say he seemed to appreciate the ideas that I had. I had good relations with all the directors I worked with. I liked 99 percent of them and I was able to please them.

DP: Would Walt ever look at a layout and say, "I don't like this movement from here to there"? Or would it ever come back to you that Walt didn't like a certain pattern or something?
KO: Walt usually didn't see the layouts to any extent until they were in a pretty finished form. He'd see the storyboards. Then the crew was supposed to translate it.

DP: My impression has been that in the ten years since Walt Disney died, the studio has been coasting. Some things have been interesting, but there haven't been many really innovative developments.
KO: I agree. When he died, he was replaced by a committee. When Rembrandt died, you couldn't have formed a committee to do what he did. It leaves a very difficult hole to fill. The natural men who got into power were the businessmen, the merchandisers. I believe they were very good at their job. But as a showman, I feel that there must eventually be a creative person or persons on the committee who are essentially showmen. It wouldn't be fair to expect the businessmen to evolve. They can't.

Floyd Gottfredson

Floyd Gottfredson, born in Kaysville, Utah, in 1905, joined the Disney
Studio staff in 1930 as an inbetweener working on the short subjects.
His initial interest was in cartoon strips, and four months after he
started at the studio, Walt asked him to take over the fledgling Mickey
Mouse cartoon strip, after Walt, Ub Iwerks, and Win Smith had
developed it. Floyd's assignment was to be temporary, but he stayed
with the strips for forty-five years. He wrote the Mickey Mouse strip
from 1930 to 1932, drew the Sunday Mickeys from 1932 to 1938, and ran
the comic strip department from 1930 to 1946. During his tenure, five
strips emerged: Mickey daily and Sunday, Donald daily and Sunday, and
a Silly Symphony Sunday, which later became *Uncle Remus*. Floyd added
new characters to the Mickey strips, including the Phantom Blot, Morty
and Ferdie Fieldmouse, Eli Squinch, Eega Beeva, Sylvester Shyster, Joe
Pipper, Captain Doberman, and Gloomy. Floyd passed away in 1986
and received a posthumous Disney Legend Award in 2003.

Floyd Gottfredson's storytelling ability in the medium of comic
strips has been widely recognized and appreciated. The possible influence of his comic-strip Mickey on the Mickey of the animated short
subjects of the 1930s is something historians can debate.

Floyd Gottfredson was a delightful person to meet and interview.
He was warm and generous and thoughtful. Before the interview at

his North Hollywood home, he sent me some publications in which he was featured. At the time I was interviewing, sources of information about Disney artists were not as widespread as today, so any information was very helpful, and I appreciated his efforts in sending the material to me. I asked many of these Disney artists to send me sketches afterwards, and Floyd sent me a beautiful color sketch of a contemporary Mickey.

This interview was conducted on September 1, 1977.

DP: Can you recall your first meeting with Walt Disney?

FG: Yes. It was pretty brief. I had been working as a projectionist, and they had torn the theater down that I was working in. I was down on what they called "film row" on Vermont Avenue, looking for another job. I saw a Mickey Mouse poster out in front of a small film exchange. I went in and talked to the fellow. He said he had heard that Walt was going back next week to New York to get artists. I didn't know at that time what type of artists, because I had never worked in animation, although that was part of the correspondence course I had taken with the Federal Schools [of Minneapolis, now Art Instruction Schools, Inc.]. They touched on animation a bit, but most of my samples were reproductions from newspapers and magazines and so on that I had brought to Los Angeles with me. So when I heard this, I rushed home, gathered up my samples, and went to the Hyperion Studio and talked to his secretary. Walt and Roy had adjoining offices with the same secretary. She took the samples in, Walt looked at them, and he was out in five minutes and called me in. He asked me what I was interested in.

I said, "I've been primarily interested in comic strips."

He said, "You don't want to get into newspaper business. It's a rat race. Animation is where it's going to be. I'd like to put you on here, if you are interested and want to train in animation."

I was anxious to get into the art business; that's why I had come down to Los Angeles in the first place, to try to get on one of the newspapers, and just didn't make it. I had been making $65 a week as a projectionist, which was pretty big money in 1928 and 1929. Walt was starting everybody, except those who were trained professionals ready to go into production, at $18 a week. I was married and I had two children, so that shook me up a little bit, but I still took it. At the time, I was doing four cartoons a month for an automotive trade journal in Terre Haute, Indiana, through the mail, so between the two jobs, we were able to make it.

DP: When you first met him, what was your impression of him? Did he strike you as being confident?

FG: He was quiet. No big front personality type. He was self-effacing, and he was interested in keeping the work going and interested in anybody who was interested in the business. One of the main reasons he hired me was because they were developing a Mickey Mouse comic strip at the time, and he said, "It looks to me like you have possibilities in animation, but in addition to that, you might be a good backup for the fellow who's doing the strip now." As it turned out, that fellow stayed only about four months.

DP: Was that Win Smith?

FG: Yes. So I did move on to the strip. This fellow, Win Smith, was doing the strip at the time. I was twenty-four and Walt was twenty-seven and Win was forty-three. We all referred to him as an old man. Interestingly enough, he drew with his right hand and wrote with his left hand. Ub drew the first eighteen strips, and Walt did the gags on those. From that time on, he tried to get Win to write the strip. Win held off for some reason. I never knew why; whether he felt that he either couldn't do it or didn't want to take on the extra work. But Walt carried the writing on to a point where King Features asked Walt to go into continuities [comic strips with continuing stories and not stand-alone gags] on the Mickey daily. He carried that on for maybe a month and a half, still trying to get Win to take over the writing. Finally, Walt called Win in and had a showdown with him. In about a half hour, Win came storming out to my desk and said, "It looks like you got a new job."

I said, "Why is this?"

He said, "No young whippersnapper is going to tell me what to do," and he walked out of the studio into oblivion. So Walt called me in and asked me if I'd take it over.

I reminded him at the time of our earlier conversation. I said, "You told me when I came in here that newspaper work and comic strips in particular were nothing to get involved with. I've become very interested in animation now, and I'd like to stay with it."

He said, "Well, just take it over for two weeks while I find someone." Then after about a month, I began to wonder if he was looking for anyone. After a couple of months, I began to worry for fear he was going to find someone.

DP: You see he was right; it didn't go very far. It only kept you going for forty-five years.
FG: Right!

DP: What was it like working at the studio during the 1930s? Was that the most exciting time when everything seemed to be developing and Disney was being recognized for the studio output?
FG: It was always exciting right up to the day I retired, because they were in a constant state of development and still are over there. In some ways, the thirties were very stimulating, because we were doing the continuities then and we were having a lot of fun with them, although they were much more work than the gag-a-day type strip. But the thing that was fun for us was the fact that we were doing everything tongue-in-cheek, and we were kidding what was then popular in the movies and so on. In that respect we did have a lot of fun with it. But there are things about that period that are embarrassing to me now when I look at them, because everything about it was so amateurish.

DP: Do you mean the strip?
FG: Yeah, I'm talking strictly about the strip now. In animation the Disney style up until the time Ub Iwerks left was really Ub Iwerks's style. When he left, the Disney product suddenly became styleless. It was pretty bad in everyone's opinion up until the time Fred Moore came along and began to develop a new Disney style. From 1936 on, the style that is now Disney began to develop and has constantly evolved right up to this day.

DP: This would be in reference to the Silly Symphonies and the Mickey Mouse cartoons?

FG: Everything they did in animation. And since we were attempting to transfer the spirit and the style of the studio into the newspaper comic strip, we were emulating them and trying to develop our own style. We were ourselves still amateurs. But it's also the sort of business where you never get through evolving and developing if you're at all critical of your own stuff.

DP: The parts you felt were amateurish, were they in story continuity?

FG: In both. We were entirely too wordy in the continuities for one thing, but then this wasn't entirely our fault. This was the style and the format in the whole comic strip industry at that time—just beat everything to death. We didn't know when we'd made our point and should move on, which we did learn later on. Toward the end of the continuities, I think we became much more professional and we tried to develop this simplistic approach up until the time I left there.

DP: Did it bother you that your name did not appear on the strip over the years?

FG: No, it didn't bother me at all. I have an interesting story that I think will completely clear this up. We all realized that we were working as ghosts there and that the product name was Walt's. That was the thing that was selling it. Early in the thirties they realized that eventually some of their animated products may die out and that they needed a name that could be a continuing name to develop the company itself. They decided early that they had to exploit Walt's name. This was very sensible, of course, and what a worldwide household name it became. It was a smart move and we all realized that. I don't know anybody who resented that, but in the mid fifties, Walt himself decided that he wanted us to share the signature—the individual artist. He himself proposed this. When he proposed it to King Features, they threw up their hands in horror back. They said no, the product, the whole studio, everything is sold as Walt Disney, and if we bring in an unknown second name and associate it with Walt, it will just confuse the readers and lessen the value of the product. So they didn't agree with that at all. Walt came back and explained it to us. We all agreed and that was the end of it.

DP: How does it feel now to have sudden celebrity status as comic strips and comic books have developed quite a following?

FG: Attending ORLANDOcon '76 [a convention in Orlando] was a heady experience and very ego building and actually fun at the time, but as I told everybody after that, once was enough for me. I've got enough to last me for the rest of my life.

DP: When you developed Mickey Mouse stories for the strip, was there any guidance from the studio? Were you allowed to create facets of Mickey's life or did they direct that? Did it have to be consistent with the films?

FG: The general content of Mickey's personality and the ethics of the studio were general throughout the studio, but after the first five or six months that I worked on the strip, Walt hardly bothered with it any more and we did go our own way. It was very seldom that we were ever criticized for straying out of the general studio path. It gave us a great range of freedom in all our continuity work that might have been a little stifling otherwise. But Walt didn't work that way. He tried to act as a spark plug all the time, to stimulate and never to stifle anything.

DP: So you didn't have to necessarily keep up on what Mickey was doing in cartoons.

FG: No, we didn't. As a matter of fact, when we got into the continuities, we moved far beyond what they were doing in the animated cartoons, so we just sort of necessarily had to go our own way.

DP: From the books I've read about Walt, the composite image I have is of someone who could be nice and could be positive and also could be very hard to deal with.

FG: Yeah.

DP: You didn't know which Walt you were going to get some times.

FG: No, you never did. And he didn't know himself. He was living in his own world all the time, and you got wherever he was in his world.

DP: The strike seems to still be an emotional issue.

FG: It is. There is no doubt about it, because for one thing, it completely disillusioned Walt. He had run the studio as a sort of a family project and had kept that sort of feeling about it. When they went out on strike and the thing got as bitter as it did, he then said to himself when it was finally settled, "Okay, if they want to make a factory out of it, that's the way it'll be." Up to that time, there had never been a time clock in the studio. That's when they were installed and why.

There's no doubt that Art Babbitt caused an awful lot of trouble at the time. Art is a great, great artist, and I have great respect for him as an animator and as a creative person, but there is no doubt in my mind—and I attended some of his meetings because everybody did at the time when he was building up this union thing—that he was associated in some way with a pinko [communist] group at the time, because this was his attitude. He was constantly quoting Marx and Lenin and socialism and the rights of these poor unpaid workers.

DP: When they made changes in Mickey, was that something that was difficult to incorporate into the strip?

FG: We didn't mind making them because we recognized them as progressive changes. For instance, the eyes especially; we knew that this was going to give Mickey a much broader and more flexible personality and a fuller personality, but it was difficult to do to start with, because we worked so long in the other pattern.

DP: In your continuities, Mickey was involved in all these adventures that were different from the cartoons. Did you ever feel that you would have liked to see the cartoons go in the direction that the strips were going?

FG: No, not really. I admired most of the things that they did in the animated cartoons, in particular, the things that Fred Moore dominated. We tried very hard to emulate his style and I think we came fairly close

to it, but we certainly didn't equal it, because he was a stylist in his own
way. So very, very great at it. Now I do feel the Mickey that we developed in the continuities necessarily was a different sort of a Mickey than
they had in the features, because he had to be a little hero in the strip
and he wasn't really the hero type in the films. But then when we went
back to gag-a-day—because of policies dictated by certain people in the
studio—I felt that they destroyed Mickey and just made him a nothing
sort of a little person when they went into the suburban family–type
thing. Neither the writers nor the artists agreed with this policy.

DP: Was this after Walt Disney died?
FG: I think they went into gag-a-day around '59, and he died in '66, but
by that time, he was so far divorced from the early strip that he paid very
little attention to what was going on.

DP: How did the continuities develop?
FG: Through most of the years that I was managing the department and
working with the writers and particularly the Mickey daily strip—we
didn't run continuities in any other strips—the writer worked right in
the room with me. Strangely enough, none of the writers—and through
the years we had five different writers—until Bill Walsh came along in
'43 were able to plot these continuities. I had no particular background
myself, but I was just in a spot where I had to do it.

DP: You mean they would have the idea, but they couldn't give you a
daily?
FG: They wouldn't even have the idea half the time. I would get the
original idea for a story and I would work up the general plot and turn it
over to them, and then from then on, they could develop the story very
well.

DP: Would they actually then break it down by panel?
FG: Yes. Once we decided on the story, the writer and I once a week
would have a bull session on what that week's work was going to be.

DP: So you were really involved quite a bit with the writing end of it, too.

FG: Yes I was. The writers would take it and break it down into panels and write the dialogue and I'd go over that and do a little editing. Up until the early fifties, I worked entirely from typewritten scripts because the writers weren't artists then. Later on toward the end, we got writers who were artists and we worked from sketches, as all of them do over there now.

DP: From your standpoint, was Bill Walsh the best one to work with over the years?

FG: He was by far the most creative of them.

DP: I've heard only good things about him.

FG: Yes. He was a genius. He had a great sense of off-beat humor that just came out of him normally and naturally.

DP: I am fascinated with Walt Disney as so many people are. Over the years of your association with him, is there a particular way that you would characterize him?

FG: Only that he had more time for you to know him in the early years. When I first started there—and in those early days they did not have a story department per se—they would have what they called a gag meeting once a week, usually on Thursday night, from eight to ten o'clock. So this was after the regular working hours, and all the animators and Carl Stalling, who was the music man at the time, would gather in the music room, and we would have a gag meeting on the picture that was in preparation at the time. I lived out in West L.A. at that time, twenty-five miles away from the studio, and I didn't have a car. I was riding the Big Red streetcars. At the second gag meeting that I attended, as the meeting was closing, Walt came up to me and said, "If you'll stick around a little while after the meeting, I'll take you home."

The studio had one car then. It was a little Model T pickup, and this was Walt's personal car and Roy's personal car and the studio's car. I protested. I said, "My gosh, it's a fifty-mile round trip."

He said, "I don't mind. I'll enjoy talking to you and getting to know you better." I'd only been there two or three weeks, I guess. And he said, "I'll enjoy the ride home. I like to be by myself sometimes and just think." So he did. He drove me out there that night and then came home. So this was the kind of time he had with people. He and his wife bought a home up in the Los Feliz Hills.

DP: Not the house on Lyric next to Roy?

FG: No. That was the home he had when I first went to the studio, and that was a smaller home. Then he bought the big home up in the Los Feliz Hills, and they built a pool there. When he got the pool finished, he was so proud of it, he came down and invited me to go up one noon and swim in it. So I took it on myself to invite Al Taliaferro and the two of us went up. He had time to do things like that, and he did do things like that then. But later on, of course, with worldwide involvement and preoccupation, he could do hardly anymore than pass you on the lot and say, "How are you? How are things going?" and that would be about it.

DP: Just out of curiosity—and this is off the subject of Disney—but what do you think of the *Peanuts* comic strip?

FG: I think it's a great strip, one of the classics of the strip business, and I think it will always be so. It ranks up somewhere near *Krazy Kat*. *Krazy Kat*, in my opinion, will always be the greatest. I don't know Schulz, but I understand that this reflects a lot of his personality and he's just as great a guy as the strip is.

Les Clark

Les Clark, born in Ogden, Utah, in 1907, had the good fortune to work at a lunch counter near the Disney Brothers Studio in 1925. He met Walt and Roy there, and two years later, Les asked Walt to look at his drawings. Walt liked what he saw and hired Les within a couple of days of his graduation from high school. Les stayed with the studio for the next forty-eight years. Les performed a variety of tasks before receiving his first animation assignment on *The Skeleton Dance*. Over the years, he animated on over a hundred shorts where he became best known as for his work on Mickey Mouse. His memorable scenes include his animation of Mickey in *The Band Concert* and later in "The Sorcerer's Apprentice" from *Fantasia*. Les became a member of Walt's famed Nine Old Men of Animation and animated on many of the classic Disney features, including *Pinocchio, Dumbo, Saludos Amigos, So Dear to My Heart, 101 Dalmatians, Song of the South, Fun and Fancy Free, Cinderella, Alice in Wonderland, Peter Pan*, and *Lady and the Tramp*. He moved into direction with *Sleeping Beauty* and then television and educational films, such as *Donald in Mathmagic Land*, before his retirement in 1976. Les passed away in 1979 and received a posthumous Disney Legend Award in 1989.

Les Clark, as one of the Nine Old Men of Animation, is well known, but his contributions may be less appreciated than some of his colleagues who had higher profiles. He left his mark on the short subjects and especially with his animation of Mickey Mouse.

Les lived in a beautiful house in the Santa Barbara hills. We recorded our interview in his living room which had several art pieces on display. Les was friendly, but reserved, and he very carefully responded to each of my questions. Not more than a minute after I turned off my tape recorder as Les was about to sign my *Mickey Mouse Club Annual*, we felt a jolt that reminded me of a sonic boom. With the next jolt, it felt like the house was being torn apart. I jumped up and ran toward the front door. Les called to his wife to get out of the house, and then they followed me outdoors. We stood there as the earthquake—measuring 5.1 to 5.5 on the Richter scale—slowly dissipated. At one point, Les said, "I don't know if those are aftershocks I am feeling or just my legs shaking." We were all shaking. When we went back into the house, many of the art objects had fallen down. But we had shared an experience that created a bond, Les seemed more relaxed, and I almost wished I could do the interview all over again. When I left his house and drove down to Highway 101, I saw that a train had derailed as a result of the earthquake.

This interview was conducted on August 13, 1978.

DP: How did you happen to go to work for Disney? I understand that you worked in a restaurant on Vermont Avenue that Walt and Roy used to frequent.

LC: Yes. It was a malt shop, confectionary store, and they served lunch and other meals. The Disney Studio at that time was right across the street on Kingswell and Vermont. This was in 1925. I skipped a year or so of high school. This was one of the years I wasn't in school for shall we say economic reasons. So I met Walt in the summer of 1925. He used to come in and have lunch almost every day. When I graduated from high school, I got in touch with him and asked him for a job. He said, "Fine. Bring some samples of your work in." So I copied some cartoons out of *College Humor* and showed them to him. I told him I copied them. He said my ink line was very good, steady, and he liked them. This was on Saturday and he said to come to work on Monday. So between graduation on

Thursday and starting work on Monday—this was in 1927—and retiring in 1975, no layoffs except vacations. Even during the hard times, Walt and Roy always saw that everybody had a paycheck which is very commendable, I think.

DP: When you went to work, was it at the Kingswell site?
LC: No, they had just moved to the Hyperion Studio maybe just a few months before. They were finishing up two or three of the Alice series and were starting Oswald the Lucky Rabbit.

DP: Were you approached by George Winkler to leave with the other staff?
LC: I was approached by the animators who did leave.

DP: They asked if you wanted to go with them?
LC: Yeah. I said, no, I was working for Walt. He hired me and I liked him regardless of what happened. That was before Jaxon [Wilfred Jackson] started working there. I think Ub and I were the only ones left in the organization except the girls.

DP: I think Jaxon came in maybe a week before they left.
LC: I think Jaxon came in shortly after that, because they had a few Oswalds to finish before they left, and during that time, Walt had Ub animate on the first Mickey. But during the completion of the Oswald series, Walt knew about their leaving.

DP: The night they ran *Steamboat Willie* with sound effects to see if it worked, was that at the studio?
LC: Yes. I was there. So was Jaxon, Johnny Cannon, Walt and Roy and their wives, Hazel Sewell and her daughter and maybe one or two other people. The picture was run in another room and we were looking through a glass window of some sort. I have forgotten how the physical set up was, but we had a lot of fun doing it, clamoring and beating on the drums and making calls.

DP: Were you the sound effects person that night?

LC: We all were. We all entered into it. It was something that was spontaneous; it wasn't prearranged. It was just something they were trying out. But the realism was there. That has become an important event now, because it was a convincing situation that showed that sound could be used and be sincere in coming from the animated characters.

DP: You each took turns going out to watch it?
LC: Yes, as I recall.

DP: From what I've heard, a bed sheet was hanging up and Roy projected the film onto it from the outside.
LC: Yes, that's right. The bed sheet was to project the film upon.

DP: I guess because it seems so primitive, that's part of what makes it seem so fascinating.
LC: Don't forget, everything was primitive in those days. As we look at cartoons as they are made today, we accept them as having been made that way forever, but we started very crudely. I mean the animation in New York was still crude then. It was Walt, whose innovations and whose desire and actually whose demand for more and more improvement developed the cartoon industry. It's all credit to Walt Disney, no one else, because all the other studios took from him what he had proven.

DP: Without him, it might just have been a novelty that might not have lasted too long.
LC: Most of the other studios were in the business to make money, and they took the money out of it and continued as they had, but Walt, any profit he made, put it back into the studio.

DP: Can you recall your first impressions of Walt Disney?
LC: No. They are the same that I have always had. I had great admiration for the man even in the early days, because he was so enthusiastic about everything. He had a beautiful gag mind, a memory like an elephant. He'd remember things you'd said to him maybe two or three years af-

terwards. I'd be startled that he would recall and I had forgotten. But he was realistic. When I was hired, he said, "Well, this may be a temporary job for you. Who knows?" A temporary job turned out to be forty-eight years. But Walt was the same then as he was later, except that he was more with the studio personnel in the beginning than he was later, because the place got so big that he couldn't give attention to personalities.

DP: The reason I ask is that having talked to fifteen or sixteen people, I have gotten a mixed image of him. At certain times he could be extremely charming, enthusiastic, and charismatic, and at other times, he was very good at putting somebody down for something they had done that he didn't like.

LC: Well, sure, he was a businessman. He expected results and if didn't get them, why he'd tell the person off. I've had several people say to me since I've retired, "Oh Walt, he was a brain-picker, wasn't he?" I'd say, "Well, no. He didn't expect any more than what he had hired a person for." He hired them to contribute to the organization, and if they had ideas, why he expected them. And he used them under his name, because he didn't think of himself as Walt Disney. He thought of Walt Disney as an entity, an organization, and he spoke of Walt Disney as an organization, for which everybody worked and not the personal part of the name. A lot of people put Walt down because they didn't get along with him or they got canned or they were chewed out by him, and naturally they probably make more or less severe remarks about him and understandably so. He had a great ego, and because of this ego, he could overcome a lot of difficulties and obstacles because he believed in himself. He believed what other people didn't believe, and he was proven right time after time after time, even with the bankers. *Snow White* was called "Disney's Folly," because what—an animated cartoon to run for over an hour? It's impossible! Nobody will sit through a cartoon that long. Well that was *Snow White and the Seven Dwarfs*.

DP: It did fairly well!

LC: It built the Burbank Studio. If it hadn't have been for the Second World War, which took all the profits and put them into the red in a way—it was the difference between making money and going below the profit mark—why the studio and its continuing production of features would have been fine.

DP: It does seem like he had an enormous amount of confidence in himself.

LC: And also confidence in the people who worked for him, because he gave his people assignments that they didn't think they could do themselves.

DP: That's what I have come to understand, that he pushed people as though he seemed to be able to analyze what somebody's abilities were more than they could tell themselves.

LC: Or at least he gave them a chance. So you see I'm very pro–Walt Disney. I imagine you've talked to others who have put him in a different light, possibly when he was demanding better quality and wasn't getting it, or when he expected a better job and wasn't getting it, or when they were fired and they didn't like it.

DP: Most of the people I've talked to stayed at the studio a long time and liked the studio and what was going on. Some saw the complexity of Walt.

LC: Walt was a complex person in a way. He considered the studio his business and also his hobby.

DP: It seemed to be almost his whole life.

LC: It was his whole life, and he had the energy to make it work.

DP: I understand that you did some animating on *The Skeleton Dance*.

LC: *The Skeleton Dance* was the first Silly Symphony, and it had the first scene which I animated all by myself, the scene where one skeleton plays the xylophone on the back vertebrae of the other skeleton. I have been asked whether I animated on *Steamboat Willie*, and I said no several times, but now I remember Ub gave me a little bit to do in one scene, but it wasn't entirely on my own. I think it was pulling up a load of hay or something for the cow. It is so vague in my mind now. I know Jaxon animated one scene, where Minnie's running along the bank of the river yelling, "Yoo-hoo." My biggest thrill was working on *The Skeleton Dance*, because it was entirely on my own with no help.

DP: Did the strike change Walt's feelings towards his staff?
LC: That changed a lot of things, because it was hard for him to realize that people could walk out. And yet, to some of those who did and who came back, he gave very important jobs, because if they could fulfill a position or create, why he didn't—

DP: He didn't hold a grudge?
LC: He didn't hold a grudge. If he did, it was in a private place, and he didn't let it interfere with the business.

DP: It seems like it was an emotion-wrenching experience.
LC: It was for him.

DP: I mean for almost everybody.
LC: It was. I know it changed my friendship with Art Babbitt, because we were very good friends at the time. He thinks that I'm not his friend anymore, which is not true. He demanded that I go out and strike with him the day that it happened. I said, no, and he said, "I'll see you never get a job again in the industry."

I said, "I'll take my chances."

My dad was standing in his doorway. He was a security officer at the studio. He said, "Do you think you're doing the right thing, son?" Because, you know, no one knew what was going to happen at the time, whether you were doing the right thing or not.

DP: You had to do what you thought was right.
LC: I did what I thought was right, and he did what he thought was right. I don't know if the strike was a good thing or a bad thing; it happened. But it cleared the air later on. Prior to the strike, there were many new people hired that were not at Hyperion and did not have the Disney loyalty or regard for making good pictures, and there was a lot of dissatisfaction amongst the newer employees.

DP: So even if you didn't have the strike, you would have had some—
LC: There would be friction.

DP: Do you recall a meeting Walt had with the staff at some point before the strike where he talked about all the problems they had gone through in forming the studio and where he poured out his feelings about the studio and about the union movement?
LC: If it is the one you are referring to, it was in the theater. He called everyone together and gave pretty much a heart-to-heart talk. It was very sincere, how he felt.

DP: Did people seem to respond positively to it?
LC: I think those who were intricate in the business, in the fulfillment and development of the animation, yes. Others, maybe not.

DP: Do you recall another meeting Walt had with the staff where he performed the whole story of *Snow White*?
LC: Yes. It was important, because it was a feature, but he used to do the same thing on shorts; he would act out or go through the motions of what he would like to see on the screen. It took on more importance in later years, because it was a feature. Walt was an actor. He could put over expressions and ideas very well, very clearly. In fact, we liked to be in meetings with him, so we'd know how he was thinking by seeing it directly from him rather than by having it passed to a story man to a director then to the animator. A lot got lost along the way. And so when he'd see something in a sweatbox, it was probably not what he'd envisioned, because something was lost in the communication between three different people.

DP: When he would act out a particular scene, was his performance vivid enough that you could remember it to incorporate it into your animation?
LC: Yes, in the early days. But as the studio grew larger, the animators did not always sit in on original story meetings as we did in the beginning, before we had a story department or when the story department

was small. We were called in only for the final meetings, but not the formative meetings that they held before they came to some decision on how the picture was to be presented.

DP: Going back even further, I have read that you would get together at Walt's house and sit around a table and have a gag meeting.
LC: Yes.

DP: Was that an exciting thing to do? Were you all caught up in the excitement of making these cartoons?
LC: Oh, yes. That was part of our job.

DP: Did those meetings ever become drudgery?
LC: No, we looked forward to them. It was something we expected to do. We'd either go to Roy's house or Walt's house and have story meetings, maybe twice a week, sometimes three times a week.

DP: At these sessions, was everybody equal as far as give and take?
LC: Yes. It was all on a very relaxed, informal basis. It was quite different in the early days, in the early development of animation. It was very exciting. As I look back on it now, it still is exciting because animation was crude by our standards today, and if we'd find out a new way of doing something, we'd pass it on to the other animators. There was no jealousy or holding things back. Everybody was working for a good result, which made it a real great place to work. The studio doesn't have it today. The animators come in today and they have all this experience that we went through handed to them. It's up to them now to take that and do what they can with it, even better it, put more heart in it. By heart, I mean realism, something that makes the figure on the screen become alive and believable rather than just moving.

DP: When you talk about these younger animators having all these things handed to them, in the early days each wave of new animators who came in seemed to top their predecessors because they didn't have to learn a lot of the things that you guys had to learn. You were the only one from your early group to become one of the Nine Old Men of Animation. Others like Freddy Moore and Norm Ferguson were tops for a while but did not stay at that level. How do you account for surviving when some of the others had such a hard time doing so?

LC: Just determination and hard work and not letting anybody else get ahead of me. A lot of them were better animators than I, but I held my own in certain areas or they didn't. Maybe I had something that they didn't have, and they had things that I didn't have. But Freddy Moore and Norm Ferguson contributed an awful lot in the early days, an awful lot. Freddy Moore was a natural-born animator. He was my assistant when he first came to the studio. He'd make beautiful drawings without any effort, while the rest of us would have to think it out or maybe make a couple of rough sketches before we got what we wanted. In fact, I think it's rather a shame that animation came so easy to him, because he let it go along without trying to research more and to develop. Walt was at fault there in giving him too much money—a young kid in his twenties. Fred left the studio, and when he came back, he just didn't have the Fred Moore approach anymore. Something had left him. And Fergy [Norm Ferguson], the same way. He came back to the studio, and animation in the few years that they were away had probably developed to a point where it was confusing to them. They were the same people, the same animators, but it's hard to realize the progress that was made from year to year to year to year. Ham Luske came in and brought in a great sense of timing we hadn't had before on *The Tortoise and the Hare*. All of these contributions from different animators added up to making things work better and progress more.

DP: You deserve a lot of credit for staying right up there.

LC: Maybe it's because Walt had confidence in me. That's all I can say. And he kept me on; he didn't fire me.

DP: I'm sure talent played a big part in that, too. Was there something special about Mickey Mouse that you became one of the best of the Mickey animators. Was there something about the character that appealed more to you than the others?

LC: Walt liked my Mickey better than the Mickeys that the fellows from New York were animating; their Mickeys were stiff and had no fluidity. So he gave me more Mickey animation to do. I animated Mickey as the conductor in *The Band Concert*. I worked on over a hundred and fifty shorts and all the features up until *The Sword in the Stone*. The only one I didn't work on was *Bambi*. I was working on *Dumbo* at the time.

DP: But with the character of Mickey, did you feel anything special about him?
LC: He was Walt to me.

DP: That says it all.
LC: I think so. Then I was directing for my last fifteen years.

DP: Did you prefer directing to animating?
LC: It was an advancement. Walt asked me twice to go into direction: first in 1940 and then a few years later. I said I'd rather animate for a while longer because I was enjoying it so. Then when we were preparing for Disneyland, he wanted me to direct a cartoon on the story of oil, which the Richfield Oil Company [ARCO today] was financing. From then on, I kept directing. I directed for *The Mickey Mouse Club*'s "Five Senses" with Jiminy Cricket as the narrator. I was a sequence director on *Sleeping Beauty* and then on educational films.

DP: I interviewed Ken O'Connor, and I know that the two of you worked together on a lot of these films. I think you were both pretty dedicated to what you were doing.
LC: Well, yes. I was a company man. By company man, I mean I believed in what I was doing, what the studio was doing.

DP: It was not just a job to you.
LC: No. God, no. As far as money was concerned in the early days, Walt had a hell of a time making ends meet at all until television and Disneyland. There were no big paychecks. What I meant to say—and I am not discounting the salaries—is that we liked what we were doing so

much, we didn't care about being rich. It didn't enter our mind. We were getting enough to live on, but we were not rich by any means. Frank Thomas and Ollie and the rest—they all felt the same way. How many jobs can one have where you get up excited the next day wondering what's going to happen?

DP: What was it like playing polo on the studio teams?
LC: That was fun. I was on Walt's team. There was Walt, Jack Cutting, Bill Cottrell, I think, and myself. Roy's team had Dick Lundy, Gunther Lessing, and I can't think of the other guy. But we had a lot of fun. We'd get up early in the morning, five o'clock, and none of us had cars. Roy Disney would come by and pick me up around five o'clock, and we drove clear out to Whitsett and Ventura. The land between the freeway and the river was an area where we played polo. Then beyond that were the riding stables. This was in the early thirties.

DP: Did you know how to ride a horse?
LC: I learned to ride playing polo.

DP: That's a precarious way to learn.
LC: But I was very lucky as far as being injured. Most everyone got hit by a ball or had a broken bone or clavicle, but I used to tumble in high school, so I took many a fall, but when I did, I'd roll and break the fall that way. I landed on my head once and my helmet was just mushy, but I didn't injure myself. We had great days playing polo. Then Walt built a practice cage with a sawhorse and a saddle on it where you hit balls during noon time. It was all fun.

DP: Were they pretty competitive games?
LC: Yeah, but, of course, I was naïve then; I am now maybe! I took the ball away from Walt once and made a goal. He gave me hell! I always thought that boss or no, you played a competitive game. He came running up to me and said, "What the hell you trying to do, Les, play the whole game by yourself?" This was Walt, laughing but still—but he was fun to play with.

DP: Was Roy a good competitor, too?

LC: Yeah. We were all equals. In a game like that, there was no—taking the ball away from your boss to make a goal would be unheard of if you were a *What Makes Sammy Run?* type.

DP: I have the impression that Walt was a more aggressive person than Roy. In a game like that, would Roy have been aggressive as well?

LC: Oh, yes. Roy was aggressive in a different way. In a business way, he was very aggressive. He was a different personality than Walt. People say he was a lot warmer than Walt. I don't think so. I think Walt was just as warm as Roy, but he didn't express it in the same way as Roy did.

DP: How would Walt have expressed it?

LC: He did an awful lot of wonderful things that people didn't know about—nice things, I mean for people, to people—at the studio and out-side the studio. I don't think Walt wanted people to get too close to him. It wasn't that Walt was not responsive or a warm person, but he was just a different personality. He had a personality for work and a personality for outside of the business, which is understandable. When you run an organization, you can't just be a good guy all the time. Roy was in a different position. He didn't have to deal personally with the animators and the creative people.

I remember the New York cartoons, *The Barnyard Fables* and *Felix the Cat*. I must have wanted to be an animator, because when I was a kid, I'd stay through two or three features just to see the cartoons over and over again, not knowing I'd be involved in animation in my later life.

DP: It was an early message I guess.

LC: I suppose. Back when I started at Disney's, I worked there a year before I did an inbetween. I worked camera, inked and painted cels—all the other jobs. I even painted a couple of line backgrounds. Then I got to do an inbetween which was quite a thrill. So it was like an apprentice-ship in a way.

DP: How long did you inbetween?

LC: Not too long, because I worked on *The Skeleton Dance* in '29 and I started in '27, so it wasn't too long before I was animating. But I was observing during the time I was working on the other things; I kept my eyes open and my ears open and I practiced myself so I knew pretty well what was going on in those days when it was so simple.

DP: What was it like to be at Disney's during the thirties—the Golden Age of Animation?
LC: It was the most exciting period of the time I was there, because we were trying to develop and find new ways of making animation work better. Look at all the shorts we worked on. We turned out one every month or six weeks. I probably worked on most of them up until *Snow White*. I was on the features at that time while shorts were still being made by other directors and other animators.

DP: Did you work on the training films?
LC: Not the technical training films like the bomb site and the weather pictures.

DP: You worked on *Donald in Mathemagic Land*. That was one of my favorite educational films.
LC: I directed one sequence in which there was a pool table.

DP: With all the triangles.
LC: Every educational film presented different problems, but once you had solved them, why you felt a sense of accomplishment.

DP: What did you work on in *Snow White*?
LC: The dwarfs mostly: Sneezy quite a bit, Happy, Grumpy, Bashful. Whichever the scenes called for.

DP: How about on *Pinocchio*?
LC: I worked on Pinocchio himself in some of the dance scenes. I was getting an awful lot of rhythm things to do, especially on early Silly Symphonies like *Springtime*.

DP: I read somewhere that you used your sister as a model for *The Goddess of Spring*.

LC: That was the first attempt to try to use live-action figures. I was very disappointed in my effort and I told Walt so. He said, "Well, do better next time," but he was looking forward to the girl in *Snow White*—getting all the flaws worked out so we'd be able to design the character so it could be animated, which the girl in *The Goddess of Spring* was not. The story department did a drawing of a girl without any design quality that you could put your hands on. That's what most of our characters are, they're designed in such a way that you can animate them easily. The original Mickey Mouse was three circles. Everything was done in circles.

Ken Anderson

Ken Anderson, born in Seattle, Washington, in 1909, joined the Disney Studio with a degree in architecture in 1934 and contributed greatly to Disney films and to Disneyland over a forty-four-year career. Ken began his career at Disney's animating on the Silly Symphonies, including *The Goddess of Spring*, *Three Orphan Kittens*, and *Ferdinand the Bull*. With the advent of feature films, Ken served as an art director on *Snow White*, *Pinocchio*, *Fantasia*, *The Reluctant Dragon*, and *The Song of the South*. He contributed to story on *Melody Time*, *Cinderella*, and *The Jungle Book*. His versatility included layouts on *Peter Pan* and *Lady and the Tramp*, production design on *Sleeping Beauty*, *101 Dalmatians*, and *The Aristocats*, and character creations for *The Jungle Book* and, much later, *Pete's Dragon*. At Disneyland, Ken's architectural background helped him to play a very important role in the development of many attractions in Fantasyland.

Ken retired in 1978 and received a posthumous Disney Legend Award in 1991. Ken Anderson is admired and recognized for the range of his work and his contributions, including his preliminary sketches for later feature films.

Ken and I talked in his office/studio at his beautiful home in La Canada. He had some Disney memorabilia in his studio, including a large three-dimensional figure of the dragon from *Pete's Dragon*. He was enthusiastic and sincere, and I was comfortable with him right from the start.

This interview was conducted on October 12, 1978.

KA: We didn't know we were great artists. We were trying to survive. There were great artists and great egos, but the greatest was Walt. As Walt once confessed, however, at a luncheon years afterwards, he could never have done it if it hadn't have been for the Depression. He wouldn't have been able to accumulate those of us that he got there. Then we found stimulation as well as competitiveness, stimulation because there was camaraderie, jealousy, and admiration—great admiration for what someone else would do. We were all acting as if there was a fire under us.

One night after we had been doing shorts, Walt gave us sixty-five cents for dinner, and the fifty of us in animation went across the street to Ma Applebaum's. I got a dinner—most of us did—for fifty cents and saved the fifteen. Then we came back to the little sound stage. Ward Kimball and I sat next to one another. Walt was in a subdued light on the main floor. At one end of this grotto-like sound stage, there were seven or eight rows of seats banked rather steeply to a projection booth behind and a little screen across. Then there was just like a dance floor, quite long and narrow, and the lights didn't completely light this auditorium. Walt had this whole thing for his stage. He had thought out and dreamed this whole *Snow White* business. We didn't know that. He spent from whatever time we got back from dinner—6:30, 7:00—until nearly midnight acting and not only describing the plot and the picture, but acting out the individual characters and the parts. He lit such a fire under those of us who were there that it never occurred to us we were ever going to do anything else in our whole lives except that picture. We worked nights and days and Saturdays and Sundays. We tacked up dollar posters all over Hollywood when we completed it. It never dawned on us, we never stopped to think that there would be another one. If there was, we knew he'd tell us another story, because it was such an *enlivening*, such a *tremendous* challenge.

He said he couldn't carry a tune, but boy he certainly knew music. And good art. He claimed no regard for art. He wasn't trying to do anything artistic or anything else; he was just trying to entertain.

The night before Disneyland opened—I'd been working for four years trying to help get that open—Lilly had a party which was pretty distressing really, but Walt ran between the party, which he didn't want to attend, and trying to see to it that all these other things got open. He was spending some time with me, and we were sitting down on the ground by the fence, listening to the music on the Mark Twain. I was pooped, because we had been working night and day, right straight through, for a week or two. There had been a lot of hanky panky going on out there. Walt turned to me and said, "You know, Ken, god damn it, I can't understand it. I hear about all these guys running out to motels. What the hell! What the hell are they majoring in women for? This is my—" He said it in almost those impassioned terms. "This is my—" what turned him on he meant. The same thing when he received accolades for *Sleeping Beauty*.

I went with him to San Francisco. They had the art society, but it was a very tony society group up there and Walt felt a little bit out of his element; a Missouri farm boy and here he was with all these stuffed shirts. They had gotten some very credible young artist to make an award for him which turned out to be a bronze. I thought a very nice bronze actually. They gave Walt a very flowery introduction, "This is a great artist who had done—" Walt got up and he denied that he was an artist, at least that he had any drive in that direction, that he was grateful people thought it was good art, but that wasn't what his drive was—it was to entertain. They didn't introduce the artist but they gave Walt his trophy. Walt looked at it and said, "I don't like to be crude, I don't want to hurt anybody's feelings, but what the hell is this thing? It looks to me like a burnt turkey." Walt said, "Maybe I could meet the young artist who did it and he could explain it."

There was shocked reaction to this vulgar way of receiving this, but the intelligence of the young artist saved the day. The artist came up, and he and Walt got along just famously. He said, "I understand how you feel, Walt. Really it isn't much different than a burnt turkey, but the thing that to me epitomizes what you've done is like the seed of civilization. It isn't representative. It just expresses the feeling of a seed with new life, and you have given that to us." Walt said that was the most complimentary thing he had ever had given to him and that he would treasure it. He said he was sorry, he didn't mean to be disrespectful in saying it looked like a burnt turkey, but damn if it doesn't look like a burnt turkey. The artist said, "Yeah, I guess it kind of does if you have to be representational." So that was the kind of guy he was. He was so honest and so able to cut through sham and hypocrisy, not only in everybody else, which is more or less easy for us to do, but in himself. He wouldn't allow himself the luxury of being hypocritical. I think he earned everyone's respect.

Those of us who were his central core are nowhere near as united, even though we've been forty-five-some years together and love one another, we're not really as cohesive now since he's gone as we were when he was here.

DP: He probably held everybody together.
KA: Yeah. How? I don't know.

DP: I guess when someone has charisma—
KA: When we finished *The Song of the South*, he took me to Atlanta, which I enjoyed. He had very little in the way of big social celebrations as far as pictures were concerned before then, and the mayor of Atlanta was throwing a big soiree for him. It was in a room where there was a raised entry about three or four steps up to a dais—maybe they used it sometimes for a platform—and the main doors were on the other side, so when you came through, those double doors opened and you stepped out on this raised platform and you came down to the dance-floor level. There probably were two or three hundred socialites—rich people, wealthy people—there. We all wore tuxes. Jaxon [Wilfred Jackson] was there and Milt Kahl, Bill Peet, Claude Coats, and myself. We were mingling in the group. Walt hadn't shown yet. I want to tell you this

because it was most dramatic. None of these people had met Walt. The doors were opening on the stage. In fact, the mayor himself had made his entrance, but the decibel level of the conversation changed very little. There was still this hum of people talking and drinking and having a big time. Other important people came in. I had my back turned, and all of a sudden, there was a dead silence. Walt's picture hadn't been published much in those times. That was 1946 and not many people knew what he looked like. He wasn't a big imposing figure anyway. He came in with two or three other people, a couple who were known in the movies but they weren't big names. The whole place stopped, and I swear you could *feel* Walt was in the room. We used to kid when we were doing *Bambi* that "Man is in the forest." We used that line from *Bambi* for Walt. When Walt was around, you could feel him.

DP: That's what I gathered. People said that they were in awe of him.
KA: He developed a cough, so he'd be—

DP: Yeah, so you'd be ready by the time he got to the room. One of my big regrets is not ever having seen him or met him. I share that with a lot of the young people who work at the studio.
KA: Walt was not a religious man in the sense that he belonged to a denomination. He resisted letting himself be called anything. He, however, devoutly believed that man is innately good, that he is moral. He has evil, sure, but basically, good conquers evil. Permeating everything he did was a hopeful upbeat feeling that man is basically good. Those of us who followed along on Walt's coattails, hung on his star, were uplifted in his unquestioning belief that man is good. Even if he slips and falls and does a lot of bad things—whatever happens—his good nature is going to win over evil. That was Roy's philosophy too, so it must have come from the family.

I feel extremely blessed that I was allowed to live my life, because I wasn't even going to start out—I knew nothing about animation. I had no idea I was going to get involved. I was in other things, but now, I'm glad I did and I think it was a hell of a lucky break for me. It was a stimulating life.

DP: You don't regret not having pursued architecture?

KA: Oh, God, no. Most of my friends who were in architecture all died of either ulcers or God knows what, because you graduated from architectural school thinking that you're going to do great things and you find out that you're a pawn of the system and that you can't do these great things unless you're just plain damn lucky. Here I was up against a guy who only demanded that I do my best. Nobody gives a damn about the architect doing his best. They want the cheapest. And here was Walt saying, "We don't give a damn,"—he was fighting the bankers all the time—"we don't care what the damn thing costs! Let's make it the best we know how!" You don't hear that anymore. When we were working at Disneyland, Walt said, "Now wait a minute. Wait a minute. This has got to be a place where people are going to be happy, where people can enjoy their dreams, where it's clean and it's the best you can think of. It's got to be the very best! And it's not going to be expensive. It's going to be something everybody can enjoy and everybody will enjoy it." This kind of spirit—

DP: That's so rare.

KA: But it was so pervasive that we who were in the business became plagues to our wives and our friends, because we couldn't get together for a social evening without branching into Walt and talking about what we were doing, what we were going to do. We were so excited. My wife would say, "Oh, for God sake, can't you shut up about the studio? Why are you always yakking about the studio? Let's talk about something else." For about five minutes we'd talk about something else, and the first thing you know, we'd be back on this thing.

DP: That's great, because so many people spend their lives working at mundane jobs.

KA: It was tremendously invigorating. On *101 Dalmatians*, I was trying something new. It was the first time we had ever used Xerox for anything other than commercials and there they had a very mannered line. We had done *Sleeping Beauty*, and Walt was really upset because it wasn't making much money and it was our last great burst of effort at self-colored ink lines and all the perfection that we had developed. It was terribly expensive, very difficult to do, and I was very aware from having animated myself, that when you had an inker make a tracing of your drawing that it lost some of the life. I found out by experimenting that you can't even make a tracing over a light board yourself of the same drawing. The tracing looks dead, but the one underneath it somehow or other has the spark of life, because it was conceived because of an idea or an emotion. I always thought that was true when we would run tests in black and white; the animation had more life to it.

So I legislated to try doing a picture in Xerox. Then I went so far as to try to make one world out of the backgrounds, too, because we'd draw things three dimensionally in characters and paint them flat, so I thought we'll draw our backgrounds three dimensionally and paint them flat, too. We will also paint them with cel paint [paint used on celluloid for animation] so that everything is the same medium. I prepared a lot of things to show Walt. Walt didn't go for that, but in the meantime, he gave me the go ahead to work on this, so we started it but without that facet. I wanted to use the line from the background and the lines on the character so they'd look like still one world and we could still paint them in watercolor. But I got into a thing where the inkers and painters were no longer needed in such great numbers and that bothered me a little bit. But at the same time *The Hollywood Reporter* and the other Hollywood paper came to me, because this was a new breakthrough and they wanted to have some sort of an introduction to it. So I gave a glowing report on how much better it was and so on. I had every inker and painter in Hollywood on me. I didn't realize what I had done because I was costing them their jobs. It turned out that most of them got their jobs back in Xerox and on the other things, so it wasn't as disastrous for them as that.

But Walt never liked the visibility of the lines. Even though they did give more life to the characters, it was the antithesis of what Walt wanted. He wanted people to believe that these things were not drawings, that these things were actually people. His whole drive had been in that direction. So when I came through with a line—outlines that were visible—that became very annoying to him. He didn't like it at all and he made several remarks that hurt me, because I had thought he liked it.

He had been so busy doing other things that he didn't know how far I'd gotten in the picture. He never really went along with it, but since then, every picture's been done that way [at least up to 1978 at the time of this interview].

I was producing the thing and I had a big unit. Walt had asked me to build this thing up and I had a whole lot of people who were painting and doing a really beautiful job on it. A lot of them had come to me and asked, "Are we employed here now? Is it all right for me to have a child?"

I said, "Why sure, Walt never fires anybody who does his job and you guys are doing your job. So don't worry. Just keep doing your job and you'll be all right."

A month or two later, Walt called me in and said, "You have to fire all these guys, Ken."

I said, "Me, fire these guys?"

He said yes. I couldn't sleep that night and I didn't come to work the next day. I had such a pressure built up inside of me that I thought I was going to explode. And sure enough, I had a stroke—

DP: My God!

KA: —a paralytic stroke and I was laid up for six months in the hospital. In fact, they gave me up as dead. Then I had another stroke after I got home. But then I began to be able to talk and I came through. Walt was fantastic. He must have sensed that it was the result of something that he said that made me have this thing, because talk about being good to me: I made more money when I was in the hospital. Walt would send me every sort of thing. Couldn't be nicer. And then I would lie in bed and think of ideas for Disneyland. I'd have a great idea, and I'd call him and tell him. Over and over again, he said, "Look it, Ken! Damn it! You get well and come back. You don't have to think of ideas now. Just forget it." He said, "When you come back, don't ever think about punching the clock, don't ever think about having to be here at any time. You will never ever have to produce another picture. You will never have to be responsible for anybody else. All I want for you to do when you come back is just sit there and create." He said, "Your time is your own. You can come and go as you please. You can just sit there and create." Gee, that's how kind he was to me when I was sick, so he must have been trying to make things right, knowing that I had taken it so badly.

DP: That must have been a tremendous recovery.
KA: I didn't accept the fact that I had a stroke and I was going to die. I knew I had some fishing I still had to do.

DP: That's probably why you survived.
KA: The fact that I could go back and not ever have to worry about vacation time or anything else, that I could come and go whenever I wanted, appealed to me enormously. As long as he was alive, which was for about another two years, that was so. But he forgot to put it in writing and never told anybody. After he died, I talked to the business manager who suggested I talk to Roy about it, but I said, "Oh, hell, how can I go tell Roy what Walt told me personally on the phone?" So I just dropped it.

DP: I have read about the story meeting where you accidentally lit Walt's mustache on fire and how after he invited you to lunch to show everyone that he wasn't still angry.
KA: His kindness, even after I put a big blister on his nose. *He* asking *me*, "What are you doing for lunch?" I can remember that.

DP: He sounds like a very rare, one-of-a-kind person.
KA: I've never known anybody like him. I mean the guy could be cruel, but his cruelty was never premeditated. It was never because he set out to be cruel. It was because he was a driving force in a certain direction and you, or something, got in his way. Also, he must have had ESP or something. Dick Irvine, John Hench, and I were working on connecting the waterway from the castle moat to the rivers system at Disneyland. Walt had given us the project and said to get a survey and natural gravity will carry it down. If we can just keep the intake around the castle, it will flow into the waterway and we will have nice fresh water there

where it is stagnant now. In getting our surveys, they discovered that there wasn't enough fall from the castle to Adventureland, so we would have to pump it.

Rather than telling Walt we needed a pump, which was tantamount to saying, "Your idea doesn't work, Walt," we came up with what we thought was a brilliant alternative scheme. We had a meeting all set up with this enormous map at the end of the room. Underneath was the other way of doing it. We flipped coins and it turned out to be Dick Irvine's job. Walt came in. He said, "Hi fellas," and sat down. Dick started to go through this thing, talking about it as if it was the way Walt had wanted it, without saying, "We came up with a new idea and here's what we are going to do, Walt." Walt began to tap his fingers. "What are you doing? It's supposed to just flow."

Then Dick had to say, "Well, we had a survey done and it shows that there isn't enough fall."

Walt said, "What in the hell are you talking about there's not enough fall? Before we ever did anything, when it was still orange trees, I walked it and it was at least a two-foot, maybe a three-foot fall." He got mad and walked out. We sat there chewing our cuds until somebody got the idea to have it resurveyed. We had it resurveyed and there was a two and a half foot fall. Exactly what he said there was.

When they built the new studio, it looked like spaghetti underneath. He had coded wires—different color codes—for all the phone services, the heat, and all that sort of thing. You wouldn't think that a man with his interests would be involved in which phone cords were which color or which heating ducts or vents went where, but he knew them all. He had a fabulous memory and he knew them so well that when people were stuck, they'd call him and ask him if he knew and he did. On top of that, he'd remember every one of my children's birthdays, because he had sent things to the hospital when they were born. Not only mine, but I think all the other guys. He would remember them all. "Why isn't it Margery's birthday tomorrow?" Now how in the hell can a guy do that?

DP: I read that somebody has said they could keep track of five or six projects, but that Walt could keep track of forty or fifty?

KA: Right. And I know he must have stayed at the studio at night to study what you would have to show him, because he didn't need any introduction to what you were talking about. He'd come in and he'd already know everything that was there.

DP: I read about two different things that took place in the 1940s that involved you. One occurred after *So Dear to My Heart*, when Walt wanted to create a setting for little miniatures. He said something about putting you on his personal payroll.
KA: Oh, he did.

DP: The other thing involved a locked room and you two were—
KA: He did that. That is part of the same story. That was one of the most interesting things that ever happened to me.

DP: It sounded fascinating.
KA: Fascinating. He took me off the regular payroll and paid me out of his pocket whenever he thought of it. We had keys to one room. He started it by saying, "You know, Ken, you can draw like Norman Rockwell. I want covers like Norman Rockwell. Americana." He said, "Damn it. You guys all do things with your hands. I can do things with my hands, too! But give me some Americana covers like Norman Rockwell does, but make them with dimension and depth so I can make dioramas." So I went into this little locked room. The first one I did was a soft-shoe dance in which he got Buddy Ebsen to do the dancing. We had Granny Kinkaid [from *So Dear to My Heart*] in the cabin. We had, I think, four or five miniature scenes that we finally finished. One of them was a barbershop quartet. The guy who was being shaved in the chair was Walt. It was an old 1850 Western barbershop from the back looking toward the front and then right in the immediate foreground was a barber chair and all these guys were customers except for the barber. They were all standing around singing. They were all caricatures of animators. Then the wall of cups on the back had the names of all his favorite animators.

DP: Who were the animators that were caricatured?

KA: Norm Ferguson, Ham Luske, Freddy Moore. I've forgotten the fourth.

DP: Was this room where you worked in the Animation Building?
KA: Yeah, on the third floor. He would forget to pay me by the week and then we'd be downtown somewhere buying some little ornamental moldings or something and he'd say, "Hey, you got a dollar?"

I'd say, "No, I'm broke."

"What the hell! I paid you, didn't I?"

I'd say, "Oh, no, you didn't."

"I didn't!" Then, my God, he'd forget how much he paid me and he'd pay me embarrassing amounts. It was such a hit-and-miss thing.

This was before Disneyland was even conceived of or at least before I knew anything about it. He said, "We'll call this Disneylandian. We'll have a traveling exhibit of these things I've made." He wanted to make the little guys move and all that sort of thing. He was upset that plastics weren't good enough in those days to make them everlasting. He wanted something when it was made to continue to exist. Everything had to be just so. He said, "We'll have like a maze. We'll set it up with little electric eyes and when a customer walks through, they can have a personal experience with this little thing I've done. If it's Granny Kinkaid, when you break the electric eye and come in there, she is making a comforter and she'll be talking to you. Out the window, out on the hillside, you can see the sheep and the chickens and they'll move."

DP: Did he record Beulah Bondi [the voice of Granny Kinkaid]? Did he get to that point?
KA: Yeah. Then it got out of hand with him again. He was trying to do all this himself, just wanted me to draw the things, and he'd decide how he was going to do them. He started out trying to carve the little characters, wood first and then clay and then he decided they would have to be cast. Then he decided he needed a machine shop at the studio. Then he thought, "Maybe I'd better get an animator working with them so we can get this thing the way we want it to work." He hired Roger Broggie. Then he decided he'd better have a sculptor to help him sculpt, so he

hired Chris D'Oro. Finally somebody made a plea for me to come back and work on the pictures. He hired Harper Goff to come in and keep doing what I had started. But when Harper came in, he wasn't hired on Walt's personal payroll—that was all ended then. He came on as a regular employee, because by that time, it had gotten out of Walt's hands again. He had hundreds of people working on his project instead of him doing it. The first one he did by himself except for the face.

DP: Was it a disappointment to you to have to go back to work on something else?

KA: It was not a disappointment, because my fellow animators and story men and layout men asked for me. To have a whole group who are your peers say, "Hey, we need Ken back," is such a compliment that you can't be unhappy about it. Besides, I was privileged to spend the first two or three months of this odyssey working very closely with him and yet never being able to completely penetrate this shell. I always knew when to call him Mister Disney or Walt or when I should laugh and when I shouldn't. It was never one of those buddy-buddy, pal-pal things. I don't know anybody that ever got that way with him, but I was closer with him than I could have been later, because later he had so many other things taking his mind. He hired many other people, and they would send people in to see me about something he had told them, but he had forgotten to tell me what to tell them. It got to be kind of difficult to handle.

He was so honest. When I first went there, I got involved in a cartoon called *Ferdinand the Bull*. Walt was gone and I was doing story and layout work in the music room at the time and was influencing the painting and the look of the thing. In my architectural studies and travels, I had been to Spain, and I had seen the hot light and the color and so on. I knew that the way they were used to handling things in shorts that it would be just a tint. There wouldn't be any of this hot color, so I enlisted Claude Coats's sympathies and another guy named Art Riley. They were working for the head of the background department who had a list of colors that Walt didn't like. It was over his dead body that we got as much color into it as we did, and it was still poopy. It was nowhere near what we were trying to do, but in order to not make the head background man mad and still do what we thought we needed to do—we weren't really thinking so much of pleasing Walt as doing the best thing we knew we should. Anyway, it came out real well. The head of the background department, who was going to have our skins, planned to profess to Walt that he had nothing to do with it, but strangely enough, before he had a chance, Walt gave him a fifty-dollar raise. Then later each of us got raises, too. But at any rate, Walt came to me and called me to one side, something he had never done before because I had had very little contact with Walt and none intimately. But after the success of the picture, he called me to one side and he said, "Ken Anderson, I want to talk to you. I want you to know right now. You're just starting here. You've only been here how long?" I said about six months. He said, "You've only been here a short time, comparatively speaking, so I want you to know that we're selling one thing at this studio and that's the name Disney. That's our trademark. We're selling Disney. You got that?" I said yes. He said, "If you want to help me sell Disney, you're my man. You can't do any wrong. You just stay with me, you're in. But if you have any idea that you want to sell the name Ken Anderson, I'm telling you now so there's time for you to do it, you can get out and there are no hard feelings. But I want you to know that if you're here, you're going to help me sell Disney." I thought that was awfully honest.

DP: How did you react to that?
KA: My feelings weren't ambivalent. I really wanted to stay there. I had worked at MGM for a short while.

DP: What kinds of things did you do there as a sketch artist?
KA: I did sketch art on Greta Garbo and *The Painted Veil* and the Helen Hayes picture, *What Every Woman Knows*. I was under [Alexander] Toluboff and Cedric Gibbons. I met Herb Ryman and subsequently was responsible for getting both Herb Ryman and Harold Miles out to Disney. As a sketch artist I designed the scenes all the way through a picture: first the big sets and then the various uses of those sets. It was an architectural offspring. I knew I could do that, and yet I found

the salary, $165 bucks a week in the Depression, was the equivalent of getting $3,000 to $4,000 a week now. At Disney's, I got $15 a week, but I preferred the $15 a week at Disney's. MGM asked me to come back, but I wouldn't go back for a $165 a week; I'd rather have the $15 because here were a bunch of poor people who had integrity and were trying to achieve something as opposed to a great organization of people.

At the other studios, nepotism was rampant. People who had no taste whatsoever and were extremely crude in many ways would trample on your work just to salve their own egos. Or if they found you a threat, they would find ways of sifting information to your superiors that you were a threat, and you hadn't done anything! You might say as Samuel Goldwyn said, "It was nerve unwracking."

Larry Clemmons

Larry Clemmons was born in Chicago in 1906, raised in Sturgess, Michigan, and graduated from the University of Michigan with a degree in architecture. He joined the Walt Disney Studio in 1932 as an inbetweener and contributed to *Mickey's Man Friday, Mickey's Circus, Hockey Champ, Practical Pig, Autograph Hound, Sea Scouts, The Volunteer Worker, Mr. Duck Steps Out, Billposters, Donald's Vacation,* and *Tugboat Mickey.* Larry moved to the nascent story department and contributed to *The Reluctant Dragon* prior to leaving the studio in the aftermath of the strike in 1941. After the war, he had an illustrious second career as a writer for Bing Crosby on radio from 1946 to 1955. Larry returned to Disney for a thirteen-week assignment that lasted for twenty-three years. He wrote for television and for feature cartoons, including *The Jungle Book, The Aristocats, Robin Hood, The Rescuers,* and *The Fox and the Hound.* Larry retired from the Disney Studio on October 31, 1978. He passed away in 1988.

Larry Clemmons is not well known among Disney historians and his interview in this book will help fill in a gap.

I entered the Animation Building at the Disney Studio and went to Larry Clemmon's office where a sign on the door read, "I am on Dialogue Stage 'B.' Pull up a chair. I'll be back in a few minutes." He was enthusiastic and spoke with a writer's flair. A good deal of the

interview—which is not included here—dealt with Larry's career as a
writer for Bing Crosby.

This interview was conducted on October 13, 1978.

DP: Prior to your association with Bing Crosby, how did you happen to
come to work for Walt Disney?

LC: Back around 1932, I got a job at Hyperion. There were only about
seventy-five people there then. I submitted a few samples. I was never a
cartoonist per se, but anybody could inbetween. So just another job and
an opportunity. I worked there for nine years and then World War II
came along. I was away for four years back home in Sturgess, Michigan.
Before the war, I had studied architecture at the University of Michigan,
so I was back to doing that but in a limited way. I didn't want to come
back to Disney's because I knew I'd never be an animator, and I didn't
particularly like it. I was a very good friend of Bill Morrow, who wrote
for Jack Benny in those halcyon days of Rochester and Phil Harris. He
said he was now going with Bing Crosby, and under his sponsorship—
Bill Morrow was considered then the best dialogue writer that had been
in radio—I made the decision to move back here. I stayed with them for
nine years. Then television came along and Bing didn't want to do that.
I got a call from the studio for a six-week assignment in 1955 and that
six-week assignment has turned into twenty-three years and no inter-
ruptions, so it looks like it's going to be a steady job. That's how I got
into this.

Then Walt put me on live-action television. He wanted to use
Disneyland as a big set, and I did some shows with Louis Armstrong
and Haley Mills and other guest stars. Story man Bill Peet left to
illustrate and write his own books, so Walt said, "Look, there's a place
on *The Jungle Book*. Go down and see Woolie Reitherman." I went to see
Woolie, and I have been on feature cartoons ever since, and that's a long
time ago. There was *The Jungle Book*, then *The Aristocats*, *Robin Hood*,
The Rescuers, and now *The Fox and the Hound*.

My way of working—I was never a sketch artist—was to start with a
live-action–type script, and I'd submit those to Walt. So Walt became a
reader. He had to; heretofore, it was all storyboards. He'd read the script,
and then he'd call me in, would make his comments, make any changes

he wanted, and I would take it back to Woolie. Walt would say, "Do the storyboards and then call me down." Having read the script, he knew what it was all about, so then he could make his changes on the storyboard. I've been using that system ever since. They would take my script and the storyboard guys would lay it out. Then we would make adjustments and changes. It was done for no particular reason, because Walt was not in a hurry. Walt never concerned himself about too much time. He wanted to get it right, to make it good. He never was a budget-minded man at all.

DP: Did you work on *The Legend of Sleepy Hollow* [from *The Adventures of Ichabod and Mr. Toad*]?

LC: Walt wanted to release the show on television and he wanted to use Bing in the opening with the boys [Gary, Phillip, Dennis, and Lindsay], who were quite young. Walt had me come in for about six weeks to do this, because I had been working with Bing and knew his style of talking. I did a little screenplay: the father wants the kids to stay home on Halloween, and they're all made up and gee, they don't want to see the old man on TV or hear his voice. The kids say, "Gosh, do we have to stay home?" And Bing turns the hose on the window of his den and the kids can't go out, it's a deluge. They're sitting there and then we just go into the show. That's all it was; it was just an opening, which was never used. Bing did the narration of *The Legend of Sleepy Hollow*. Did a good job, too. Walt always admired Bing.

DP: Yes, and Bing admired Walt. We exchanged letters about his time at the studio, and he wrote about his admiration for Walt. Do you recall any conversations you had with Walt about Bing?

LC: He admired the way that Bing handled himself in Hollywood: he was a good father, he had a big family, and he came up the hard way— Walt did too—and he was a good talent, a good casual actor. I think all people liked the way Bing handled himself. He was so natural.

DP: When I interviewed Ben Sharpsteen, who had been the production supervisor on *The Legend of Sleepy Hollow*, he mentioned an episode that happened during the recording session:

The most outstanding thing of the whole episode with Bing Crosby occurred when he came to record. The man who was directing him said, "Now Bing, would you do that again for us please?" Bing stopped short. He said, "Do it again? Didn't I do it right?" "Oh yes, Bing, it was good, but we think it could be a little better." It upset the man no end, because he really was just fishing, hoping that Bing would do it again with another take. But Bing was such an out-and-out professional that he had done it the way he thought it should be done and there was not any other way to do it, not any other way to him unless somebody could point out to him the wisdom of it.

LC: I think it was Ed Penner, the gentleman directing it. Well, take after take after take. They wear it out. At the time I worked at Disney, a lot of people thought, "If they do it fifteen times, it's fifteen times better." That's not true. Sometimes, the very first take is the best. If there is something wrong, if they blow a line, they all know it and they play it back, they'll do it over again. No, that quote's right. Bing didn't abruptly say, "I liked what I did. That's it. Let's do the next one." But "Where did I go wrong?" They liked to work with Crosby. You know, that aura, because at that time, they never worked with any big people. They worked with voices like Billy Gilbert and Donald Duck [Clarence Nash], so when they get someone big, the guy wants to live a little bit and say, "Look Bing, let's do it over again."

DP: I liked the voices used in *The Jungle Book*, especially Phil Harris. I thought the vultures with British accents were very funny.
LC: I suggested to Walt getting Snozzle [Jimmie] Durante for the head vulture, because the head vulture is sort of dumb. He said good idea. We tried to contact him but nobody ever got to Durante personally. You always had to go through people. If we could have gotten to Jimmie, he would have said, "We'll do it! I got a million of 'em!" I wrote the whole thing for Durante and I was so let down when we couldn't get him. I never knew Jimmie, but we did some shows with him and Bing. I'm sure he would have done it. "What have you got for Jimmie?" "We want him to play a vulture." They would say, "A vulture?" and hang

up. I've always felt that our casting should say, "We want them to play themselves." The animators can put them in a vulture suit, make them a lion or a tiger.

Walt had heard Phil Harris down at a Palm Springs affair. He said, "Gee, Phil comes on, he's bright, he's breezy. The audience loved him. Let's see if we can get him for *The Jungle Book*." Well, they got him.

They were cutting some dialogue, just a page or two, as sort of an audition test. I got a call from Woolie Reitherman. He said, "Can you come on down to the sound stage?"

I said, "Why?"

He said, "Phil's down here, and we are having a little trouble." Phil was on the stage talking to these guys he had with him.

I said, "What is it?"

Woolie says, "Phil says he can't do this. He says he can't play a bear. I think we're going to lose him."

So I introduced myself to Phil. I said, "Any problems, Phil?"

He said, "I can't do the zoobies, zoobies, zabies. What is this? Zoobie-zoobie-doobie-doo, like a bear."

I said, "Phil, we don't want a bear. We want Phil Harris like on *The Jack Benny Show*."

He said, "That I can do!" Well, we couldn't keep him away from here!

From then on, we'd never tell a guy to play a jack-rabbit or an owl. We had one guy here for the voice of a hound dog. He said, "I've got to think how a hound dog would say it."

I said, "Don't think hound dog. Don't think dog. Think yourself. How would you play this? I mean you're a character in this." It makes it easier if they don't think they've got to sound like a dog. I said, "The animators will do that." You get better performances that way, a natural performance.

DP: I can't see Bob Newhart [*The Rescuers*] sounding like a mouse!
LC: Someone said, "Bob is a typical mouse." He sort of took umbrage at that. Bob is a nice guy. A delightful guy to work with. He's a doll to work with.

DP: What were your first impressions of Walt Disney?

LC: Walt was not the easiest guy to work with. He never quit working. You felt a little bit of strain, because you knew you had to please Walt. He was very patient up to a point. You only had to say one thing to Walt. He'd say, "How are you coming along?"

You'd say, "Walt, I'm having a little trouble. I think I need your help."

Right away, you know, "Come on in."

But if you said, "I'm doing great."

"Oh you are?"

Or "When you see it, you'll like it."

"Oh, you think I will, huh?"

But he had so many things going himself that he liked to overlap assignments. He wouldn't think what you're doing. He'd never say, "Are you busy?" He didn't give a damn what you're doing. I had about three things going and I was winding them up. I was walking in and he was walking out. We stopped. He said, "What are you doing now?"

I said, "Well, I just finished so-and-so, I'm wrapping up on this, and then I'm well into this and this."

He said, "Four things? You're not busy."

Walt was never a guy to pat you on the back. I think if you kept working here then you knew you were doing a good job. He didn't throw off compliments like that. Didn't have time for it and I don't think that was Walt's nature. A lot of guys were afraid to open their mouth in front of Walt. Walt was aware of that and couldn't understand why. But that's in any organization. "Gee, if I say something, I may be wrong. I'd better keep my mouth shut." Walt would say, "What good are you to me if you don't express yourself?"

DP: I gather that he didn't like "yes men" either.

LC: Oh, no. He could see through, he could see one coming a mile away.

DP: You worked here during what has been described as the Golden Age of Animation. How would you characterize that period as far as being one of the team at Disney?

LC: It was an unhappy time for me. Inbetweening is a drudge, but you're always hoping to be an assistant and then an animator. I knew I'd never be an animator, not a good one who would get the crowd scenes and the special effects and all that. I just wasn't happy. But it was a sinecure at the time and something to work. We didn't have a story department, but I'd had lunch with Freddie Moore and Norm Ferguson and Bill Cottrell and we'd kid back and forth. Someone told Walt that they thought I had potential as a story or a gag man. He called me in one day and said, "I understand that you're supposed to be pretty funny." He said it with a crooked smile. "Well, why don't you go to work with Bill Cottrell and let's see." I was happy about that, but there was no story department then, not like now.

DP: Were you here during the strike? Were you on strike?
LC: No. I had a family and I thought what the heck, striking—nobody wins. You always lose in a strike. They closed the studio, because they had to have an arbitrator out here and then they had to settle on who's going to be hired back. The war was coming along. We weren't in it then, but we had too many people here. Gunther Lessing, who was Walt and Roy's original attorney, said, "All of you who haven't had your vacation yet, you might as well take it now." So I went home. Then I got a wire from them that said don't return to the studio until further notice. Thirteen years go by! I hired myself to an aircraft factory—war work—and then I had a chance to go back to my hometown. My father had a factory back there.

Herb Ryman

Herb Ryman, born June 28, 1910, in Vernon, Illinois, and a graduate of the Chicago Art Institute, made his first mark in Hollywood as a storyboard illustrator at Metro-Goldwyn-Mayer on *Mutiny on the Bounty*, *David Copperfield*, *The Good Earth*, and other films. Herb took leave from MGM at the urging of actor Donald Crisp and traveled around the world in 1937. In 1938, he met Walt Disney, and his legendary career at Disney began. He was an art director on *Fantasia* and *Dumbo* and worked on other features such as *Victory Through Air Power* as well. He left the studio to work at Twentieth Century-Fox and returned in 1953 when Walt asked him to draw the first detailed conceptual rendition of Disneyland over a single weekend. Herb contributed enormously to Disneyland with designs for Main Street, Sleeping Beauty's Castle, New Orleans Square, Tomorrowland, the Jungle Cruise, Pirates of the Caribbean, and many other aspects of the park. He also contributed to the design of attractions for the New York World's Fair in 1964–65. Herb continued even after retirement to contribute conceptual drawings for EPCOT, Walt Disney World, and Tokyo Disneyland. He was working on concepts for Disneyland Paris at the time of his death. Herb passed away in 1989 and received a posthumous Disney Legend Award in 1990.

Herb Ryman is a highly regarded artist, well known especially for his atmospheric sketches used in the planning and development of Disneyland and other Disney theme parks.

When I completed back-to-back interviews with X. Atencio and Bill Justice at WED (now Walt Disney Imagineering), X. said to me by way of introduction to Herb who happened to be walking by, "If you really want to know what Walt was like, you should talk to Herb Ryman. He spent holidays with the Disney Family." I met Herb, and after a bit of conversation, he agreed to an interview a couple of days later when our schedules mutually permitted. As I was coming back to pick up a drawing from Bill Justice the next day, Herb said he would leave me a map to his Van Nuys house. I hate to admit it, but I knew very little about Herb at the time or about his brilliant career at the studio. The next day, I picked up Bill's wonderful drawing of Chip and Dale, and with it was a detailed map full of flourishes to Herb's house and a signed spiral-bound book of his art which contained a biographical essay. That essay was enormously helpful as preparation for my interview. I met Herb at his house, and we had an in-depth interview that practically bowled me over. He was most generous with his time, and I am grateful that we had a serendipitous meeting at WED. At the end of our interview, he said that he had told me more about Walt Disney than he had told any other writer. I know Herb had many interviews after mine, but still at the time, that was very flattering to hear.

This interview was conducted on October 15, 1978.

HR: There isn't any one person who would know and who could tell all of the facets of the Walt Disney story: Walt Disney himself, his relationship to his employees, his relationship to life, to the world, his relationship to his brothers. You still have the privilege and the opportunity of doing something that has never been done if you wish to pursue a biographical account. Men have gone to great lengths to interview and to get people out for lunch to talk about Walt and their reminiscences. Many times there are prejudices and there are biased attitudes, which are part of the Walt Disney story. Many times these things overshadow and make an inaccuracy in the total story.

As you know by now, Walt Disney was a rather unsophisticated, quite simple person. Not a world-renowned philosopher, not a do-gooder, not a religious fanatic, but a very normal, ordinary person with a genius for knowing and caring what people wanted and what they would enjoy. Most of all, he was a businessman and a very astute businessman: very, very methodical in eliminating all of the things that would in any way conflict with the total concept of entertainment. His idea was the three-year-old, the two-year-old, the ninety-nine-year-old great grandparents—if they could all be made aware of beauty and fun—most of all fun—and amusement and laughter and then along with that, if they could learn. We can all learn as long as we live.

One thing was brought to my attention several months ago, which I had not heard Walt say precisely in this way, but I am sure that he did say it when responding to the question, "What is your idea regarding education and what is your idea regarding entertainment?"

He said, "I would rather entertain them and hope that they will learn than to teach them and hope that they will be entertained." This is a very simple statement, but if our colleges, if our universities, if our educators, had a little bit of that philosophy, our schools would be better schools.

Walt was a good friend to many of us who worked with him and for him. He was able to bring out hidden energies. Walt's enthusiasm and his curiosity and his affection for life and for all things were very deep, and he plumbed into the depths of talents around him, which sometimes I thought were rather ordinary talents. But out of these talents—by encouragement, by stimulation, and sometimes by insult—Walt could bring things that were phenomenal. He had an ability, a very uncanny ability, of just pointing his finger at someone and saying, for instance, "Now, Don, you will conduct the music." And as Don would stammer, Walt would say, "No, Don, you will conduct the music, and Jack, you will do this, and Fergy [Norm Ferguson], you will do this, and Herb, you will do the backgrounds" and so forth. All of a sudden, you were not only put on the spot, you were being made responsible, but somehow you were being complimented by a person who thought you could do it. So consequently, rather than go out and cut your throat or commit suicide, you would actually try to do it. Now I won't say there weren't failures in the process, but I think this idea of expecting something from people, especially young people with imagination and sensitivity and talent, expecting something beyond their capabilities, is a very healthy thing. It makes them grow and makes them work. The reward is in virtue itself: the accomplishment of the thing.

Walt Disney had a tremendous respect for great men, great inventors, great thinkers. It would be a mistake to consider Walt Disney merely an entertainer or merely a motion picture tycoon. He was a much broader person than that. He'd spend all of his time, all of his waking hours, with a very intense curiosity and a great affection. He loved the little animals—the little horses, ponies, and mules—that were really the first employees at Disneyland. The trains, the construction, the workmanship on the wagons—everything was top quality. No expense was spared in anything Walt ever did. No steamship that ever plied the Mississippi River was as elegant as that little jewel that Walt built for Disneyland. I was there one day when the head of a tugboat company from New York Harbor asked to visit the *Mark Twain*. He said to me, "I am so excited to see someone who's done this with live steam, to go to this trouble."

Then Walt joined us later and we went into the Golden Horseshoe. I don't know whether anyone has ever told you or not about the furnishings of the Golden Horseshoe. Just before the Golden Horseshoe was ready, Walt asked about the whiskey bottles on the back bar. I said, "They are the bottles of the turn of the century. I think it has a very good feeling of authenticity."

Walt said, "We've got to change the labels on those bottles." When I protested, he said, "Herb, there are going to be a lot of people coming here. I would like it if they didn't see anything that anyone could disapprove of." So we changed the bottles.

Walt was never concerned or never worried about criticism from the critics. Some very severe criticisms of his films would make some of us think, "That's too bad. That film is going to be a flop." Walt, when questioned about it, would say, "I don't care what the critics think. If the public likes it and pays money to see it, that's all I care about."

DP: The more that I have read about Walt Disney and the more that I've talked to people, the more complex my image of him becomes. Since I never met him and never saw him, I realize that I am at a terrific disadvantage.

HR: No, you're at a greater advantage, because you can look at it through detached historical perspective.

DP: Several people told me that you would be one of the best to talk to, because you knew him better than so many others.

HR: I won't say that I knew him better, but Walt and I did have a good, friendly relationship. It was due to several aspects. Lilly's sister Hazel and Bill Cottrell and Margery [Hazel's daughter from her first marriage] lived near me, and so it happened that Lilly and Walt came out very often to the valley even though they lived over in town. And then after our South American trip [a goodwill tour of South America at the behest of the State Department for Walt and a group of his artists provided an opportunity to gather material for two films]—there were seventeen of us all together, and I was one of those chosen to do the backgrounds and color—naturally, we were all very close. I saw Walt often in a personal way with Bill Cottrell and Hazel. My mother was living then, and she'd invite Walt and Lilly and Hazel and Bill over here and we would have chicken fries here during the summertime. Walt was a guest in my home many, many times, and then I was a guest in his home many, many times.

One night, Walt said, "Come on out in the kitchen, Herb. I want to talk to you." He said, "Say Herb, you know Sharon is going to be sixteen years old. I want you to do a portrait of her. Will you do it?"

I said, "Well Walt, that's very flattering that you want me to do a portrait of her, but you could get anybody in the country." [Norman Rockwell had already created portraits of Diane and Sharon.]

Walt said, "Yes, I know I can get other people to do it, but I want you to do it."

I said, "All right, I'll do it." So I did the portrait of Sharon. She was sixteen at the time.

When Diane was sixteen, Walt had commissioned a very famous woman, American illustrator Neysa McMein, to do a portrait of Diane.

Neysa McMein died before the portrait was finished. It was a rather casual portrait in the sense that, I think, Diane had on a turtleneck sweater. But I liked it very much. It was a fine job, but it really wasn't finished. I had quite a task on my hands. I had to do a portrait of the second daughter not to compete with the first portrait. That meant that I couldn't make it larger and I couldn't make it smaller. I had to use the exact size and I had to use a somewhat similar pose. It was kind of a political thing, and I knew it was difficult to please Walt. All during the summer, Sharon came out here and posed. It took me quite a while to get what I wanted. Her hair was short at the time, kind of in a pageboy bob. She had on a rather formal red dress that made the sixteen-year-old girl look more like a twenty-year-old woman. But still I had a lot of fun with it and during that time, I got to know Sharon very well.

One day, the portrait was done. So I thought I would take it to their home in the Holmby Hills in the afternoon and leave it with Lilly. I said, "I hope it's okay. I think it's very good. It's as good as I can do." Knowing that Walt never left the studio until after six or seven o'clock, I could miss Walt. I thought that was very clever of me to avoid having Walt make some remark about the mouth or something. Portraits are very tough things to do for everybody, because there is always someone who can say the nose isn't quite right or why did you do the eyes that way? So I took the portrait out there and Lilly seemed to be pleased with it. Just as I was going to leave, Walt came in through the back door and it was not even five o'clock! He had some premonition or else Lilly had called him and told him I was going to be over there.

I said, "I'm just leaving."

He said, "Oh don't leave. We can sit down and have a drink." He gave the portrait a glance, not much of a look at it. I thought, "Well maybe he doesn't even care about it."

So we talked about other things and finally I said, "Well here it is. I've got to be on my way, so if there's anything you want me to do, why let me know. You're the doctor."

He said, "Hell, I'm not the doctor. My wife is the doctor."

"Well," I said, "just whoever has any remarks to make; I'll try to make everybody happy."

Walt didn't like the shadow on one side of her face. I said that that was the way that I wanted it, but that I could put the whole face in direct light if he wanted me to. But he never forced that upon me and so I let it stand as it was.

From then on my relationship with Walt was that of a friend. I never saw Walt as the stern, harsh executive. I didn't know that man. I knew the other Walt, the family man. Now there was the other Walt as some people learned to their dismay, because he could be tough and he could be totally ruthless. That Walt I observed from a distance, but I never knew that Walt. I knew the Walt that was warm and friendly, but also the mercurial person who could change moods in a second.

One day we were out at Carolwood [Walt and Lilly's home] after Walt had built the little train. It was a beautiful little train. He used to ask me, "Herb, why don't you run the train?"

I said, "No, I'm not going to run the train. I might break it and then I'd never hear the end of it."

So I never did run the train. The train became a marvelous toy, but you see Walt was also planning ahead. He didn't want the train just for himself; he was figuring out how to make things work for Disneyland. All this maneuvering was calculated to prove or disprove certain things that would be working at Disneyland. His whole drive and the whole force of his character was directed toward this dream that he believed in. Now the rest of us didn't believe in it quite so much, although we were delighted to work on it. It was fun. I enjoyed it because it was creative. I could draw any kind of impossible things. Walt would come in and he'd say, "Can we do that?"

I'd say, "Well, sure, we can do anything."

He'd say, "Good, let's go ahead with that." Sometimes Walt would introduce me, "Herb is one of our artists here. Sometimes he's practical."

I'd say, "Well if I was practical all the time, I wouldn't be creative." So I'm not known for being practical. In fact, my whole life isn't very practical. I've ended up in a very impractical way, but I can't go back and relive it. I've had a very pleasant time.

DP: Tell me about your pre-Disney career.

HR: I was twenty-one when I started working at Metro-Goldwyn-Mayer. All the men who graduated with me from the Chicago Art Institute— talented though they were—couldn't get a job even at $10 a week. And here I was, the only artist at MGM making $165 a week. From 1932–35, I was the only artist there. My illustrative work was used to create scenes for some of the most expensive films and some of the finest films ever made, such as *A Tale of Two Cities*, *Anna Karenina*, *Queen Christina*, *The Good Earth*, and *Little Old New York*. I helped to design exteriors and interiors and made illustrations for them. These were all brought before the producer, the director, the cameraman, and Cedric Gibbons, the head of the art department. Then we built these sets, and we made the picture become real.

It was a great thrill for a young man. There was one drawback—there were twelve art directors and only one me. Sometimes I worked seven days a week and I usually worked ten to twenty-two hours a day. One time I worked for thirteen weeks, working twelve to twenty-two hours a day. I never worked twenty-four hours a day, but I would work twenty-two hours a day three and four days in succession. But I was very proud, and I was happy to be able to do it, because there were plenty of men who could take my place and be very happy to do it. Three years of this kind of work developed and trained me and sharpened my faculties. At one time, I had fifteen weeks' pay stuffed in my pocket that I could not go to the bank to deposit.

One January during the rains, Clark Gable, Charles Laughton, Franchot Tone, and Donald Crisp were sitting outside of my studio on the back lot. They wanted a sun bath, but there wasn't any sun. They were the principle actors in *Mutiny on the Bounty*. I was a young kid, and they'd come up and see my work, so we became kind of close. Donald Crisp asked me one day if I ever did any traveling. I said no, I have been busy drawing pictures.

"Didn't you go to China when they were doing the second unit preparatory work for *The Good Earth*?"

I said, "No, I didn't get to go anywhere."

Donald Crisp said, "At your age, you ought to travel and you should see the world, and you should do it before you get married and have a family and get tied down."

So I began to think about that. I began to think, "I'm exhausted
and I'm tired of looking at artificial scenery." Right across from me was
New York Street with brownstone fronts. You would open the door
and behind it was a bunch of weeds and telephone poles. No interiors,
all artificial. I went home that night to my little apartment in Culver
City, and there was a letter on my table. It was from my cousin, Halvern
Norris, who was the American Counsel in Bangkok, Siam. He invited
me to visit him. What a coincidence! Donald Crisp wanted me to travel
and here is this letter from my cousin in Bangkok. This is more than
coincidence—this is an imperative demand. Two days later, I went down
to the shipping company and bought passage around the world for two
years. My first-class fare, including stopovers, cost me the enormous sum
of $879. I lived in Peking. I became a friend of Colonel Stillwell, later
General Stillwell, and I became a close friend of the author of *Anna and
the King of Siam*, Margaret Landon. (Much later, I worked on the black
and white film of the book.)

That was part of my preparatory background for my work at the
Disney Studio. I had not met Walt Disney at this time. I was living in
Paris and whenever I'd go to a party, people would ask me if I knew
Walt Disney. I had to say, "No, no, I don't." They would look at me as
though, "And you're from Hollywood? You're from the film industry and
you don't know Walt Disney?" They weren't interested in the fact that I
knew Greta Garbo or Clark Gable or Lionel or John Barrymore. They
were only interested in Walt Disney. So I thought, "Well, it's easy for me
to say that I'm a good friend of Walt Disney's." So I did. I said, "Yeah,
I know him very well. He's a good friend of mine." I'd never even seen
him at that time!

When I returned, I had an exhibition in New York at the MacBeth
Gallery along with, at that time an unknown, Andrew Wyeth. I would
have stayed in New York and continued in the realm of fine art except
that Fred Hope, a friend at MGM, wanted me to come back and work
with him on *Gone with the Wind*. Unfortunately, Fred passed away, so I
didn't work on that film. But I did return to MGM and worked on a few
films. Then Vern Caldwell, who was the head of the Chouinard Art Institute and a friend of Walt Disney's, asked me if I would ever go to work

at the Disney Studio. He explained that Walt wanted more quality all the time, because he had a dream of doing very sophisticated artistic films, such as *Pinocchio* and *Fantasia*. I said I would be interested, but I am not a cartoonist. "There's no place for me at the Walt Disney Studio." Vern wanted me to have an exhibit of my work over there, so I did in what was called the Annex at the old Hyperion Studio. This was in 1937. After the exhibit, the people at the studio asked me to come over for an interview. They liked my work and they hired me. I took a 50 percent cut in my salary to go to work there because I thought it was a challenge.

DP: Did you meet Walt Disney then?
HR: No, I didn't meet Walt until later. He didn't interview me.

DP: When you finally did meet Walt, what were your impressions of him?
HR: I was very impressed, because naturally Walt was a world-recognized figure at that time. The films that he had done—*Three Little Pigs*, *The Old Mill*, and the other Silly Symphonies—I had seen almost every one of them and I loved them. And after traveling for two years and seeing and talking to people in China and Japan and India and Europe, I knew that Walt Disney was the most beloved living man of this time. So I was prepared to be in great awe of him and, of course, I was. Then I got to know him as a friend, as a very intimate person that I could be with, talk with. I suppose one of the reasons Walt liked me—aside from my talent—was that I never asked him for anything or demanded anything. So we got along very well. A lot of people took advantage of Walt's friendship and asked for raises. Consequently, I never made very much money at the Disney Studio, but it was a very good arrangement because I still don't need a lot of money. All I want is to know that I'm developing and improving and that the quality of my work is progressing, and it still is.

Walt had a very affectionate, ingratiating smile. Very contagious enthusiasm. He could look at you and talk to you, and he had an almost hypnotic enthusiasm.

One day, Vern Caldwell came in and said, "Say, Herb, your name is on the list to go to South America." I asked why. He said, "Ben

Sharpsteen recommended you and a lot of other people have recommended you. Walt has been asked by the State Department to go to South America on a goodwill tour. You're one of the people to go." A couple of days later, Walt called me in along with Frank Thomas, Norm Ferguson, Lee and Mary Blair, Chuck Wolcott, Larry Lansburgh, Ted Sears, Jim Bodrero, and Jack Smith [and Bill Cottrell and Hazel, Jeanette Lansburgh, John Rose, Jack Cutting, Jack Miller, Webb Smith]. That's about all. We all went to South America, and we had a lot of fun down there. For three months, we never went to bed. When we came back, we started to work on *Saludos Amigos*. In fact, Walt Disney was probably responsible for bringing about this tremendous affection and enthusiasm for Brazilian music. We were introduced to the samba and other rhythms.

When we were going to do *Victory through Air Power*, based on a book by Alexander de Seversky, Walt took it upon himself to be a leader in this crusade because he believed in it. One afternoon, he called us all into one of the projection rooms. I didn't know what the talk was going to be about, but I happened to be in the front row on the right-hand side. Seversky, the great Russian pilot and advocate of long-range, land-based bombing, gave his talk on the book. Walt then explained that he had bought the rights to the book, and he was going to do a film of it. He sat right in front of me about ten feet away. He looked at me and he looked at the others, and he explained what we were going to do. I was absolutely horrified to hear that we were going to do a film that I knew would consist of maps and arrows and technical tricks and so on. Walt looked right at me and no doubt in my face he saw consternation, amazement, disbelief, and fear. After the announcement, we all went back to our respective rooms.

A few minutes later, Walt appeared in the doorway. He said, "Herb, does that sound awfully dull to you?"

Of course, I knew that he had been watching me. I said, "No, no, no. I think it's a great idea." So I lied! I didn't think it was a great idea at all.

He took his hand, and he banged on the door jam and said, "Well, we're going to do it, and you're going to be the art director."

I said, "Fine," but I thought, "Oh boy! This is worse than ever, because now I have to work with this thing." Ken Anderson and I worked on the preliminaries for it. It really wasn't as dull as it could have been, but it wasn't one of the big pictures that Walt ever did.

DP: Several people have said that he was not somebody who engaged much in small talk. Others have said that he was not always easy to be with because he was always thinking so much about projects and what was going on at the studio. When you were with him socially, were those things true?

HR: Yes, that is correct. You couldn't engage him in any small talk whatsoever. I knew the subjects, and I knew what he *would* talk about that would be applicable to the work that we were doing at the studio. You couldn't say it was shop talk. For instance, he was always interested in little anecdotes about Abraham Lincoln, because he was a great admirer of Lincoln. Then there were times when he'd tell you a joke. It would just come out of nowhere. Some joke that he'd heard that had no application to any situation. The average person who didn't know Walt would think that he was in a jovial mood and that it was a time to tell jokes. Well, it was not a time to tell jokes and you'd better not tell him a joke, because if you told him a joke, he'd just look at you and look bored and never recognize the fact that you'd told him a joke. And never answer you. So in that respect, he was impossible to penetrate. He'd be thinking about the next move or the next thing that was on his mind. When he came back from London and had this degree from Oxford, naturally we were all very proud that Walt had this recognition. In a way, it was a compliment for us, too, because we had helped. I saw him in the hallway and I couldn't help congratulating him. I said, "Walt, we're very proud that you've had such recognition. It must have been a very exciting experience, and I want to congratulate you."

He looked at me and he said, "Oh Herb, we've got things to do! Don't talk about that."

DP: When you would go to Hazel's house or when he would be over here or you'd be at his house, would he be fun to be with or would he still be thinking about the studio? Would he join in?

HR: He would join in on anything. He was a great participant. He was not cold. He was not aloof. But there was always a limit that you could not take advantage of and you couldn't step across the line. If you stepped across the line and took up his time to relate something outside his interest, he would just go completely dead. He didn't want to hear any dirty jokes, and he would not tell any dirty jokes, although now and then, he would come in and explode some risqué joke in order to shock you so you'd think, "Wow! Did that come from Walt?" But then if you'd start to tell him a joke, then that was the end of it. Absolutely the end of it. He'd just walk on by. So any little risqué joke that Walt ever told was told not because he enjoyed the joke, but just to kind of stun you into something.

Walt had a unique way of acting out things; he could tell any story and he could become a frog or a toad or a mouse or an elephant. He was able to project himself into these personalities. In fact, I never saw this as much as the animators did, because he would say, "I want the elephant to do this or I want the stork to do this," and then he would become whatever it was. This is probably the basic quality of the anthropomorphic interpretation which is symbolic of all Disney films: trying to humanize a toothbrush or a bowl or a fork or even a push pin. It was Walt's projection into this anthropomorphism that made these things come to life.

It is my conviction that the lack of sophistication and the lack of a sophisticated education in the case of Walt Disney, the fact that he was a common man and a Missouri farm boy with a very limited education—he didn't graduate from high school and he was embarrassed by it and always had a lot of respect for people who had degrees—contributed to his worldwide success, because he became a person who could feel the pulse of the world. One of the supreme examples, before I ever knew Walt Disney, at the height of the Depression, was *Three Little Pigs*. It came out and made such an impact on all society all over a world that was wallowing in the deepest darkest Depression and there was no hope. Everything was going wrong financially, economically, spiritually, morally, and here came this happy little film of the little pigs. "Who's Afraid of the Big Bad Wolf" seemed to be symbolic of something and people would whistle and sing it. Even at MGM, in our sophisticated art department, we'd sing and whistle it. Now this had an impact on the whole world that Walt didn't intend. He wasn't preaching any moral thing, he wasn't trying to revive the flagging spirits of a dejected

world. He just was making a film, but the feeling that he had for what
people would go for, what they wanted, this was the genius of Walt
Disney.

And to bring it up to date, Disneyland, EPCOT, each of these
totally innovative things, these were concepts that Walt and Walt alone
could do. People say to me that they know I had quite a bit to do with
the beginning of Disneyland, and I did, but it was Walt's concept and
it was Walt's motivation that permitted you to go ahead with it. And
if he didn't approve of it, you didn't go ahead with it. It was Walt's
leadership at every turn of the road. I worked on Disneyland with
Walt's permission. But I did start a lot of things. I started New
Orleans Square. John Hench and I were given the assignment one year.
We wanted an area fronted on the river—the Rivers of America—and
we thought New Orleans Square would fit into that area. We must
have made a hundred drawings. I'm very proud of the way the Pirates
of the Caribbean has turned out. I made many trips to New Orleans
with Walt and Lilly. I developed a lot of things. Of course after I
worked on it, Marc and Alice Davis perfected the details of the ride.
So did Fred Joerger and Harriet Burns. I always say that Marc Davis
did the Pirates of the Caribbean and Bill Martin did the architecture
for the street in New Orleans Square. I can't very well stand up and
say, "Look what I did," because there were quite a few others, but I
think I got it started.

So each person that you talk to and each person you interview will
have a little part of the puzzle, the jigsaw puzzle, that goes into the
portrait of Walt Disney. But it's of such a vast scope—the picture of
Walt—and I would also like to go on record as saying that Walt was
not a deity. Walt was not a superman. Walt was just a regular, live,
flesh-and-blood person, and I have no doubt at all that the fame he
established during his lifetime will live and grow for several hundred
years and that Walt Disney will become and already is a legend. It is
for people like yourself to have the privilege and the duty of presenting
Walt as a human being and a person who can be known, a person who
you can be close to. Walt loved children. He loved everyone. He could
meet people. Walt had a marvelous rapport with young and old. He was
not an aloof person at all.

One day we were walking down the street together in New Orleans. This was one of our trips when we were developing the concept for New Orleans Square at Disneyland, because Walt began to realize that it could really be something. It was a Sunday morning, not many people on the street, but as we walked along, I looked across the street and I saw four women who had spotted Walt. I thought, "This is the end of our peaceful walk, because they are going to come over and get his autograph." I was curious what his attitude would be.

One of the women came up behind us and tapped Walt on the shoulder. She said, "Pardon me, but you're Walt Disney."

He turned around and I thought he was going to be mad or something, because we had been concentrating on ideas for the park, but he gave them all a big smile and he said, "Hello there." He shook hands with the woman and he said, "How are you?"

The woman was embarrassed. She said, "You don't know me."

He said, "Well, I do now."

She said, "We wanted to know if you'd sign our book."

He said, "Why I'd be delighted to." So he signed the four autograph books that these tourists had. He surprised me, because I thought he would say that he was not giving out any autographs. But he was delighted and this was the way he could be. This was the way when he went to Europe, when he traveled with his family, and when he first had his own plane, and we went to Puerto Rico. I noticed that Walt was the first guy off of the plane, and he would take care of the luggage. Walt would assume kind of fatherly duties and make the reservations at the desk for everybody. He was very capable in assuming all these duties, and this same guy could also make films.

When you interview other people, I think what would help most would be to get a cross-section, get a slice, of the meaning or the significance of Walt's personality to make the figure come to life. There's something I want to mention about life and death. Back in 1955, I had been commissioned to do a mural at Forest Lawn on the theme of the Resurrection. A mural on the Crucifixion was already in place. Walt wanted to see that mural and the Great Hall at Forest Lawn. As we were driving over, we were talking about death and cemeteries and such things. Somebody said, "I don't like Forest Lawn. I think it's a commercial cemetery."

Walt said, "Well, now, don't say that. I used to bring my father and mother over here. I'd let them off on a Sunday and they'd walk around inside and then I'd come back and pick them up. I remember how much it meant to them. It means a lot to a lot of people."

Then somebody said a thing that I was very shocked to hear, "Walt, what's going to happen to you when you die?" I thought, "Boy, what a question."

Walt was sitting next to me. He took both of his hands and BANG he hit the back of the front seat. He said, "Well, for one thing, when I go I don't want anything left around. Now this means monuments."

I never said anything, but I thought at the time, "You will have something left around whether you like it or not. You're going to have the Walt Disney films, you're going to have Disneyland, and you're going to have something in Florida, Walt Disney World, so whether you like it or not, you are going to have monuments." But this was the modesty of Walt.

In 1952, I had a letter from Doubleday. They said that Thomas Costaine had recommended that they ask me to illustrate his book, *The Black Rose*. I was flattered. I was working on Disneyland at the time, so I asked Walt if I could leave to work on the book illustration and he said okay. When I returned, Disneyland was still under development, and Dick Irvine took me to see Walt. As we approached Walt, Dick yelled, "Hey, Walt, Herbie's back."

Walt turned around and looked at me, and he said, "Hi, Herbie. I just wanted to let you know that we could get along without you."

I said, "I knew you could Walt. That's the reason I left." And that was the end of that conversation.

DP: I read where you talked about Walt's endless curiosity and enthusiasm. It seems to me that that really applies to you, too.
HR: I suppose we had that in common. The people that I gravitate to, my friends, are people who are building something, doing something. Walt was one of those people, so naturally we were very close. I don't think Walt ever heard a complaint out of me, and I never heard any from him,

so our relationship was to go ahead and to build, to go forward and do something different, do something new.

DP: Did you ever meet Walt's parents?

HR: No, I never met them. His father died when we were in Argentina. He said they were beautiful, wonderful people. He said he never could do enough for them. One thing that's interesting, there was a man who had assembled the Washington, D.C., capitol in king stone, and it was on exhibit at Robinson's Department Store. It was eleven feet long, all beautifully done. The man resembled Walt's father. Walt met him and liked him. He said, "I am going to buy that."

I said, "What are you going to do with it?"

He said, "I don't know, but we'll find something." It became part of the pre-show area at "Great Moments with Mister Lincoln" at Disneyland.

People ask me, "If Walt were alive, what would he be doing now?" Well nobody knows what he would be doing, because you couldn't guess what he was going to do when he was alive. He could come in and say, "You're not working on that, are you?"

"Yeah, I'm working on that."

He'd say, "Oh, forget that. We're going to junk that."

I said, "Walt, you spent $500,000 on this. You're going to scrap it?"

"Of course!"

I said, "You didn't sound like that last week."

And he would say, "Well I can change my mind. My wife does it all the time."

DP: I have a couple of more questions about Walt in party settings. Theses are minor, but they are part of my effort to get a feel for what he was like. If you were at a party and somebody started playing the piano and people were singing along, would he participate in something like that?

HR: That would depend on if it was a family group. If it were Bill Cottrell and Hazel and Margery [Hazel's daughter] and Marvin [Davis, Margery's husband], he'd participate in anything.

DP: I have never heard anybody say whether Walt Disney ever sang?

HR: Oh, yeah. We had Christmas Eve and we had New Year's Eve. I was always flattered that I was included in those things, because they were just family and I was not a member of the family, but I was treated as such. Walt wasn't Walt Disney—the businessman. He would sing or he would relax or he'd help make the punch. He was a very normal person with his family. In fact as far as he could be permitted, he would be normal wherever he went. But you see, one of the things that occurred—and this was inevitable after his fame and world renown and recognition— he might be walking the deck of a ship crossing the Atlantic, and there were always these people who would find out who he was and they'd walk up to him and say, "Oh, you're Walt Disney. Well I have an aunt who's written a story about a monkey and a grasshopper. It would make a delightful feature-length film. You're so fortunate that you're on this ship, because I just happen to have the script with me." This was always boring to Walt, and it wasn't that he wanted to reject them, but it got so tiresome. He was approached by all of these people and there wasn't any way to cut them off. He was just helpless.

DP: When people would give him scripts, would he read them?

HR: No, he couldn't do it because he couldn't take the time, and invariably these were not great works of art.

DP: Did you once leave Disney's to go to Twentieth Century–Fox and then later come back?

HR: Yes, I did. How do you know that?

DP: I read it somewhere.

HR: Well, you're the only person who knows that. I'll tell you how that happened. The war was still on, and I was working on a film, *Food Will Win the War*. I was the art director on this film, working with Ed Penner. I heard that my friend Margaret Landon's best-selling book, *Anna and the King of Siam*, was going to be made into a film with Rex Harrison and Irene Dunne. I thought to myself, "Gee, I used to do films. There was a time when I was thought talented enough to contribute something to a

major motion picture, and here I am doing potatoes and lettuce and cab-
bage and carrots and limes." A friend, Phil Dike, encouraged me to contact the art department at Twentieth Century–Fox so I did. I called Lyle
Wheeler, the head of the department and an old friend of mine. I said, "I
lived in Siam and I was a friend of Margaret Landon and I've got quite a
library on Siamese, Thai, Malaysian, Burmese, and Cambodian history. I
think I know as much about it as anybody in the country. Besides, I can
still draw. Suppose there's a chance for me to work on the film?"

Lyle said, "Well, my god, Herb, there's not only a chance, this would
be wonderful if you would. But I thought you were tied up at the Disney
Studio or I would have called you a long time ago."

I said, "I am tied up at the Disney Studio, but I never signed a
contract." Walt asked me one time why I never signed a contract and I
said, "The reason I won't sign a contract is that I don't want to be held
and bound. I want to be free." So I went to Walt and I said, "I am sick
and tired of doing vegetables. I have had an offer to go to Twentieth
Century–Fox to work on *Anna and the King of Siam*. I was a friend of
Margaret Landon, and Lyle Wheeler wants me to be part technical
advisor and art illustrator for the whole picture and lay it all out."

He said, "Well, Herb, you're not going to leave us without finishing
what you've started on?"

I said, "No, I won't do that, but I want to leave to work on this
picture because it's an honor and it's a challenge and these vegetables are
not a challenge. I just hope it's okay with you."

He said, "Yeah, Herb, as long as you finish what you are doing, go
ahead." So I left and stayed at Twentieth Century–Fox until 1949 when
I had an invitation to travel with Ringling Brothers Circus. I wouldn't
turn anything like that down. So I left Twentieth Century–Fox and
traveled with the circus for two summers.

Later, when Walt used to introduce me to celebrities visiting the
studio, he'd say, "I want you to meet Herb Ryman. Herb traveled with
the circus."

I told him, "Can't you think of anything else to say about me except
that I traveled with the circus?" He meant that as a big compliment
because he'd always wanted to travel with a circus.

DP: Did you continue to see him socially during this time?
HR: Yeah, all the time.

DP: So it didn't have any affect on your friendship?
HR: Oh no, no, no. No affect at all. No alienation. No breach. On Saturday, September 23, 1953, I had a call from Walt. He said, "Herbie, what are you doing?"

I said, "I'm working on my circus pictures."

He said, "Can you come over and see me?" He was at the studio.

I said, "Yeah. Sure."

He said, "I'll be out in front to meet you."

When I drove up, he was out there. As we started to walk in together, I said, "What's on your mind?"

He said, "Oh, I want to talk to you about an amusement park."

I said, "You mean you're going ahead with this idea of the amusement park across the street?"

He said, "No, it's bigger than that."

I said, "Where are you going to put it?"

He said, "We don't know yet. I've got some people researching it. We don't know where it's going to be."

I said, "What are you going to call it?"

He said, "Disneyland."

I said, "That's kind of an egotistical thing to call it, isn't it?" He said no and I said, "I guess you're right. I guess it's a good name." I was joking with him. He knew that. He wasn't insulted.

He said, "It's a good name," and it was. Then he said, "Herbie, my brother Roy has got to go to New York on Monday morning. He's got to talk to the bankers. It's going to take $17 million to get this thing started."

I said, "Gee, that's a lot of money."

He said, "Yeah, it is. If we don't have the money, we can't do anything."

I asked, "What's the park going to be like?"

He said, "It's going to have a lot of rides and it's going to have a train. You remember the train we talked about? It's going to have a lot of things, a whole lot of things. A lot of people. Very exciting. Roy has got to take a drawing with him on Monday morning to show the bankers. You know the bankers don't have any imagination."

I said, "Well where are the drawings? I'd like to see them."

He said, "Oh, you're going to make them."

I said, "No, I'm not. This is the first I ever heard about this. I can't do anything between now and Monday morning. You'd better forget about it."

He said, "Well, if I stay here with you, will you do something?"

I said, "Yeah, if you stay here." So he stayed. We had sandwiches, and we talked about how big it ought to be and what there ought to be. He knew he wanted a castle. He knew he wanted a railroad. Marvin Davis had a little map that he and Dick Irvine had worked out where you were going to go inside under a tunnel by the railroad station and there was going to be a hub and a castle and a kind of frontier land and a land of the future. The word "tomorrow" was never used. I did the map and got it started.

One day after I'd been working on Disneyland for a while and they had gotten the money and the go ahead, Walt asked me, "Herbie, would you stay with us and help us on the project?"

I said, "Yeah, I will stay with you, Walt, as long as it is interesting."

He said, "I'll try to make it interesting."

So I stayed. I was assigned to Tomorrowland or to the Land of the Future, which I hated and which Walt hated. Walt never liked the Land of the Future, although he knew it had to be there, because if you have the Land of Fantasy and the Land of Adventure and Frontierland, you've got to have the future. So I was working on it for several weeks, and I had rockets and funny little things. Nobody knew what to do with it. It was very embarrassing until one day I did a rendering with a fountain, a molecular fountain—a protein molecule—that was going to symbolize the entrance to the Land of the Future. It was a fountain that squirted water and everything. I wrote on top of it "Entrance to Tomorrowland," because I didn't want to write "Entrance to the Future." At a meeting, I brought this thing in and put it up on the wall. Walt spotted it right away. He said, "What are you trying to do? Are you trying to name the land?"

I said, "No, I'm not trying to name the land. You name the land, that's your prerogative."

He said, "Well, you're calling it Tomorrowland."

I said, "The name of the park is Disneyland. You've got Fantasyland, Frontierland, and Adventureland; the name of this area should be Tomorrowland."

He looked at me and he said, "Yeah, and people will get used to saying it and they won't think anything about it. Yeah, that's all right, we'll call it Tomorrowland."

So in a way, I have been quite a bit of help when I look back, although without Roger Broggie, without Bill Cottrell, without Dick Irvine, without Marvin Davis, without Marty Sklar, without a lot of people, you wouldn't have anything. It was a team that had to work. Most of the animators and most of the young people who came in the early days of the Walt Disney Studio were just out of high school. The Depression was on and the $15–$20-a-week salary was a good salary, so they never went to college because they had a job and they had fun. And a lot of them are still there. They didn't have to go to China. They didn't have to work at MGM. They didn't have to do a lot of things. They were protected. They were secure. They were safe, and they were doing a product that they enjoyed making. However, I wouldn't trade places with them. I don't regret my schooling and I don't regret trips and all of that.

DP: Some people have said that Walt was difficult to be with for a long period of time, partly because they were concerned with maybe saying the wrong thing.

HR: I tried to avoid being with him on trips. If I could, I'd let somebody else sit next to him. In meetings, I'd let somebody else sit across the table, and I would sit on the same side as Walt, because he could become the businessman any minute and you were supposed to react, like with *Victory Through Air Power*.

DP: If you were with him socially, did you have to be on your guard?

HR: Oh, no. No.

DP: But on trips, you did?

HR: On trips where there were other people and where there was business, then I would be just like one of them. I wouldn't be a personal friend, and I wouldn't act like a personal friend. I would act like I'm here on business. If I could, I'd let somebody else sit and have breakfast with him. If I could avoid it, I wouldn't sit next to him on an airplane because it might be awkward.

DP: Somebody referred to it as avoiding being the moth dancing too close to the flame.

HR: I didn't have any fear, but it was totally unpredictable on these business trips. So I would try to stay out on the fringe, and if Walt wanted to see me, he knew where I was.

DP: In your writings [*Herbert Ryman: Paintings and Drawings*, a spiral-bound booklet], you said something that I found fascinating:

> I do sometimes wonder if such a simple piece of art as a drawing or a watercolor or a portrait which hangs in a man's home and is seen and enjoyed by only his family and possibly a few friends and neighbors—, I wonder if that is really of more consequence than some of the living conceptions that we've done for the public enjoyment and education— something again done anonymously and yet reaches millions of people.

HR: I mean that. That is not an insincere statement. Any one of the things I have done for myself is a better piece of true art than New Orleans Square; however, very few people will ever see them, very few people will ever understand them, and very few people will live or be enriched by them, but everyday, people are delighted with the visit to the Pirates of the Caribbean and the atmosphere of Tom Sawyer's Island. Whenever I go there, I sit and watch them, and I realize that if it wasn't me that got some of these things started, it would have been someone else. It would have been the person that Walt permitted to work on it. So this is only an accident of being at the right time and at the right place. The ninth chapter of Ecclesiastes says, "And I returned and saw that the race is not to the swift nor the battle to the strong, nor yet bread to the wise, nor riches to me of understanding, nor reward to men of goodwill, but time and chance happenth to them all." I have seen time and chance happen. I have seen men who don't deserve success have tremendous success. I've seen singers sell records by the millions who in my opinion shouldn't sell at all. I have seen men who were good, kind, brilliant, educated, witty, go down as total failures. I have seen lots of that. Now Walt Disney represents time and chance. You take Walt Disney and lay him back a hundred years and there would have been no Disneyland, no film, because there was no such thing as the electric light. Disneyland came just at the time when the public needed this amusement park. You could say, "Well, did Walt know that?" I don't know, but he was there and it was his idea and it was nobody else's idea. I merely had the privilege of helping him, and if I hadn't been at home that Saturday morning, Harper Goff or John Hench or someone else could have done the drawing that started it.

DP: You are right about time and chance. I appreciate you taking so much of your time to talk with me.

HR: I'm very glad to. If anything that I say contributes to the fabric of the reality of the Walt Disney legend, I'd be very happy, because you can get a wrong concept of Walt Disney, just as you can get a wrong concept of anyone. We are about to embark upon the next twenty-five years, fifty years, wherein Walt Disney will become a legend. Luckily today you've got the recorded voice of Walt Disney and you've got good photographs of him, good stills, motion pictures, from the front, back, sides. He is a tangible reality. He's not something that you have to invent, and he's not an image that you have to pad. People can look at the Disney films, look at Disneyland, they can see the things that have been accomplished, due to his persuasive impetus. You can say, "Yeah, this is the way he was."

Jack Cutting

Jack Cutting's career at the Walt Disney Studios spanned forty-six years. He was born in New York City in 1908 and a fellow alumnus of the Otis Art Institute (with Wilfred Jackson and other soon-to-be Disney artists). He joined a staff of nineteen at the Disney Studio in 1929. Jack began as an assistant animator and contributed to twenty-five of the Mickey Mouse and Silly Symphony cartoons, before he became the first assistant director under the tutelage of Dave Hand. In 1938 Jack directed *Farmyard Symphony* and in 1939 the Academy Award-winning *The Ugly Duckling*.

Jack evolved into casting voice talents as well as supervising the translations of films into foreign languages. He traveled to Latin America where he served as foreign supervisor on the feature films *Saludos Amigos* and *The Three Caballeros*. By 1944, he was named the Manager of Foreign Relations. He traveled extensively for the studio in this capacity, overseeing the dubbing of television, theatrical, and educational films into many languages. In many ways, he became a goodwill ambassador for the studio. Jack retired in October 1975 and passed away in 1988.

Jack Cutting is not as well known as he should be and probably underrated. His early career in animation is overshadowed by his pioneering work in the foreign language dubbing and distribution of Disney films.

Jack was not an easy person for me to get access to simply because he did not grant many interviews. But he called Dick Huemer who told him he should talk with me and he did. Jack chose as the setting for our interview his North Hollywood backyard which had a commanding view of the Burbank Airport. Unfortunately, we were also under the path of approaching and departing planes, so at regular intervals the drone of the planes would smother our recorded conversation. But Jack was an early aviation pilot, known as "Ace" Cutting to his friends, so this was a favorite spot for him. We had a great interview and Jack warmed up as we went along. We talked about getting together a second time to talk exclusively about Roy O. Disney, whom he greatly admired, but regrettably, I let that opportunity slip by.

This interview was conducted on April 24, 1979.

JC: Walt had a great reserve about him. It wouldn't be the thing to do at all to walk down the hall with your arm on Walt's shoulder. Not because he was Walt, because remember some of us came there when he was very young and we were all very young, but it was just that he seemed to draw back from it, whereas his brother Roy, if he knew you well enough, would walk along with his arm on your shoulder or take your arm.

DP: Let's talk about another Roy, Roy Williams.
JC: I was at the studio when Roy arrived. He was given a desk next to me, so we started out very close together. Roy had played football in school. He had this wonderful face, and he was powerfully built and very big, very strong when he was young. He arrived with a turtleneck sweater. You couldn't decide at first whether he was off the docks. He was a great one for mugging and putting on things, so he could look very tough. He was a gifted guy, an extremely gifted guy, but he appeared as a buffoon to many people. Underneath he was shrewd and sharp in his appraisal of people. You've heard all the stories I'm sure about how if he was given an assignment, he'd dash out story gags like

they were coming out of an IBM computer. Maybe you couldn't use many of them, but they'd be there. Things rolled out; many of them bizarre, but bizarre in my opinion in a delightful way. They had a certain plastic quality that was marvelous.

There was a funny period in the early days with Roy. Roy claimed to be approached by the wrestling syndicate from the old Olympic Auditorium in Los Angeles. They wanted him to come and wrestle as part of the routine. He had a great gag going for him in connection with it. He was going to be the cartoon wrestler, and when he got his opponent down, he was going to take these grease pencils out and draw on their backs.

Roy had an adoration for Walt that you can't believe. Others had it too. He once told Walt if anybody bothered him to let him know.

DP: When I interviewed him, he said, "I loved Walt more than anything in the world. He was God-on-earth to me." I thought that pretty well summed up his view.
JC: He was very proud of the fact that as time went on, Walt was fond of him. Walt was very faithful to people that he liked and had been around there a long time. When things were slow, he thought of this business of Roy playing the Big Mooseketeer on the *Mickey Mouse Club*. Roy had never attempted to perform in any way, shape, or form, but he succeeded at that in his way.

DP: I read that you had attended the Otis Art Institute. Were you there at the same time as Wilfred Jackson?
JC: Yes, I was there when Jaxon and Jane, Jaxon's wife, and Bill Herwig were there, and John Hench was there. There must have been a half dozen of us—

DP: —who all came over to Disney's.
JC: —but at different times. Jaxon had come over the year before.

DP: Was he your Disney connection?
JC: No, I had none at all. I had gone briefly to the old Chouinard's Art Institute on Eighth Street, and then I went to Otis. My father was helping

me to go to art school, but one day he wasn't sympathetic anymore. He told me he thought my running around with a bunch of "Bohemians," as they called them in those days, would come to no good end. He offered to pay all my expenses for law school, but I said, "I'm not interested. I want to draw. I want to be an artist."

So he said, "You're on your own."

I felt I had to go out and get a job. I had a friend at art school, and we had been talking like so many young students do about maybe going to Europe to study. That's the romantic period in your life and you want to do those things. Someone I knew said that there was a little cartoon studio over on Hyperion Boulevard. I laughed. I was so smug, because I thought it would be wonderful to be an illustrator. When he said "cartoon," I said, "I'm not a cartoonist."

He said, "Well, you can draw."

I took a few samples and I went in and said, "I'd like to talk to somebody, because I want to get a job." And I was there over forty-six years.

DP: Who did you talk to?
JC: I think it was Ub Iwerks. That would have been at the end of July 1929. I started to work there the first week of August 1929. Bill Cottrell was there. Merle Gilson was there. Ub, of course, was there, and Les Clark and Johnny Cannon. Did you ever meet Les Clark? He's a nice guy.

DP: I interviewed him in August, right at the time that a major earthquake hit Santa Barbara [where Les lived].
JC: He's a first-rate man. He's also self-effacing. He deserves more consideration than he gets from people who write about the studio.

DP: Do you remember your first impressions of the studio? I assume you had a change of heart about being an animator.
JC: Well, no, I still thought, "I'll work and save what money I can and then later on, I'll go back." But once I got inside the place—you see the group was very young: Walt was twenty-seven, I was just twenty-one, many of them were in their early twenties. A few from New York, like Ben Sharpsteen and then later Bert Gillett and a few others, were older.

DP: The experienced animators.

JC: He hired them from the East. He had to start bringing in people because you know the story about Oswald. And then later Ub left. Norm Ferguson—Fergie—was brought out from the East. Tom Harmon, Jack King, they all came later.

DP: What about Dave Hand?

JC: Dave Hand, yes. I was the first assistant director they had in the studio, and I was Dave's assistant for quite a while. He was a colorful, interesting personality. Later, Dave just roared right on past everybody and his brother.

There was a great charm to some of the early animation; I always looked at it, and especially as I got older, as an art form special in itself. When I see some of the old pictures, I'm still delighted, because they have a special quality. It's akin to when you see some clever children make drawings. You sit down and try to imitate them, and it is damn hard. And there was a certain naïveness about the animation of that time and the drawing that delights me. Then, as it was bound to do, it became more refined and sophisticated, and that was another period.

DP: I think you're right. There is a certain energy and vitality to the early cartoons.

JC: That was because everybody believed in what they were doing. I don't remember anybody being cynical in that young group. And also it wasn't a great business—you made no money at all—but there was that feeling among some of us who were younger that just to be there working on these pictures, just to finally see something come out, was wonderful. You didn't think about all the long hours or that you weren't getting paid for this—the Disneys were too poor anyway. You were helping to make a picture. That was the wonderful part.

DP: When you went there, were they still having night gag meetings at Walt's house?

JC: No, they had them at the studio. If your gag was accepted, you would get two or three dollars or maybe five dollars. Everybody joined in as best they could on that. Some didn't have the flair for it, but everybody tried.

DP: What were your first impressions of Walt Disney?

JC: I was surprised the first time I saw him that he was as young as he was. I somehow expected him to be older. He was only twenty-seven. One of the first definite impressions I had about him was that he seemed very serious and he seemed to be older; he had a strange kind of maturity. Strange is perhaps not the right word, but you had a feeling that there was some part of him that was either more mature than most people his age or he had a fixation about something. Maybe it was the fixation, because he seemed hellbent on doing something, but doing something that Walt wanted to do. He was not prone to say, "Well, what'll we do?" From the beginning I had that feeling that this man wants things his way. I think that is why he was able to dominate the older men. He didn't allow them to come close to him except on his terms.

DP: Some people who came from the other studios talked about how he took the whole business more seriously than some at the New York studios.

JC: Oh, yes.

DP: With Walt it wasn't a matter of pumping pictures out to make money. He wanted to perfect things and his staff appreciated that quality about him, having been in the business and seeing how other studios did things.

JC: He's certainly to be forever remembered for that, because he wanted to move onto different levels. And he was the right man, because he had this innate sense that told him—he was highly selective and that was the big thing. If you did something and I did something and we put it on the storyboard, he'd take one or the other and we may not agree, or when he'd come in and look at the storyboard and he'd be disgruntled or dissatisfied—no one bats a thousand as they say in baseball, but he had a high track record. He was a top-flight editor. People around him could draw far better than he. He did very little animation, but he could spot talents and appreciate them and do something with them. When something started to take form, he had tremendous sensibilities about discerning what was meaningful or what was not meaningful or what had something that would be valid for an audience.

DP: He seemed to have an uncanny ability to know what people would like.
JC: Yes, he had that to a marked degree. He was not a man who could sit down and talk about art per se. He didn't know the story of this painter or that painter or the different schools of art. I used to save my pennies, because I was interested in illustration. I'd buy these nice editions of illustrated books by Arthur Rackham, Edmund Dulac, and people of that caliber that were so wonderful at illustration. It was the golden age of illustration. So I had a number of these books and one day I took some to the studio. I showed them to Walt. I said, "Wouldn't it be wonderful if someday we could animate like this?"

He didn't say, "Oh, hell, no," or anything. He didn't knock it down. He was rather pensive. He looked at the books and said, "Yeah, it's nice," but you could feel the wheels going around, that he was receptive to anything like that. He was letting things come in from all angles. Sometimes he didn't know what to do, but he put ideas away and he had a great retentive memory. He did that with people. He pigeon-holed people and put them away and used them later.

Once in later years, there was someone at the studio on the live-action production side who Walt had paid a great deal of interest in when he first came. One day, this man said to me, "I don't know. I used to be called up to Walt's office and we'd talk about this and I'd be in on this, and I seldom see him anymore. I don't know why."

I said, "Well, you're still here. That's the number one point of importance." He laughed about that because he was a highly qualified man in his profession, but he was sensitive. I said, "Don't be disturbed about it, because over the years, Walt collects talents and people. He's become a rich kid now, so he's got a whole room full of toys. He doesn't have time to play with all of them, but he keeps them and then suddenly it will dawn on him that 'I could use this one' and he takes it off the shelf. But he's keeps them busy doing something."

I think part of the survival there was to be a good student of Walt. When I say you had to study him, I don't mean this in a contrived way, that you were trying to get ahead and make good points, because you couldn't do that with him anyway. I meant you had to study him, because there was quite a bit in knowing, having the right feeling about when to approach him. He was a complex man in some ways, simple in others. But his emotional nature was very mercurial.

DP: You mentioned before we started that sometimes when you passed him in the hall, he would be very warm and other times ignore you.
JC: I think he was preoccupied. After all, as time went on, let's face it, he was human and so he began to believe a lot of these legends.

DP: I imagine it would be hard not to.
JC: For any of us. But he had a lot of sensitive, profound people around him, and some with big egos. In fact, some with the big egos had violent conflicts with themselves and ultimately with him. Joe Grant was one, a talented guy. But they'd get so frustrated they'd almost become ill, because they wanted to dominate—

DP: And Walt didn't want anybody to—
JC: —and he wouldn't let anyone. He couldn't because it's a pyramid and he was alone up there and there was no room. [Concerning the change of the studio name from The Disney Brothers to Walt Disney], in the end, maybe he was right, because having Walt Disney as a symbol—the studio as well as the individual—may in the long run have been the best way. But I think initially, it was certainly his ego. He was determined. He wasn't going to let anybody get in his way. I'm sure he had some unhappy times because of that. You've got to be on guard all the time and you don't let people come too close.

DP: Do you think Roy was able to develop an attitude that allowed him to lose some battles and still remain enthusiastic? I mean do you think it was just brotherly love or do you think he understood Walt?
JC: I think the basis of it was brotherly love. He had great devotion for his younger brother. I'm convinced of it. I think the other part was that

Roy never considered himself a so-called creative person. He became
more and more susceptible to the living legend idea: Walt was a genius.
Not only did he love him, but "my brother is *it*." Roy could be very
aggressive in negotiations, very smart and concise and extremely honest
and forthright. But I think he eventually gave up quarreling with his
brother, and there were times when he was unhappy about it. I have
always contended that one of the most fortunate things that ever
happened to Walt was that he had a brother like Roy, because I'm sure if
he had had just a partner, with his temperament more than one partner
would have said, "Well, to hell with you," and it wouldn't have been so
easy. Roy complemented him and did a lot of things that relieved Walt
of doing them, like going to the banks. Walt loved to throw the line,
"We'll let Roy worry about getting the money." It wasn't until later years
that I noticed that Walt began to make more gestures and say, "Look, my
brother's done this and that." But Walt was a paradox: he could be very
gracious and charming, but he could be very heavy handed.

DP: Did you see both sides of him at times?
JC: Oh, sure, everybody did. Some of us, not knowing whether we were
going to be out the next day or not, let him know that we weren't a
whipping boy, and once you did that, I always had the feeling that he
may not be your pal, but he was not going to push you around. But some
people made the mistake of standing up to him in front of others. If
you did that, it was embarrassing not only to his ego but to his position.
He couldn't accept it, so you had to go. I think sometimes he needed
somebody to push around because he was frustrated when things weren't
right. There were quite a few people who were fine talents and lovely
people, and I'm sure he had affection for them, but he would just take
out after them.

DP: When you played polo, was he the boss?
JC: No. I remember in one game, I rode him off quite aggressively, as I
would anybody—because it's a game—and he made some remark. But
he liked the game, and he made it possible for some of us to play who
never could have played. We wouldn't have had the means to play. I'm

grateful for that. He was very serious about it, and he got into it more and more and he became quite competent at polo.

DP: I imagine that would have been really fun. It would also be a chance to see the people you worked with, including Walt, in a different way.
JC: Yes. And then I saw him in other ways, too. Whenever you interview people, they're going to tell you about the elephant from the view in which they saw him.

DP: Yes, I know.
JC: You'll hear so-and-so was very close to him for years. Well, but how close? Some that didn't see him often were sometimes closer. It's a complex question. Did anybody really know him? I think he revealed himself in brief intervals to people, almost spontaneously. I worked for the company in Europe for a few years, and he came over a number of times. I had some experiences with him in another ambience, which was enlightening. He came out to the house quite a few times over the years when I was living in Paris.

DP: Was he more relaxed or different in Europe, or was he still the head of the studio?
JC: It was not always predictable. He asked me about this famous old book shop in Paris. It had been there for years, and he'd heard about it. One day he said, "Let's go," and we spent the whole afternoon browsing around.

DP: Would he buy books?
JC: Yes, he would. But then again, he was so changeable. When he got wind to do something, he didn't dwell much on what it cost. But if suddenly he was not in the mood, then anything could be expensive.

DP: That must have been a great opportunity to be in Europe working for the company.
JC: Yeah. I didn't work with Walt in Europe the way Perce Pearce did. He went over and lived in England for a few years and acted as a producer for Walt. Perce had a love/hate relationship with Walt. Crazy

about him and yet the closer he was to him, the more he would get upset about things. Walt had the capacity for doing that with some people. And then there were some people who played it another way. They got to the point where they didn't do too much until they had their ear to the ground to find out what Walt thought. That's not good either.

DP: I understand that he didn't like "yes men."
JC: No. On the other hand, there were many people who had good spots, and unless he came and expressed opinions, they marked time; they didn't do anything. I don't believe in that. I'd rather stand up and be counted. Part of the trouble was that many of the talents there were gifted people, cultivated people, but with no background whatsoever in making a living in a commercial sense. And here was this wonderful environment that was set up, because he had taste and he wanted to do these things, but he was like Svengali; he needed Trilby. So he had all of this talent, and they were in a lovely ambience, because the master made it possible. In a sense, he shielded everybody. There were some fine talents who could go out tomorrow and get a job, but there were some who didn't want to come away from this Never Land. It was fun there. They knew there were other places, but they weren't like this place.

In the later years, I wasn't as close to him as the top animators and the different people he was working with, because I was working on other projects which came under Roy. But something wonderful about both of them was that if they knew you and had confidence in you, they gave you a lot of latitude. They didn't stand over you and tell you what to do. Out of the blue, Walt would call me and ask me to do a special assignment for him. If the end result was good, he was great about it. That pleased my ego; I was flattered that he had confidence in me. Naturally, we were all devoted to him. I could tell, as the years went by and as I was changing—and we all change in the passing years—I could see something about his character development, too.

DP: Was he more distant because it wasn't like the early days when there were only a handful of people there? Was he more businesslike or was he more relaxed because he was more successful?

JC: In the early days, it was all very friendly. There was something interesting about that; Walt and Roy did have a nice way of making the old timers feel that they were part of the family. He was never stiff with any of us that had been around there. We in turn weren't with him. As far as being at ease talking with him, in some ways it was much better.

DP: How did you move from animation to the foreign film distribution?

JC: I went through different stages. Like many of us—Jackson, Dick Lundy, and others—when we first came, the studio was very little and we did everything; we did inking and painting, we became inbetweeners, and when we had to, we'd shoot the camera tests ourselves. Then we had to learn to be assistants. They have scene planning now, but in those days, the animator liked it if the assistant could figure out the camera pan moves and all the simple mechanics that they wouldn't have to bother with. Then some of us got to do bits of animation. A group of us who Walt hoped to build into animators worked under Ben in one section of the studio for a few years. This group included Jack Kinney, Roy Williams, Ken Anderson, Joe D'Igalo, and Hardie Gramatky. Some of us didn't make it. I sensed that I never was going to be a great animator. I knew that the day Freddy Moore come into the studio. He first sat next to me, and it seemed that overnight, he was animating. He didn't know it was supposed to be difficult. If ever anyone was born to be an animator, it was Freddy Moore.

I didn't want to spend the rest of my days just being at a certain level, so when Dave Hand was made a director, and he was very ambitious taking on multiple pictures, I said, "Dave, couldn't you use an assistant because you've got all this work to do?" Low and behold, a short time later he got in touch with me. He said he had spoken to Walt about it and Walt said why not try it. So I became his assistant. That gave me an opportunity to learn about cartoon direction and I got some experience in editing and other things, including recording. Then he began to have me lay out some of the scenes and then there was a short period there where I got a crack at directing several of the shorts.

DP: Which ones did you direct?

JC: *The Ugly Duckling* and *The Barnyard Symphony* and so on. But then the studio expanded, and after *Snow White*, they had to give some thought to the foreign markets. Dubbing was very little known yet, because sound hadn't been in long.

DP: Prior to this, the shorts had not been dubbed?

JC: The shorts had not been dubbed. Later on, we did a few. There were so many visual gags in them, you didn't need to. But they brought in a man from outside, Buchanan, who had been a producer of radio shows, and he was given the assignment of getting *Snow White* adapted into some foreign languages because they couldn't get off the ground without it. I was intrigued by this, and I asked Roy if I could work with Buchanan. I was given an opportunity to go with him to South America in 1939 or 1940. Some things happened during that trip that resulted in Walt and Roy firing Buchanan and putting me in charge. Roy said, "I've been talking to Walt, and Walt says, 'Let Jack do it.'" That's all the directive I ever got. That was again so typical of Walt. I had to learn a lot, because nobody knew much. There was nobody around to teach me. Today, it's done all over the world and the technique is known, but I had something to do with a lot of the developments and how they did things later, because I was in it early. That's how it happened. I was curious.

DP: I appreciate you allowing me this time for an interview.

JC: I've only done this twice before. The reason I agreed to see you was because Dick Huemer—who's an old friend and I'm very close to Dick—said, "Oh, talk to him." Dick spoke highly of you. And it's been a pleasant experience to talk to you, because I have a good feeling that you're sincere about what you are doing.

Harper Goff

A mutual interest in model trains brought Harper Goff and Walt Disney together in a London shop and led to Harper joining the Disney staff in the early 1950s. Harper, born March 16, 1911, in Fort Collins, Colorado, already had a distinguished career as a magazine illustrator and as a set designer for such Warner Bros. films as *Sergeant York*, *Casablanca*, *Charge of the Light Brigade*, *Captain Blood*, associate producer and art director on *The Vikings*, and art director on *Pete Kelly's Blues* and later, *Willy Wonka and the Chocolate Factory*. At Disney, Harper designed the *Nautilus* for *20,000 Leagues under the Sea*, worked on Walt's miniature exhibits that turned out to be a precursor for Disneyland, and developed conceptual plans for Disneyland, including Main Street and the Jungle Cruise. He also played banjo in the Firehouse Five Plus Two Dixieland Jazz band. Harper received a Disney Legend Award in 1993 and passed away that same year.

Harper Goff is not widely known, but he left an indelible mark with his design of the *Nautilus* and for his drawings and research that were instrumental in bringing Disneyland to its successful development.

Harper lived very close to Jack Cutting in North Hollywood. He and I sat in his living room, where I saw an impressive model of the *Nautilus*. He was very cooperative, and we covered some non-Disney topics as well, including his fascinating association with Errol Flynn.

This interview was conducted on April 24, 1979.

DP: Can you tell me a bit about your pre-Disney career?

HG: I started to work in 1935 at Warner Bros., and the first thing I did was *A Midsummer Night's Dream*. It was the black and white and the definitive one up to that time. I worked many years at Warner's and I worked up to become art director.

DP: Did you begin as a sketch artist?

HG: I started as a sketch artist and then I worked on up. Then we had a lot of strikes. Finally, there were too many strikes, so during the war, I did camouflage for the Douglas plant and some of the other plants around.

I knew Donald Douglas and tried to get permission from him to make paintings for historical reasons of the Rosie the Riveters [female workers in World War II-related industries]. In doing camouflage, I had to be inside the plant, and I saw the planes being built and the gals. The planes all had this yellow anti-rust paint on them, corrosion paint—it was very decorative. But he wanted to see some of my work. I had done a lot of work on aviation subjects, and he said no, he wanted me to do paintings of Douglas aircraft in combat around the world. So I did pictures for his own use, and they were printed in various magazines. A New York agent saw my paintings, and the war was still on, so he wanted me to go into magazine illustration. So I did that. During the magazine illustration period, I did things for the big gate-fold inside magazines that had nudes. I would do automobile races and early aviation history and things like that for the back side.

In 1951, my wife and I were in London. I was always a miniature train fan, so I went to Bassett-Lowke, Ltd., a company that had been in business since the turn of the century, manufacturing miniature live steam and electric locomotives. I was trying to find something I could afford to bring back as an antique. I found one, and the man said, "There's a gentleman coming in this evening who's shown some interest in that. I can't sell it to you, because I think he may think it's being saved for him. But if you come back in the evening, why maybe you can have it."

When I came back, I recognized the man; it was Walt Disney. We got to talking. He kept saying the name's familiar, the name's familiar. I said, "I can't think where you'd know me from."

He invited my wife and me out to dinner that night at a gambling and dining club that had been the Rothschild home. It was a very beautiful place. He had Bill Walsh with him. We later became very good friends. When we were sitting at dinner, Bill Walsh said, "Didn't you do some illustrations for *Esquire* that were on the back of the nudes?"

I said yes. Walt said, "I'm probably the only man that takes those nudes out of the magazine and pins them up backwards with the nudes to the wall. I've got all your pictures. I'd be very much interested if you would like to come work for me." So that was the start of it. He was surprised to know that I had done work in films.

DP: That's interesting. What year would this have been?
HG: This was about 1951.

DP: What were your impressions of him that night?
HG: Well, I had known him a little bit. A friend of mine, Ward Kimball, has his own train out here in the valley. I had met Walt out there amongst other people, but he met a million people out there and I was just one more guy. But he knew me a little bit, too, because I was a member of the Firehouse Five [Plus Two]. I had come over and played in Kimball's office. But he hadn't really recognized me.

When we went to the Ambassadors, I didn't have a tuxedo or tails or anything with me. When Walt said, "I want to go there," Bill Walsh said, "You're supposed to dress."

Walt said, "Well, how am I going to dress? I never take any of that sort of stuff with me." So we walked in and, of course, what could they do? They were very glad to see Walt Disney, but there was nothing they could do. His attitude was "take it or leave it." So they tried to take us up to a little private room.

Walt wouldn't hear of it. He went to the maitre d' and said, "Now, wait a minute. I've got guests here. I've got Mr. and Mrs. Harper Goff here and so and so. We want to do down to the room where they dance."

So we went down there. He was that way and I liked him. He was my host. I would never in the world have gone into a place like that. I probably couldn't have gotten in if I wanted to, because they expected everybody to lose their shirt gambling and, of course, Walt wasn't going to do that.

When I came back to America, I didn't act upon it immediately, but I finally got interested in the idea and went over. He said, "I've got something that I think you'd like." It was Disneyland. It wasn't called Disneyland then, but it was a totally different operation. One idea that he had in mind and that I was put on immediately was a traveling exhibit that would travel through the country. He wanted to have something here permanently, but he also wanted to put a show on the road. It would be called "Walt Disney's Americana." In those early days he was interested in animatronic figures, although the name "audioanimatronic figures" had not been created. He wanted something like, as he put it, a series of jukeboxes that could be loaded on express cars, and in little towns people could walk through the train, starting at the last car and walking up to the front, and see miniature scenes, beginning with the discovery of America right up through recent times. Everything would be played for them there in miniature. I designed a little barbershop where you could look out the window and look across the street and see things going on. You saw it from the inside. Then we had a newspaper office where they were printing a paper, and you looked out and saw the barbershop across the street.

He wanted to pursue that, but I barely got started before he had to go to England to set up a number of pictures: *Robin Hood*, *Treasure Island*, and *Rob Roy*. He said, "Start working on this Disneyland thing while I'm gone. I want you to do an underwater True-Life Adventure type thing, because we've got some wonderful footage shot by Dr. McGinnity down at CalTech Oceanographic. This man can provide us a lot of stuff. It's shot in miniature tanks. Find a way to put it into some kind of a story. I've always wanted to do *20,000 Leagues under the Sea* as an animated cartoon, and maybe we could cut this in as background material or incidental." He went away and he stayed away, and I saw that he wasn't going to come back for weeks and weeks and weeks. I was only answerable to Walt Disney. He told me everything he wanted to do, and I didn't have anybody between me and Walt. I didn't like the idea of making it, because I'd never had any animation experience, but I laid out about thirty storyboards based on live action.

When he came back, he was really upset because I had gone off on this tangent and he was really out of patience with me. But subsequently I noticed when I'd come back from lunch, he'd be sitting there looking at the storyboards. One day, his secretary, Dolores Voght, called me and said, "Walt wants to talk to you."

He said, "Do you know what A.R.I. is?"

I said, "Not exactly."

He said, "Well, it's an audience reaction indicator." They had a mechanical way of people pressing buttons if they liked something. They weren't wired up. They would get a cross section of people— filling-station operators, char people, artists, professors—and they would get an idea of the average. If people were laughing and enjoying it, it would register, and they would know what scenes were playing. Walt wanted to use a later version where people filled out cards like preview cards on whether they liked something. They still called it A.R.I.

He wanted me to do another storyboard, a live-action storyboard, this time for *The Great Locomotive Chase*. Then we would bring these exhibitors through and see which they wanted us to do, because they were clamoring for product—Disney product—but it took too long to make animation products. I quickly made *The Great Locomotive Chase* storyboard because he loved trains. But for some reason or other, the preponderant number of exhibitor association groups was very high on *20,000 Leagues under the Sea*. So I digressed from Disneyland long enough to do that. We got that out of the way and then I came back and worked on Disneyland.

DP: You did a marvelous job with the design of the *Nautilus*.

HG: The picture was very good. We had to build sound stages and tank stages. Walt was terribly upset when he saw great big trucks coming in with truckloads of plywood. He knew that cost a lot. We had to build flats for sets and things that we knew we'd have to have. Walt wanted to start easy, but he didn't realize we had to have at least one big stage for the big long *Nautilus*. There wasn't really any way to start easy. But from having footage turned out with an animation board and light board in a small room to suddenly this thing—it was a rather traumatic experience, I imagine! But he had the courage of his conviction, and he was the most courageous man that I've ever seen that way. Because he had courage and he had confidence in himself, he inspired confidence in people around him that this picture was going to go. There were skeptics naturally who felt that he wasn't well advised to go into this. What did he know about it, particularly when he refused to hire a well-known director? He always seemed to get somebody that was less expensive and less famous. I've always felt that he figured that anybody could produce a picture with William Wyler directing it and it was going to be successful. But if nobody had ever heard of the director, nobody had ever heard of the screen writer, and the actors were second echelon people, then they had to assume that the reason it was a good picture was because it was a Walt Disney picture. That's exactly what he wanted. And it worked!

DP: But that was one movie where he used the biggest names—
HG: The biggest names that he probably ever used. I remember he came to me and said, "Do you know an actor by the name of Kirk Douglas?"

I said, "Yes, it so happens that I've worked with him a couple or three times."

He said, "Well, my daughter is just crazy about him." I forget which daughter it was. He said, "I don't recall seeing him, and I guess I'll have to get a picture to view. She says he would be a great Ned Land."

Walt wanted to put Disneyland right across the street from the studio in Burbank where the freeway runs. He figured he had enough land for Walt Disney's Kiddieland, or whatever he was going to call it. His sights were lower then. But he didn't know where people were going to park. There were some narrow strips of land around there that weren't being used, so he went to the Burbank City Council to see if he could get a kind of trade off to bring this big attraction to Burbank in exchange for a ten-year or twenty-year okay to use certain property for parking without having to buy it. He'd be kind of leasing it. Some of the city council sneered at us. They didn't want to bring a carnival to Burbank. They didn't want the kind of people that followed carnivals. I know that Walt was very disgusted.

DP: I'm sure they could kick themselves for that decision.

HG: I think that he took a great deal of pleasure in taking it elsewhere after the reception he got.

My wife and I traveled thousands of miles all over the United States, trying to find information about, for example, what proportion should there be of men's toilets to women's toilets. How many do you need and how often do you need them? How much thievery? How much destruction? How many people come in a car? How big a parking lot? We knew what that would be for a theater that was sold out, but for this kind of a place?

DP: Lots of questions that most of us wouldn't think about.

HG: Now it's all tabled. So Walt sent my wife and I all over the United States. Because his name was very big, he could get our foot in the door. He would write a letter to Williamsburg and Mount Vernon and Luna Park and Coney Island and Palisades Park and throughout the Midwest and Florida, and we were always welcomed there. We asked all kinds of questions about turnstiles and all sorts of things.

DP: Did they ask you what you were developing?

HG: Yeah, we told them roughly what we had in mind. We were far enough away that nobody thought there was any competition in those days.

DP: Did you get encouraging responses from people or was it pretty much negative? I gather that people didn't think Disney could pull this off without a Ferris wheel and things like that.

HG: I think everyone thought, "He's doing fine in film. Why is he trying to get into our racket?" I don't think there was any fear engendered at all, but they probably thought he was going to lose his shirt and he'd be sorry. Anybody that was in the amusement business figured it was going to be very much like their own. They couldn't see the difference in quality, cleanliness, a non-carnival atmosphere with no barkers, a clean family park. But everyone was very polite.

I found out that you could work for anybody in the world—I mean people like Charlie Chaplin and Cecil B. DeMille—but nobody was as magical as Walt, whether you were in this country or in Europe. One time I got in a place where I was in a bad way, and I didn't have a passport. I had left the passport in the hotel. They wanted some kind of identification. I searched and I brought out this card: "Harper Goff, Vice President, Carolwood Pacific Railroad." Walt had made me an honorary vice president of the railroad that he had at his home. The card was signed by Walt Disney.

They said, "Does he own a railroad?"

I said, "Yes."

"And you're the vice president?"

"Yes."

"Oh."

I didn't have the passport, but this was just as good! Disney and the card were magic. I've had Warner Bros. cards, I've had cards from every kind of organization. It didn't mean a thing. So what! But Walt Disney! It was totally different.

But anyhow, I mainly worked on Disneyland, particularly Adventureland. I was interested in the vegetation part and the jungle. I became the coordinator between the studio and Evans and Reeves, the landscape designers and architects. We worked together, and I was coordinator of the whole park.

DP: I understand that there was an agreement that you had to keep two palm trees that had been in front of a house or a farm on the property in the pre-Disneyland days.

HG: That was no problem because that's the reason we spotted Adventureland where it was. Many many years ago—I imagine in 1910 or something like that—there was a real estate company in town and also a farm insurance company. One of them, or perhaps it was even a title and guarantee company, gave you a palm tree to plant if you did business with them. A big Phoenix canariensis. It is a date palm but it doesn't bear dates that you can eat. Another option was a monkey puzzle tree, which is a strange-looking pine tree, an exotic tree that grows to a great height and has a very geometric pattern. The great old farms of that era still have these great big date palms. They didn't belong anywhere else in Disneyland except Adventureland. And we had good walnuts and oranges on that particular corner down there.

DP: Was Walt as involved with the planning of Disneyland as he had been with his animated films?
HG: Oh, yes. It was his toy, his hobby. We were helping him enjoy his hobby.

DP: Did he make it clear what he wanted in a particular area or were you allowed a certain amount of freedom?
HG: I had been the art director on *20,000 Leagues under the Sea,* and I came up with this method of doing the giant squid. It was really a giant puppet, run by wires and compressed air and everything. It had scale and size and we owned it. We were originally talking about a submarine ride, but we decided to wait until we could build it out of income instead of advance cash. We realized that we would have to have absolutely clear water to see anything, so we would need a great filtration plant. That would have to come later. At about that time, I had seen Bogart and Hepburn's *The African Queen.* They had all these encounters with animals alongside of the boat. So I got to thinking. We couldn't make animals run, so I thought that aquatic animals—hippos and rhinos—if they are standing in the water or standing in the brush or elephants, if they just stood still and did something, or giraffes, if their heads could come over the top, or alligators in the water where you didn't see the mechanism under the water—this was the ideal thing. Walt agreed. So we did that.

Now Walt had a definite idea about the whole thing, but a lot of it was maybe an idea that he hadn't crystallized visually. I was always a three-dimensional man, so I had a great big table brought in and I made something like a sandbox where we could fool around with shapes of the ride contours. Walt had been to the Bois de Boulogne, north of Paris, and he had seen the gravity canal boat ride. We were thinking of things like that. Walt had all of his film stuff to do, all of his TV to do—he was a very busy man and he didn't get around to you. You keep wondering where he is, why doesn't he come by, but he knew just about where you were when he last saw you and he was expecting a lot of work, so you sat there and worked. But as I recall, everything was pretty acceptable. He had very pertinent suggestions, and he was very much in on it. Most of his ideas were keen and observant and telling.

He never would say, "I don't like what you're doing," but unbeknownst to you, he would get somebody else working alone—and they didn't know that you were doing this—to parallel you. If they took off in a different route, he would watch and see. For example, I was under the impression at one time that I was the only one working on Disneyland, unnamed Disneyland at that time, but on this project. I was interested in having a boat. There was one of the Disney guys that had a boat. I used to go down and visit him. I'd say, "What are you doing?"

He said, "I'm kind of doing a special thing for Walt. What are you doing?"

I said, "Well, I'm kind of doing something."

He said, "He's got more secrets." Then later on, we found out that we were both working on the same thing, but we knew each other and we were close lipped. We never told anybody what we were doing.

DP: Was that frustrating to find out?

HG: A little bit. It would have been more frustrating if you'd found out that he eventually went the way the other guy was doing than your way. But there was no way to find out what the other guy was doing, so he would just watch these divergent things, and then he'd get a reaction, and finally he'd call one of them off. He always could put his finger on the weak thing, and he always was able to improve. But it was his hobby. He never seemed to lose interest, but with Walt, as he went around from television to the *Mickey Mouse Club* to his live-action films to animation and then to Disneyland, wherever he was, you had the feeling that that's where his interest really was. I understand later on that some of the people that were in film thought that he no longer had any interest in the film, that he only was interested in Disneyland, but when I was there, that was not true.

DP: He seemed to have a marvelous capacity for all of those things.

HG: He had an understanding of the public. He came up with the idea of the True-Life Adventures. I was around where I heard these things. Ub Iwerks said, "You cannot run sixteen millimeter pictures on the big screen. You'll have to blow them up to 35 millimeter and then the grain will start and people will not hold still. They're used to 35 millimeter quality." I thought that Ub was right.

But Walt [objecting to the 35 millimeter filming on the basis of maneuverability, power sources, film cost] said, "Put it together. Now let's blow it up and go to a big theater and let's look at it."

We looked at it in our own theater, and I thought, "God, look at those scratches in it."

But we did our regular publicity, and a big beautiful theater like Grauman's Chinese Theater ran this special True-Life Adventure and it knocked the people right in their bloody hat. Nobody even noticed the lousy film. Walt said, "If they look at the quality of the film, we're dead! But they're going to be so entranced with these animals." He was right. So he knew. He knew.

DP: I suppose, after a while, people reached a point where they didn't argue with him, because he was usually right.

HG: He was a difficult man. There's no getting away from that. He was a difficult man and a frightening man. And I don't know why. I worked for important men, but I never admired or respected anybody any more than I did Walt. Consequently, I think that I have dreamed about Walt Disney more than any man. And it has been kind of a nervous dream. Even after I no longer worked for him, he was a man that I wanted to please. But he could be very damning without being cruel. He could just raise one eyebrow like, "You're not seriously telling me this is the way you want to do this thing," and all he did was raise one eyebrow. He often seemed to deliberately forget something that had been discussed in the past if for any reason it wasn't convenient. He'd leave you out on a limb. You never knew when this was going to happen. He was a great one to come in and talk to you alone and then come back later and say [referring to a drawing], "Well, why have you brought this man in here and shown him doing this?"

I'd say, "That's the way we discussed it."

He'd say, "We who?"

"You and I."

"We never discussed this."

I don't know why he did it. Either he really forgot that he had discussed it, or he now realized it was such a bad idea that he didn't want anybody to think that at one time he thought it was good. I've heard this so often that I know it didn't just happen to me. He did forget sometimes. He'd forget things that he had said that he would do to prepare the way for us. Then when we would go in and say, "Now where is this that you were going to get us?"

He'd say, "I don't know what you mean." And you could see that look, "Oh, God, I forgot to get that." Then he'd deny it. He'd say, "You didn't ask me for that" or something like that.

Everybody had a day when Walt came in to see the thing that he'd been working on for six weeks or so. Walt would do two or three of those visits on a day. So you'd come out of A.R.I. or something, and somebody would ask, "How's Walt?"

Someone else would answer, "He's got his wounded bear suit on today," and that meant that he was snapping out at everybody. Or "He's a sweetheart today," and he liked everything. He'd say, "Oh, I like that. I don't know about you, but I think this is coming along really well." And boy, everything was good! But on the other days, I never heard of a day when somebody started off and had a bad thing that everybody that day didn't have a bad thing. You just knew you were in for it.

When we were working down at the Pan Pacific [Festival of California Living at the Pan-Pacific Auditorium in Los Angeles] showcasing the miniature Granny's Cabin from *So Dear to My Heart*, Walt would come in at night and watch two or three of the shows and hear what was going on, and he'd take us over to Dupar's restaurant for a late supper. Flossie [Harper's wife] and I had been with Walt a lot of times like that. He was so completely different, so wonderful and friendly and appreciative, and he told us things. I remember he said, "The firm is in the red. Well, I don't feel like I'm not a success. When I look at all the people that I'm supporting over there, all the animators and all of the cameramen and the ink-and-paint girls and the writers and the sketch artists and everybody, they are having babies, they're paying for homes and cars, they've got their kids in schools and going to college, and all out of the Disney operation. So we lost eighty thousand dollars. I feel like I'm a roaring success."

I drove him many times to Disneyland. I was supervising down there, so I went every day after a morning at the studio. I imagine over two years we made about fifteen to twenty trips over there. We wouldn't talk business on the way down. At about this time, we just found out that the Russians had the atomic bomb. Walt thought it was a good thing. He said now there was going to be a standoff. We'll be afraid to use it, and they'll be afraid to use it. He was dead right there. We talked about forming the school.

DP: CalArts?

HG: CalArts. It didn't turn out the way he wanted it, I'll tell you that. But we talked about things like that. Sometimes he'd get a ride back with somebody, but the times he rode back with me, then we talked about the work on the way back, because we had just seen things that he wanted to change.

DP: Then it was business.

HG: It was business. If I wasn't there and he walked in and saw something I was responsible for that he didn't like—whether it was the placing of a grass hut or the size of a grass hut or something—he would call over the carpenter who was building it and tell him that he wanted it to be twice that big or that it had to be over here. I'd come back and the thing would be gone. I'd give the guy hell, and he'd always say Walt Disney did it. Usually we had a reason—like that was the only place we could have a big speaker, so we were trying to hide the speaker with something and that's why this shack was put right there. But the guy who was doing it never had the guts to say anything so he would just move it. We had all sorts of funny things like that happen. Nobody knew what was going on, but Walt did not have the courtesy to call the guy that was responsible and say, "I would suggest that you move that" or "Is there any reason why?" He'd just move it and sometimes it was drastic.

DP: Would you then contact him and tell him why you had done it?
HG: We'd explain it to him. He'd say, "Oh, well, I don't like it where it is."
I'd say, "It's there for a reason."

He'd say, "Can't you move the speaker?" If the sound people said no, that's where it has to be, he would acquiesce but never enthusiastically. But he was trapped and he didn't like to be trapped. He never liked to admit that we had a better reason for doing something than he had. So he was a little bit upset when he had to go back and do it the way we'd done it. But that will happen to anybody.

DP: Can you tell me about your experiences with the press on Opening Day at Disneyland?
HG: On Opening Day we had a situation with no liquor [for the attending press]. We didn't know whether we dared to have any liquor because of Anaheim's old-standing laws, and we hadn't gotten an adjudication on it. So Walt decided if the press wanted to bring it, they could, but we were not going to serve it or have it for sale. The press got there and they had all the mixings and the smorgasbord, but no liquor. They got mad. They were sitting around talking about what they were going to do. I was the host in the press room. I was supposed to see that everything was all right. They said, "Dumb bastard! Where's the liquor?" They tried to get out of the park, but so many people were coming in they couldn't get out.

"Where's the nearest liquor store?"
"Well, this is Anaheim."

So one guy said, "I'm going to sit down here and say that a father and mother with two kids came and left and it cost them two hundred dollars. Everything is so expensive." Another guy said, "Well I'll make it worse than that." They were sitting around saying, "He always thinks he's had good press, but he'll learn."

There was an old movie columnist who went by the name Jimmy Starr, and he said, "Well, fellas, it isn't fair. We've only got seven rides going. If they all cost five dollars, you couldn't spend that much money. And there are not that many restaurants open."

They said, "Who cares? They'll read us. Who are they going to believe, Disney or us?" That's a fact. Some guys write what they think will make a good story.

Eric Larson

Eric Larson, born in Cleveland, Utah, in 1905, joined the Disney
Studio in 1933, with a degree from the University of Utah in journalism
and recent experience in freelance journalism. He became an assistant
animator and quickly rose through the ranks as an animator, contributing to *Snow White, Fantasia, Bambi, Cinderella, Alice in Wonderland,
Peter Pan, Lady and the Tramp, Sleeping Beauty*, and *The Jungle Book*
and to twenty shorts and six television specials as one of Walt's famed
Nine Old Men of Animation. In later years Eric, with Don Duckwall, helped keep Walt's dream alive by training and mentoring a new
generation of animators and artists to fill the gap as the veteran animators began retiring or passing away. Eric expanded the studio's Talent
Program which still exists today. He retired after fifty-two years with
the Disney Studio. He passed away in 1988 and received a posthumous
Disney Legend Award in 1989.

Eric Larson, another of the Nine Old Men of Animation, is
widely known and appreciated for his wonderful character animation
in a long career at the Disney Studio. Among the successive generation of animators, he is beloved as a mentor and a teacher and a
friend.

When I first sat across from Eric in a meeting room at the Disney
Studio, he looked serious and gruff and I thought that this was going

to be a difficult interview. But once he began to talk, I was captivated
by his warmth and compassion. Even though he was working on an
autobiography, he generously shared his stories with me.

I associate another event with Eric that took place about a year
after our interview. I had mentioned to Frank Thomas that I had
with me a recently purchased Super 8 millimeter home movie version
of a 1937 RKO Pathe newsreel that included a promotion for the
soon-to-be-released *Snow White and the Seven Dwarfs*. He invited
me to bring it to the studio. I walked in one morning with the film
and my Super 8 projector. We hung a piece of paper on the back of
a door, and I showed the film to Frank, Ollie Johnston, and another
long-time Disney employee, Lou Debney. They wanted to see it
again and called in Eric Larson. All of them enthused over the scenes
and named the various artists as they appeared. This was a wonderful
moment to share with this august group. At the conclusion of
the film, Frank called the Archives to make certain they had a
copy of it.

This interview was conducted on April 25, 1979.

DP: How did you happen to come here?
EL: This is the last place I expected to be. Journalism was the thing
I wanted to follow. In school, I had written quite a few things and I
had sold quite a few things. I had an adventure story, *The Trail of the
Viking*, and it was suggested that I come down and go to KHJ and see
what they thought of it. This was radio days. So I did and they liked
it, but they said, "You don't know anything about radio writing?" I
said no. They said, "Well, we have a fellow who just defected and went
over to Disney, who was one of our best writers. His name is Richard
Creedon. Go over and see if he will help bring this thing into radio
writing, so that it will be presentable in dialogue from the radio standpoint." The story had a lot of guts and a lot of adventure and some
love interest. It would have made a typical good radio serial, but they
wanted to see if we could get a few episodes for radio presentation, and
then they would put it on experimentally as a sustaining thing and see
how it went.

I went over to see Creedon. He read it and he liked it, but he said, "It's going to take some time, because I have outside commitments. I'm committed here at the studio. We may be able to work on it maybe one night a week."

I said, "Okay, that's all right with me, because I'm in no particular hurry as long as I can sell stuff freelance."

He said, "Walt's looking for new talent. He wants to do classics in feature cartoons, and he's going to need a lot of good qualified talent." Of course I drew as well as wrote. The idea was to write and illustrate my own things from an adventure standpoint, which is my long suit. He said, "Why don't you try out here and see if you like it."

I said, "This is the most mechanical business I know of, and I don't think I want anything to do with it."

He said, "I'll promise you one thing: it will challenge any creative ability you have." So he got me interested. They said I could try out for a few days and see how I got along.

A couple of days went by—three days I think it was—and they said, "You're on the payroll if you want."

I said, "Okay," thinking that Creedon and I could do one night a week, but also thinking about what he had said about the possibilities in animation and what Walt wanted to do.

DP: What year would this have been?

EL: 1933. I knew very well there would be a chance to draw, there would be a chance to write, there would be a chance for almost anything. After about five weeks of the low-man-on-the-totem-pole stuff— inbetweening—Ham Luske asked if he could have me for an assistant. That started me in animation, and it was the most exciting experience I had ever had. I fell in love with the business and here I am.

DP: You were here during the whole *Snow White* period and the buildup to it. I've read many things about the excitement of being here during the thirties.

EL: I never met a person like Walt. I guess, next to my dad, he's probably the most influential person that ever came along, much more than any

professors I've ever had or anything. This man could sit down and in
five minutes tell you the whole story of *Snow White* and could raise your
enthusiasm to the ceiling. Another thing that caught me completely off
guard, but I enjoyed, was the fact that here were these men that he had
collected around him, including Ben [Sharpsteen], who were so talented
in the things they were doing, and they didn't want to hide their talents.
They wanted to share them with you. Anything they knew, they would
be happy to let you in on. This was something I hadn't experienced.
I hadn't been in the business world, but I always felt that the creative
person always did his stuff and didn't let anybody see it for fear that they
would copy it. But these guys—all of them—were so anxious to help
you. Here you were, a neophyte, and they just swept you into their arms.
It was the most exciting thing I had experienced. And so the studio—
with Walt, of course, as the key—just became a fascination with me and
it's been an emotional thing ever since. It's had a lot of ups, it's had a lot
of downs—I mean my personal feelings and my personal experiences—
but I look back, and I didn't get treated quite as badly as I thought I did
at times. In retrospect, at the time I thought I was really getting kicked
in the butt, but that's creativity.

DP: What were your first impressions of Walt Disney?
EL: My first impression was "Here's a guy that can scowl better than
anybody I've ever seen in my life!" I never did get real close to Walt,
although I was close to him in production. But I never became a guy
who would go up to his office at the drop of a hat or anything like that.
I was out at his place by invitation and went to New Mexico with him,
but I always felt that there should be a certain distance. I think it was
just my awe of the guy. He could excite people. Just listening to him in
some story meetings or hearing him talk in the hall to people before I
really got to know him, it was exciting. This I think is my first impression of him: here's excitement. This guy knows what he wants to do
and he has the ability to make other people grow into the attitudes that
he himself had. He was very insistent. He said, "You guys are a lot of
egos, but I want you to remember one thing and that is that you're a
team. And only a team effort will get a result on the screen." But the

enthusiasm you talk about on *Snow White*—I got married shortly after
I started here, and we got onto *Snow White* and that meant working
nights. All we got was a fifty-cent chit for the place across the street—
Ma somebody—and we'd go over there and have dinner and get back
at six and work until nine. You'd take home your enthusiasm to such a
degree that your wife didn't even find fault with the idea. I thought that
was pretty darn good. She and Walt got along fine. She had the same
love and respect for the guy, and they got along fine whether it was
playing slot machines or whatever it was they were doing. She had no
fears. I did.

DP: You were the employee.
EL: I was the employee. She could say anything she wanted. But the
enthusiasm was just absolutely—I don't know where you'd find that
kind of enthusiasm. I hadn't found it, but then again, I hadn't been out
in business, I hadn't been out in the world. I knew it didn't exist in my
dad's business. He had good employees, but not the kind of enthusiasm
I found here.

DP: It sounds like it was a pretty rare thing.
EL: To me very rare, and I still don't find it any place. I wish there were
more of it here now than there is, but times change, people change. Walt
isn't here, and we try to pass on to these people the tradition, the enthusiasm that Walt passed on to us, so you get a second generation print as
it were. It would delight us if we could get them to take hold as Walt got
us to take hold.

DP: I've talked to about twenty-five people so far and the enthusiasm
that people have felt talking about him is to the point where I feel
almost the same way and I wasn't here, I never met Walt Disney,
but I feel like I almost knew him and can appreciate what he was able
to do.
EL: And it wasn't only on us. It was on anybody he associated with. He
could go into a meeting with a bunch of tycoons and take complete control.

DP: This is a broad question, but several different historians on animation or on Disney have selected different points at which they feel the zenith of animation was reached. I was wondering if you feel that it has been reached and if so, where?

EL: I guess taking everything in graph form, you have to have your undulations; you just can't keep going up and up and up. Many things contribute to that. One would be your story material, and I don't think we are any better than the story that we have to do. When I say story, I'm talking about not only story line but the characters involved. Another thing would be the enthusiasm of people. I have to look back at certain years as being a golden era or a golden age, because they were the times when I found myself so excited about the business. I came from a zero, a negative, to a very positive. So they have to be considered exceptional years.

I look back on *Fantasia*, and I had a hell of a time on *Fantasia*. I worked on "The Pastorale" section and the only thing that I feel happy about are the flying horses and the beauty of the design, the rhythm, and the flow of everything. I look back at the Centaurs, and I kick myself and could kick anybody else, because this was a case of lack of analysis. How much nicer an effect the picture would have gotten if we had studied circus horses and what they could do to music and let the horses have horse action and then the man part of him could be a man and do what he wants to do. Instead of that, Ken Anderson, myself, and a heavy-set story man named Don got out on a sound stage one night and the three of us carried baskets on our backs and we skipped around like Centaurs, but we were skipping like human beings, not like horses. So to me, that has always been a very bad stage of analysis. We missed it and I think it could have been a much more charming thing.

DP: I think the section with the Centaurs has been criticized.

EL: It has to be. It isn't honest. But that's one thing this business teaches you to do and that is to analyze and not to let it go by the boards. At least I feel it did, because horses don't skip like human beings for

Heaven's sake! They do dance, though, and they can dance to any rhythm you want to put them to.

DP: When you said circus horses, I had a visual image of them prancing.
EL: Oh, yeah. Beautiful things. The human part could still dump the grapes and gesture and do anything they wanted to do, but you'd have a horse action carrying them.

DP: It would have been interesting to see how that would have worked out.
EL: It would. It would have been a heck of a challenge, but on the other hand, it wouldn't have been any more difficult than what we did. But I think we leveled off after *Cinderella*. I don't know; *101 Dalmatians* is a good picture. *Lady and the Tramp* is a hell of a good picture. I feel we've gone downhill a little bit, and we're starting to pick back up on *The Rescuers*. I think we could reach a crescendo again. You can't get up to a point and just sustain that. Creatively, it isn't possible. A very interesting thing is happening now. I directed quite a bit of *Sleeping Beauty*, better than half of it, maybe two thirds of it. I always felt it was one heck of a powerful good picture. When we started on it, Walt said, "I want a moving illustration." That's what we tried to give him. The picture has been badmouthed ever since we put it out until recently. Now people are starting to take hold of it again. So anyway, let's say that maybe we went downhill a little bit.

We want to remember, too, a lot of your top men begin to retire after *The Sword in the Stone*. When I came into this business, Frank [Thomas] and Ollie [Johnston] and Marc Davis and Ward Kimball and John Lounsbery all came about the same time. Hal King and a few more came then, too. There was a group of us who developed, and Walt started putting a certain amount of responsibility on us in a way. But we came through what we called the unit system: each one of us came up through a very strong animator. These are the men I spoke of a little while ago when I said that here were such great talents and yet they opened up their arms to you to let you have everything they had: Ham Luske, Norm Ferguson, Bill Roberts, Wilfred Jackson, Ben Sharpsteen,

Freddy Moore, and then just a little bit later Bill Tytla. Good gosh, what more could you ask for! We came up under those men, being taught, you might say, with them looking over our shoulders. A number of years ago, we dissolved the unit system. Don't ask me why because I can't answer. It's the biggest mistake we made. Now we are trying to set up units again. Like on *Bambi*, I had ten animators plus all their assistants working with me. I spent most of my time up here in this room and then would go down and animate at night. But you could keep control of certain things. You learn by working with somebody who has gone through the mill. But you're always learning. There's no such thing as graduation in an animation class.

DP: I suppose that's probably healthy.
EL: Oh, sure it is. It is amazing how much inspiration you get out of these young people who don't know a doggone thing about animation, but sometimes they come up with an idea that clicks and you get excited about it.

DP: Reminiscent perhaps of the kind of excitement of the thirties?
EL: The thirties were great years, there's no question about that. You had your short subjects which really were a training ground for new animators in a way and also a peak performance for the animators who were already here, like the ones I mentioned. Some of us took our turns getting in and out of animation. We'd go into direction and then we'd go back into animation. But it was a tight nucleus for a long time, even to the point where we got the idea that nobody ever retires, nobody ever dies, and this thing can go on forever. And suddenly you were caught. But I feel we certainly had a little downward trend as far as our performance goes. We reached a certain peak and then we dropped a little bit, but then you start lifting back up again.

DP: When you did the "He's a Tramp" sequence in *Lady and the Tramp*, did you have any feeling that that was going to become such a classic?
EL: No, I didn't. I got quite well acquainted with Peggy Lee at the time. Voices come in, you know, and she was an inspiration. She did some of her gestures as she went through the dialogue. I thought,

"God, if I could get a lot of that in that dog, I could at least have some fun with it." But she turned out to be a very real gal of the street.

DP: Yeah, that's one of the sexiest dogs I have ever seen.
EL: It was a case of trying to understand the anatomy of a dog and then putting in all the human "come on" and attitudes—half-closed eyes for sexy stuff, tilts of the head, brow lifts—things that make her come on.

DP: You did that very well.
EL: It was a real fun sequence.

DP: Have you ever found a famous voice to be a hindrance to animating?
EL: Not when the voice has the quality that hers had.

DP: It seems that in recent years all the voices have been identifiable to the audience.
EL: I don't think that's necessary, but then there's a difference of opinion there. You have to go back to the dwarfs. None of those people were well known. They were old vaudevillians, except Pinto Colvig, who was at the studio as a gag man and had been a circus performer. But they were voices with quality and personality and sincerity. These guys were used to telling stories over the footlights; they would have to emote to put over their points to an audience sitting out there saying "Show me." They just enjoyed doing it. It was a beautiful thing.

DP: In *Pinocchio*, you are listed as a director of animation. Do you recall what your sequences were?
EL: I worked on quite a few of them. I did a lot with planning and developing the character of Figaro and also Cleo. I worked on Lampwick turning into a donkey and Pinocchio finding himself starting to turn into a donkey. The scene where Stromboli first presented him and figured he was going to be a flop but hoped he wouldn't and he got mixed up with the marionette dolls. I did all of the doll stuff except the

Mad Russians, which Woolie [Reitherman] did. The stuff of Figaro and Gepetto, and Figaro in the body of the whale. I did a lot of the Figaro stuff, but three other animators, including Don Hudson, worked with me on Figaro. We were scattered pretty well through the whole picture. Here's one clue as far as I am concerned, as far as all the guys are concerned: you're looking for personality. In Figaro, for instance, you had a cat to deal with, but this cat was also a four-year-old little brat, and he was spunky and he had tantrums and he had reactions that a kid would have. This is a charm of animation, to put the human interpretation of emotion and character into in that case a four-legged animal. There has to be a relationship with what we put on the screen to the audience or else we don't succeed.

Walt was always insistent that we stick to realism, but once you know what it is, caricature it for all it's worth, get everything you can out of it.

DP: But have that basis in realism.
EL: But have a basis that is honest and sincere, that has a reality to it.

DP: That sounds like a pretty good idea.
EL: It worked for him. When we start getting off that kind of thing, we get into trouble. We don't very often get off of it now, but we haven't been developing them with the quality that we would with him standing guard over us.

DP: I suppose one of the hardest things about having somebody like Walt Disney who was so involved with everything and such a powerful figure, is to not have him here, but to work as he would want you to if he were here.
EL: Yeah. When you looked at the thing, it was not will it please me, but will it please Walt. Now we try to please ourselves.

DP: Have you ever had the feeling that a voice is going to come down someday—

EL: Yes, sir. I imagine there are a lot of tremors up there! "Why don't those guys do this or do that or something."

DP: Maybe because I've done so much research in this area, but with some films like *Snow White*, I can almost see beyond the movie. The movie reflects the good feeling at the studio and the excitement of everything coming together and people putting in hours and hours of overtime and loving it, because they were excited about what they were doing.

EL: Ward Kimball did a whole soup eating sequence that got into the rough stage and almost finished, and then it was cut out. I did about half a sequence of building a bed, and that was cut out. There was no need for it in the picture. But the enthusiasm kept you going to animate it without any idea that it would be thrown out. When it was thrown out, you said, "Well, I'll help you on something else, and we'll get the doggone thing out, and it will be a good picture."

DP: I understand one of the thrills of the premiere of *Snow White* was seeing the audience reacting not just to the humor but to the other emotional scenes.

EL: Those scenes of Frank Thomas's with the little dwarfs around the bier of Snow White, that really grabs hold of me. I think one of the most moving things I ever experienced though was *Fantasia*. It ran at the Cathay Circle Theater—all this beautiful sound, multiple speakers, and it finished with "Ave Maria." It was just as quiet as this room right now. I thought, "Oh, brother, all of that and then no response." It seemed like about an hour, but it must have only been about fifteen or twenty seconds, and then all of a sudden the applause broke loose and there was a standing ovation. Glory, that thing just threw me to the top of the theater! They were so taken. When "Night on Bald Mountain" was on, you had maybe six or seven speakers, and you got the gripping quality of the music and Bill Tytla's devil—that's a masterpiece. Then you go from that into "Ave Maria" and the sainted quality of the straight trees that became leaded windows and pretty soon the chorus begins to come in. They start opening up those speakers clear around the theater. Finally as the chorus is booming out, you are completely surrounded with a heavenly chorus. There's no question about it! You try to analyze it, and you can understand why people just couldn't do anything. They were just numb. And then all of a sudden it broke loose. But boy, I'll never forget as those speakers opened up and the sound just started to travel from here and go clear around the theater and come down out of heaven.

DP: It's too bad that it hasn't been seen that way, because it was designed that way.
EL: Only a very limited number of theaters had that sound system, Fantasound, because it cost about $60,000 even at that time to get the equipment installed.

DP: I have always liked the "Ave Maria" sequence, too, even though a lot of critics have not.
EL: It is a pictorial thing and emotionally it does take hold of you, but Wilfred Jackson had a hell of a job of sustaining those constant pan moves through the whole thing. That camera was constantly moving—trucking, panning, and there wasn't a still moment set in it. To design things that would pictorially blend so beautifully was a heck of a challenge for somebody. Jackson directed the sequence. I just don't see how anybody can say that isn't emotionally—maybe it isn't entertaining, but it's emotionally powerful. When I say entertaining, there's nothing to laugh at.

DP: It's almost that moving illustration that you were talking about.
EL: But you feel an atmosphere that just takes over.

DP: There is a calmness and a peace—
EL: Calmness is the word. The serenity of the whole thing; after all that devil stuff, then this takes over. To me it's a hell of a change in emotion. Visually I liked it because I like that kind of thing. I'm inclined to be a bit of a dreamer.

DP: Well, that's good!

EL: I like good music and that was good music. Beautifully designed. What a challenge to the cameramen and the people who designed it and to Jackson, because the music had already been recorded!

DP: You couldn't do much about that.

EL: Nope!

Don Duckwall

Don Duckwall came to the Disney Studio in 1939 fresh from a stint with the Pacific edition of the *Wall Street Journal* and with a business degree from Kansas State. He worked as an assistant director in the Mickey and Pluto unit through the strike in 1941. He returned to the studio in 1955, again as an assistant director and over time became the Director of Animation Administration where he remained until his retirement in 1981. Don's screen credits include production manager on *The Jungle Book*, *Robin Hood*, *The Many Adventures of Winnie the Pooh*, and *The Fox and the Hound*, and producer on *The Rescuers*. He passed away in 1986.

Don Duckwall is not well known among Disney historians and this interview will help fill a gap. Don himself felt that his greatest achievement was in creating, with Eric Larson, a training program for animators to replace the original team of animators, who were beginning to leave the studio.

The first time I met Don, we conversed in his office at the studio, and I was impressed by the drawings on his walls. He had a completed animation scene from each of the Nine Old Men of Animation (Frank Thomas, Ollie Johnston, Les Clark, Eric Larson, Ward Kimball, Milt Kahl, Marc Davis, John Lounsbery and Woolie Reitherman). There

was a framed cartoon of an exasperated Donald Duck standing outside
a door that read "Donald Duckwall" and screaming, "There is always
a wall between me and that guy," or words to that effect. Don had
personalized scratch pads with a drawing of Donald Duck in Spanish
garb under the name "Don Duckwall."

Don and I met several times at the studio. At one time I thought
I would like to work at the studio, and through the urgings of Frank
Thomas and Ollie Johnston, Don took me around to meet the heads
of many of the departments. Don was always very gracious and generous with his time. The interview that appears here was recorded at
Don's home in Studio City after he retired, and it happened to be on
my thirty-first birthday. I had planned my trip to Southern California
so I could also attend Disneyland's twenty-fifth birthday celebration
the next day.

This interview was conducted on July 16, 1980.

DP: How did you happen to go to work for Disney?

DD: I got a degree in business administration from Kansas State College
[now Kansas State University]. My first job in 1938 was with the *Wall
Street Journal*, Pacific Coast edition. I didn't know a soul in Los Angeles.
I also didn't know that the *Wall Street Journal* at that time was nearly
going broke. In the eleven western states, we had three thousand sub-
scribers. It was rough. If you left your desk—everybody had a desk lamp,
there were no ceiling lights—and you didn't turn off the desk lamp, the
president of the Pacific Coast edition would lecture you for ten minutes
on waste. It was not what I had pictured as a student graduating. I was a
serious student of business administration, so I was frankly not happy.

I was bowling one night with a fellow from Kansas State, and
another guy showed up, Dan Price, who had married a Disney in Ellis,
Kansas. I can only imagine that she might have been a niece of Walt's.
He said, "Why don't you come out to the studio, because we're just
expanding like mad?" This is when they were still on Hyperion.

I said, "I don't know anything about the studio."

"That's okay. They're really expanding. They need guys that have a
good head on their shoulders, and you've got a college degree and that
ought to help."

So he set up an appointment with the personnel manager. The man offered me a job as his assistant in the personnel office at $125 a month. (At the *Journal*, I was making $100 a month plus 10 percent of any advertising I sold.) Part of my job would be to make certain that the correct animators were working with the correct directors, because as he explained it to me, a person does a better job if they are happy and they respect the person they are working for. So I jumped at it. The *Wall Street Journal* was coming out with a special edition, and I asked if I could stay two more weeks, but he said, "No way. This job is open. We've been looking for a guy. It's open next Monday. If you're here, you've got the job. If you're not here, you don't have it." So I took the job and had to face this president of the Pacific Coast edition and tell him I was leaving short of the special edition. It was a really bad scene when I left.

So the next Monday, I went to the studio. The personnel manager had a strange look on his face. He said, "You know, I hardly know how to tell you this but Walt had an efficiency outfit from New York working here. I knew they were in the studio, but I didn't know they were checking me. I am reduced to myself and my secretary. That's all the money I've got, so there isn't a job." Well, I can't go back to the journal now! He said, "The only thing I can offer you is traffic at $16 a week. It's carrying mail around, but there's a little shack out there we call the Dog House that has a hand-operated mimeograph. I'll put you there, and then I'll get you out just as soon as I can." So for maybe a month or so, I ground out mimeographs day after day. Then suddenly this guy's on the phone. He said, "Get over to the annex. They just fired an assistant director and they need a new guy. Report to Harry Tytle."

I said, "What's an assistant director? I don't know anything about the film business."

He said, "Just get over there. They'll tell you what to do."

So I started with Harry and then very shortly and very fortunately was assigned to Dick Lundy. Dick was a natural-born teacher. The only picture he ever directed was *The Riveter*, and he used to come back at night and work with me and teach me assistant directing. There'd never been a director in the history of the motion picture business who would have done that, but Dick did. He was terribly knowledgeable. He knew lots of good short cuts that you could take that would save you time but not endanger the product. He gave me a thorough grounding in the job of assistant director.

Consequently, when Harry Tytle was made head of shorts, I was put in the biggest shorts unit, which was Gerry Geronimi's. We used to handle eight shorts at a time, which was not a feature, but it was getting up there. We tried to kick one out every six weeks, and when one would go out, then we'd have a new story come in. We had a whole wing of the Animation Building—1B—and we were on Mickeys and Plutos. Gerry's system was to have supervising animator Nick Nichols pose every scene. So Nick really controlled the action with his poses. He didn't have time to do too many poses, but then he would sweatbox the first rough coming back from the animator. When it was ready for Gerry to see, Nick would always be there with the animator. It was a pretty good system. As time went on, Gerry trusted me enough that I sweatboxed with Nick to begin with, and when the two of us thought it was there, we would bring in Gerry. We moved good volume.

When I was assigned to Harry, he was working under Jack King on *The Autograph Hound*, which cost, I believe, $115,000 in 1939. That was a tremendous amount of money. Dave Hand, who was the studio manager under Walt, said, "Okay, this has got to stop. We've got to get shorts out for something like $30,000–$35,000." I think we started at $35,000. We ultimately worked down to where *The Pantry Pirate* was done for $27,000. This was before unions and we had cash bonuses. If Herb Lamb, who was the budget man, would budget it for $32,000 and we got the thing out for $27,000, then Walt in essence would say, "I'm going to spend what the budget man says. So you people in the music room [where the unit worked] have the spread between $27,000 and $32,000 to divide amongst you." The director got the lion share and on down. As an assistant, I got $75, but every six weeks we had a new one and 75 bucks in 1939–40 was really appreciated. It was a great system which ended when the strike came along.

DP: Did Walt Disney spend much time with the shorts? Did he come into any of the sweatboxes?

DD: He came in when we called him. He saw every story before it went into production. He okayed every story. The procedure was that the two story men would get an idea, and they would sell it to the director. Then if he said, "Okay, I think we ought to go on that," he would tell Walt. If Walt said it didn't sound like a good one, that was where it stopped. If he bought it, then the story went into work. Harry Reeves was the head of story and he would get involved. Then they would work the story over. I sat in there many times and heard the two story men and they would call Harry. They'd also call Jack Hannah from the Duck Unit or somebody else and talk to them. They would look for every way in the world to tighten up that little eight-minute short so there was no air in it. It had to be just perfect. Then they'd call Walt, and he'd come in cold, never having seen the storyboards, and would sit down there. These were instances where you developed total respect for Walt Disney. There are lots of stories about Walt wandering the halls at nights and so on, but whether he did or not, he still was able to sit there, look at those boards, and let the story man go all the way through. You heard I'm sure about the many times a guy would be telling a board over here and Walt would be looking over here, and then soon he's sitting there drumming his fingers which makes everybody nervous as a cat. But in the end, he would put his finger right on something that was so obvious, and you would just say, "Why didn't I think of that!" Everybody should have thought of it. Amazing!

DP: Would he see each of these cartoons before they were released?
DD: It depended on Walt's way of working with the directors as individuals and his confidence in them. If the director felt uneasy about the story, he could call Walt anytime. You could reach him. He was a very approachable guy. You send him a note and you got a telephone call back. That was true his whole life long.

DP: I wasn't aware of that.
DD: Oh, yeah. I admired him tremendously. I've seen plenty of other administrators in that studio that you couldn't even get in their offices to talk to them. That was never true with Walt. If he was in the studio,

maybe he'd be tied up right then, but you could bank on it, he would return your call. He would make time. You would see him. And if you sent him something on paper that he liked, and you made it short but tried to put the essence down, you got a phone call back. It was zip. Amazingly fast.

DP: During the period when you were first there, when feature films were in production, did you sit through some of the sweatboxes with Walt present?

DD: Yeah. He was quite critical of any director who called him in when it was so late that he couldn't do anything. If the dang thing is all cleaned up, all you've got to do is ink it and paint it, why are you calling me now? So if you were going to call him in on it, give him a chance. Get him in there when it was still in pencil, when you can still make changes, because that's the purpose of doing it. But ultimately with Gerry, on most of our pictures he would look at them somewhere along the line before the whole thing was ready to clean up. Then he would not see it again until we got an answer print back from the lab in color, all finished. Then it was the assistant director's job to find a theater—usually the Alex in Glendale or somewhere close like that—and you called the manager to get permission to sneak this thing between features, at 9:00 say, and you would not tell anybody about that other than Walt, the director, the story man, and myself. You just put the answer print under your arm and took it to the projectionist, and you were there at 9:00 when it ran. At the end of the running, the group went straight outside the theater to the sidewalk and that's where you heard from the boss, how he felt about it.

I will never forget *Mister Mouse Takes a Trip*, because he just lectured us. He didn't like it. As a matter of fact, we really didn't ever see what Walt saw in the story. He was enthusiastic about the story and somehow he didn't convey it to anybody in the unit, because we used to fret about it because it didn't seem that great. I did my daggondest to give them the absolute, the ultimate, just the living end, in realistic train sound effects. I used to park and listen to the train crossing trestles and coming into the Glendale station, because we had all decided to make these sound effects, which had to be from the first to the last frame, real. It turned out they shouldn't have been. It seemed to me like Walt pounded on my nose for ten minutes out there on the curb. Oh, boy! It makes the hair stand along the back of my neck now!

DP: I think your experience with him is one that a lot of people had, because I remember Ben Sharpsteen telling me about Dave Hand in the early days actually trying to sneak out of the theater and getting caught in the parking lot by Walt who chewed him out about a film that he didn't like.

DD: Just like a father. When you were a little kid, do you remember how your dad sometimes would just say it and say it and say it again and again and again, and you'd think, "Lord, I know! I'm sorry!" Incidentally, I never saw *Mister Mouse Takes a Trip* again until maybe the last year I was at the studio. I thought, "I'm going to go stand in the back of the room and just see how terrible that thing is." I stood by the door so I could run. And it wasn't that bad! It's not a great short, but it's not that bad.

DP: Did Walt seem any more critical of a Mickey Mouse short than say a Pluto or any of the others?

DD: No, no. That was his baby, but I don't think so. There was another part of that bonus thing that I should tell you. You only got the bonus at the end of the picture if Walt approved it, which meant he had to approve your short. Now if he did not approve it—as he sure in the world didn't approve *Mister Mouse Takes a Trip*, then the rule was you had to get the next three shorts in the black to start with and Walt had to approve the next three before you qualified to get bonuses again. So it hurt when you didn't get approved.

DP: Ben Sharpsteen said that in the thirties, before features started, that a director could tell how much weight Walt was giving to a cartoon by what animators he would assign to it. If he wanted Mickey Mouse to be better in it, he might assign Les Clark for Mickey and maybe an animator of lesser quality for Donald.

DD: Yeah.

DP: Within these units, did you have that kind of system with the animators?

DD: No, by this time, we had our units, and pretty much everybody stayed. Now occasionally, some guy would do an outstanding job and they would move him up to features. We had our team, and Jack Kinney had his. They were doing Goofys at the time. Jack King did the Ducks. Each one had his own unit.

DP: Was there a feeling at all that the features were the majors—

DD: Oh, definitely! No question. Every single person who worked on shorts was not only aware, you were doing your double darndest. You weren't just working for bonuses; you were working to get yourself onto a feature.

DP: Did Walt regard them this way?

DD: Definitely. No question.

DP: So even though he would have the time to sit in on the shorts, at that point, they wouldn't have been as important to him as the features.

DD: That's true. He made no bones about it. It's a way of life that we've gotten away from in the last twenty years or so, and I'm not sure we're right, this business of never putting anybody down. The same thing was true, you could almost say, in our studio, because for Walt, the feature was *the* thing. If you were worth your salt, you were going to make it onto that feature before long. It was just a matter of time. You had to start young, you had to start low perhaps, and you had to start where you could.

DP: It seems like it would be a great system to bring people in and test them to see whether they were going to last without committing them to a feature.

DD: I have said that a thousand thousand times over there in our training program: if we only had shorts. It's ideal because our young people today, as much training as we give them and as strong a people as they are—we really search for strong people to begin with and we give them our best—I'm talking like I'm still there all of a sudden!—but still, they never experience the broadness that shorts have. They are into all the little niceties and little finesses that are in feature making, and certainly it's great and they have to have it. I'm not saying it's wrong, but a person is better for having a total, full-rounded thing, and everyone of these real strong animators that we talked about worked on shorts in the old days. Not only that, during the late forties, Walt made all of those package films like *Make Mine Music*, that were really groups of shorts put together, and all of our top animators worked on those. So, yeah, you bet, it's a great training ground.

DP: I know they have become expensive to make and the return is little, but it would be interesting if a group of shorts was made by the young animators and then shown on the Disney TV show. They could use the budget they would have spent on that hour's programming to pay for the shorts.
DD: They cost too much, Don. I've lived through that every way you can think of. I've done the very things you are saying. My ideal was to take Eric Larson and the trainees and see if we couldn't make little eight-minute pieces to string together for a television show. Or is there a way that we could put them in education films? When I touched bases with the education people, my golly, they turned handsprings. They gave us five concepts, and we divided the trainees up into teams and came up with some dandy storyboards. There was one with the Pooh characters that I just loved. But the budget people said that in a hundred years we couldn't get our money out of them in education. During my ten years with the training program—it was ten years from the time I kicked it off until I retired—time after time I went to Bill Anderson and Ron Miller with another attempt to see if we couldn't work out something. And every time, they were amenable—just work up something—and every time, the cost would just torpedo us.

DP: Do you remember when you first met Walt and what your first impressions were?
DD: I was dumbfounded that he knew my name. But he worked hard at that. I suppose I must have been with Dick Lundy on *The Riveter*, but I can't honestly say that I remember the incident. Just, "He knew my name," you know, bottom-of-the-heap me!

DP: When you went there, did Walt seem to fit the image you had? Or when you met this guy that you bowled with, did he mention anything about Walt?

DD: He didn't know him personally. I don't doubt that he got his job through his relationship. Probably the girl's father called Walt at home or something. He was an animation checker. He wound up on the picket line. I worked all the way through the strike as about 50 percent of us did. But he was in the picket line, and not only was he out there; he was really vocal to the extent that I wrote him off personally at that point. No friend of mine would talk to me that way. I would never have anything to do with him. Interestingly enough, he was not one of the ones that was hired back when Walt began hiring people back.

DP: It must have been awkward in the family.

DD: Yes, I should have thought so.

DP: Was that a tense time, going through the strike?

DD: Oh, terribly, because those are your friends out there and there are so many things that get involved there. It was hard. You see, this was 1941. We weren't yet in the war. Times were still pretty tough and here were young people who never had an opportunity to save any money, even though our salaries had gone up considerably—oh, I don't know, from $20.00 to $40.00 a week. We didn't have children at that time, but we were married and didn't have any spare cash. St. Joe's [Providence St. Joseph Medical Center directly across Buena Vista Street from the Walt Disney Studio] wasn't there, and the union opened a soup kitchen under the trees over in that vacant lot for people and their families. The strike lasted three months, which is a long time, and it wasn't easy to just go and get a job at a filling station or something, because times were hard.

DP: Still the Depression.

DD: You bet. There were soup lines downtown, and people weren't able to get a job anywhere, so it was really heartbreaking to see the strike. I can understand the intenseness. I can understand how this guy, for example, felt so vehement. I just can't understand a man calling somebody the names that he called me when I thought he was a friend. That I can't understand. Now I had friends out there who were gentlemen. When you ran a picket line, there were not laws like there are now, so they made a loop in front of the gate and you were completely surrounded. We used to park somewhere three or four blocks away and gang up and get a whole car full to run it, because you came up to the line and they didn't stop. You just had to nudge people out of the way, and then you were *totally* surrounded by them all yelling everything they could think of. And then you had to run, pushing them out as you went through. Now, these were your friends. I remember Jack King had a brand new black Cadillac sedan, and somebody scraped a nail along the whole side of it. There was tremendous bitterness before it was over. And afterwards, inside the studio was bitterness. Some animators refused to work with some directors.

DP: Art Babbitt was one that I gather there were a lot of bad feelings about.

DD: Yeah. He was a strong character and he led people into a union. Of course, Art's mellowed, too. I see him at the Academy, and he's a nice old guy. You'd like him. And a good animator I should say. But the thing I didn't like about Art at that time was his accepting his paycheck week after week. I was an assistant on shorts and he was on features, and I could see him in and out of people's rooms and up and down the hall. He was never at his board. Now what's he getting paid for? That was morally wrong to me and I didn't like it. I liked him until this came, and then I wrote him off. There were people in the picket line who went out on strike that I liked before, during, and after the strike. A lot of them. A lot of them.

DP: You could retain your friendship and yet disagree on how you felt about the strike?

DD: Yeah. Plus the fact that assistant directors we were told would not fall under the union because we were executives. I don't know how much I was making at that time, but it wasn't very much, but I was an executive as every assistant director was. None of us went out, I think, and there were about eighteen assistant directors.

DP: Somebody said that during the strike Roy Williams put a railroad tie on the front of his car and drove right through the strikers.

DD: Could be. Roy was unpredictable. Roy was a man of wild stories and a lot of them could have been true.

DP: I would think that a lot of strikers would have been afraid to have harassed him too much.

DD: He was frightening because he had tremendous physical strength and not the best judgment. So even as a friend, I didn't ever want him mad at me!

DP: Did you leave right after the strike?

DD: Yeah, the studio closed. I have a clear memory that the strike lasted for three months. My memory is that the studio would not have been open more than about two months, and then it was closed *very suddenly.* Absolutely shut down. It was a bad scene. Not the happy place that it had been. There were too many hard feelings, really deep-seated feelings there. The day that it was shut down, Gerry Geronimi and his secretary, Esther Newell Bochet, and I were in the theater. We were dubbing a short and had gone back in after lunch, and we spent the whole afternoon in there. We came out at 5:00, and it was the darndest feeling. It was like a ship that came to port with the tables all set, the coffee half drunk, and so on and nobody aboard. There wasn't a soul on the lot. Normally at 5:00, everybody would be leaving the lot and so on. We walked across to the animation building and went in and we didn't see a soul in the whole building. We got on the elevator, went up to the second floor (we were in the 2-F wing), and went down the hall without seeing or hearing a sound. When we got to our wing, the double doors were closed and there was a memo. I couldn't begin to quote, but in essence it said something like "The government can tell me *how* I have to run my business, but they can't tell me that I have to run it. The studio is closed until further notice." And that meant everybody—Roy and Walt and everyone else.

As I said earlier, at the time of the strike, none of us young people had saved any money. We were pretty close to Geronimi and his wife.

We used to go to his house and go swimming. We'd go over there and I'd say to Gerry, "I just can't hang in here."

He kept saying, "I'm seeing Roy, and they're going to open up again. We're going to get our unit back, so hang in there."

After about two or three weeks, I said, "I can't hang in there anymore." So I went out and took a test at Lockheed and started to work that night at midnight. Then Gerry did call me, but by then I felt I was Draft bait. Gerry even got me a nice raise if I would come back, but I decided that I would stay because by that time I was enrolled in a class learning to repair aircraft instruments in Glendale. Then I went overseas as an automatic pilot guy.

DP: Were you drafted?
DD: No, I was a civilian attached to the Eighth Air Force. This was my specialty, and I got civilian overseas pay and 90 percent of it deposited at home. When I got out in 1944, I had cash. Four of us guys who had met overseas started an export business.

DP: Did you have any interest during any of this time of going back to Disney?
DD: No, I thought that was behind me. I stayed in the export business, but eventually I sold my share and looked for a little business to run by myself. On impulse one day, I called Bonnard Dyer at the studio, whom I had known before the war at Lockheed. He said to call Ken Sealy. So I called Ken and we didn't even talk money. I just needed something eight to five, a tie down, some work to do. I asked him if there were any openings that a guy like I could fill. He said sure. "Nick Nichols is directing now and he needs an assistant right now. If you can come tomorrow, you can start." I went thinking sometime within the next six months or a year, I'll find that business to run. Well, you know that place: once you're in there, you don't do anything else.

DP: Were you glad you came back?
DD: Yeah. I never regretted anything.

DP: I have heard that Walt had a different attitude towards those who were loyal during the strike versus those who weren't. Did you find that to be true?

DD: I never felt it, and I always thought of Ken Peterson. Ken was in the picket line. He was also head of animation when Harry went to Europe in the sixties. So you see, I don't think that's true. I honestly don't think Walt would have ever allowed Art Babbitt back—

DP: I think that was more personal.

DD: Yeah, you bet it was.

DP: I love the story about Ken Anderson walking with Walt on the path between the sound stage and the theater.

DD: Ken told it as an insight into Walt, that you absolutely could not secondguess the man. He said he got out of his car at the parking lot and started to walk in and Walt was right there, so they walked along together. They were walking side by side and talking as they went. As they were cutting across between the sound stage and the theater, the sidewalk got down to one-person wide in there, and Ken stepped back, but Walt said, "Go ahead, Ken. Go ahead."

All the way along Ken listened to Walt behind him mumbling, "Why in the hell, this Goddamn place, you'd think they'd have a sidewalk wide enough for people to walk on."

They got to the other end and Ken, trying to be agreeable, said, "Yeah, Walt, it does look like they'd have made that sidewalk wide enough for two people to walk on."

Walt bristled, "Jesus Christ, Ken! A guy building a studio can't think of everything!"

DP: You were saying earlier that you were involved in the training program for ten years. Did that begin with a decision to start building up the animation department after cuts had been made in it?

DD: No, Walt cut the animation department down to the size that it was primarily due to the costs. He was into the parks and he was into live action—he was spread too thin. So he was the guy who cut it down, and he told us at the time he did it, "Now just make a feature every three or four years. You can do that forever and you just keep the nucleus here. You just keep your top people and hang on to those people as best you can and keep turning out good features. Just let it ride." Okay. There was a period after *Sleeping Beauty*, when it wasn't well received, that the scuttlebutt was that Walt was thinking of stopping animation. I've set that aside as not true, but I do know that he cut it down. But that's fine. He cut it down to boy's size. He explained to us how and why we could continue functioning well and efficiently—more efficiently probably.

As head of that thing, so as far as I was concerned, that was my directive until the things began to make so much money, when Woolie Reitherman was putting out those things and Card Walker [president of Walt Disney Productions at the time] was pounding the table, "Why can't we have more of them. Let's double the department"—like you could just go out and hire.

Ron Miller, who was my boss, said, "Okay, we've got to get these people."

I said, "Ron, they don't exist. We kept our top people and sure, we could get some people back maybe for money. I'm not sure. But bear in mind, they're not replacements for these. In the first place, they're as old as the people we're dealing with." So it was my suggestion originally, and I first had to sell Card, that we start a training program for young people right out of art school. My first and best move was to get Eric Larson sprung from animation production to teach them, because my biggest concern at that point—and we were thinking animators, animators, animators—was how in the world can you teach these guys to do what those old timers did on *Pinocchio* and *Bambi* and so on? How can we teach them and still get production out? I was still thinking the old way: a bull pen of inbetweeners and when a guy gets good enough, you put him with an animator. Finally it dawned on me we can't do it that way; we've got too small a team and we are going to upset our apple cart. So we have to lose one animator and he's going to get them going that way, so that when they do get assigned to Milt Kahl or Frank Thomas or one of those people, they are going to be worth something.

I began reviewing portfolios and I think I got pretty doggone good at it. I broke Ed Hanson [later head of the animation department after Don retired] into it that way. We averaged about one applicant a month that we took into the program during the ten years. But we just couldn't find them. I mean we were making the effort. Every letter got a direct answer. A lot of times these people sent us absolute junk, but in their mind it was quality work. You cannot put them down and you don't dare destroy them, so you've got to answer them in a way that lets them live and believe in themselves and still not hurt you. My contention was that you don't ever stop the training program. I don't care if you double the size of the department, you don't stop. You simply raise your standards. But anybody who could meet that standard, you're an idiot not to take them. I think I have them convinced that that is the way to go.

That was my baby. If I made any major contribution to that studio, it is the training program. That is writing—I read everything that anybody sent us—that's painting, that's layout drawing, and that's animation. It's making it happen, making it function and meaningful. That was my baby, it was my dream, and I built it and I made it work, and nobody else did that. Now it couldn't have happened without Eric.

DP: If you hadn't started the program when you did, a lot of the people who are gone now would never have had a chance to work with the trainees and the whole Disney way of doing something would have—
DD: It would have been lost.

DP: I have been impressed with how nice everyone has been that I have interviewed. It has been a great experience.
DD: I have always said I was one of the younger old timers, because I started in '39. When the group in the thirties started—Eric was a little older than Milt, but not by much I think—in general, they were all in their younger twenties, right out of school! Walt was the old man and he was in his thirties, for crying out loud! So he was like a father image to a lot of us. I think it would be fair to say that he actually influenced our lives because he influenced the way we thought.

DP: I imagine his charismatic nature carried over beyond work, too.

DD: Charismatic, charming, and hard as nails, all in one guy.

DP: I am interested in two people who have followed Walt in leadership roles and whom I know very little about: Card Walker and Ron Miller.

DD: I enjoyed working with Ron. I never worked with Card very much. Card was in publicity and the other side of the business, although I've known him since he was Blackie in the camera department before the war. Ron I've worked with ever since he came into the picture as being in charge of anything that had to do with animation. I admire Ron and I have a lot of regard for him. I think Ron is a deceptive person to meet or see, because he is so big and there is something about that big football player image, but he's got a mind like a steel trap. He is quick and sharp and a good thinker. I am wide open with how I feel and I was always that way with Ron, and he always heard me out, which I credit him with. In story meetings, Ron was sensitive where he should be [to story elements]. I was amazed how much Walt rubbed off on Ron in that short period of time. Walt was pushing Ron awful hard, but every so often, there would be something that came out of Ron that would take me aback, because it was just as if Walt had made the decision. There are people that would not agree with me on that, but this was my experience. He was wonderful for me to deal with when I retired. He has always been wonderful for me to deal with. He gave me my head, maybe even more than I should have had in animation, I don't know, but I ran that daggone department.

DP: After Walt Disney passed away, did things change a lot at the studio? Did it feel leaderless?

DD: I was working terribly closely with Woolie through those years and Woolie was strong. Thank God he was strong. He's done so much for that studio. A lot of people find fault with Woolie because he can also be very hard, but he is strong and I am a great admirer of Woolie Reitherman. And I thank God for him, because I don't know that we would have come through. With Walt's death, I didn't know whether we could make an animated feature without him. We never had! He was such a good story man. It is true that we did not make features as good, because they didn't have an A to Z story line. They were episodic, but fortunately they made money, and they were entertaining. Yes, I would say there was a tremendous hole there, but there was also a tremendous rallying around. Just great strength of the people who worked with Walt. You felt it.

DP: Was having Roy O. Disney there a big plus?
DD: We always looked at Roy as a money man and I never saw him in any other light. He never did move into pictures. A nice man.

Index

Printed in the USA
CPSIA information can be obtained
at www.ICGtesting.com
CBHW031049250724
12099CB00001B/41